Early Praise for *The Baby Decision*

"Bombardieri is magic. In this book, she takes you by the hand into the depths of the scary and sometimes overwhelming baby decision and step by step, she helps you find clarity. *The Baby Decision* is a must read for everyone of child-bearing age."
—Mara Altman, Author of *Thanks for Coming,*
Baby Steps, and *Bearded Lady*

"The intelligence and generosity of Bombardieri's perspectives are a gift to all women and men; she deeply honors individuality while reminding us of the compassion that is all of our potential."
—Bina Venkataraman, writer and climate
policy expert

"I am so excited about *The Baby Decision.* Being thirty-one, my peers are beginning to struggle with this question in a big way. When I read about the distinction between 'growth' and 'safety' needs, a light bulb went off over my head. You broke that down so clearly and so quickly. This is such an important book!"
—Katie O'Reilly, Journalist, memoirist, contributor
to **atlantic.com**, *BuzzFeed,* and *Bitch*

"*The Baby Decision* is an indispensable guide to greater awareness and freedom for anyone wrestling with one of life's most important decisions. Bombardieri provides a lens that illuminates the archi-tecture of healthy decision-making. Brimming with humanity and respect, informed by research and infused with clinical wisdom, this book is a gem."
—Stephanie Morgan, MSW, Psy.D. Psychologist,
Private Practice. Co-author, *Mindfulness and*
Psychotherapy, and *Compassion and Wisdom in*
Psychotherapy.

"A perfect guidebook for any person making the life changing decision to have a child, or be childfree. Merle Bombardieri offers cogent, insightful, practical, and always deeply kind suggestions to help her readers make their own best decision with clarity, courage, and peace."

—Deborah Rozelle, Psy.D., clinical psychologist, trauma and adoption expert; co-editor and author of *Mindfulness-Oriented Interventions for Trauma: Integrating Contemplative Practices*

"This book is an invaluable tool for anyone making this enormous life decision . . . In clear and compassionate prose, *The Baby Decision* guides productive thought and discussion. Most important, it makes two things clear: first, it's OK to feel uncertain and conflicted. And second, you CAN come to a decision and move forward."

—Jenna Russell, *Boston Globe* reporter, co-author *New York Times* Bestseller, *Last Lion,* and *Long Mile Home*

"Intelligent, sensitive, and exceptionally useful support to all in the process of the conscious decision making about transition to parenthood or childfree living. A tremendous contribution!"

—Janet Surrey, Ph.D., Clinical Psychologist and Meditation Teacher specializing in Diversity, Mothering, Adoption, and Substance Abuse. Her latest book is *The Buddha's Wife: The Path of Awakening Together*

"Bombardieri is a master at teasing apart the details of the decision-making process. Her thoughtful and thorough exploration of each facet of the decision-making process—among the array of parenting options, is an invaluable resource for those contemplating parenthood, and professionals who help them work through the process."
>—Carol Sheingold, MSW, LICSW—adoption
>professional and bio-adoptive parent.

"This book offers an accessible, doable, and empathic approach for any person struggling with the *baby decision*."
>—Phyllis B. Fitzpatrick, LICSW, Private Practice,
>Former Adoption Social Worker

"This is the essential guide for any person or couple considering parenthood."
>—Kayla Sheets, Genetic Counselor, Founder of
>Vibrant Gene

Praise for the first edition of *The Baby Decision*

"I think the millions of young women turning the decision over in their heads could profit by reading it. . . . Full of sentences you'll chew over and savor. Best book on the subject."
>—Ann Ulmschneider, Childfree Advocate

"Imaginative and sensitive . . . Millions could profit from reading this book."
>—Caroline Bird, pioneering feminist economist
>and author of *The Two-Paycheck Marriage* and
>*Born Female*

THE BABY DECISION

*How to Make
The Most Important Choice
of Your Life*

SECOND EDITION, REVISED AND UPDATED

Merle Bombardieri
MSW, LICSW

ORCHARD VIEW PRESS
STOW, MASSACHUSETTS

Published by
Orchard View Press
Stow, MA 01775
www.orchardviewpress.com
Author Contact:
www.thebabydecision.com
Follow us on Twitter: @thebabydecision
Like us on Facebook: www.facebook.com/thebabydecision

Printed in the United States
First Printing, 2016

Paperback ISBN 978-0-9975007-0-7
ePub ISBN 978-0-9975007-3-8
Kindle ISBN 978-0-9975007-2-1

Edited by Andi Cumbo-Floyd
www.andilit.com
Cover and interior design by Barbara Aronica-Buck
www.bookdesigner.com

To Rocco

✦ CONTENTS ✦

✦ INTRODUCTION ✦
THE GREAT CRADLE DEBATE

Laura and Michael Rose have everything they could possibly want, or do they? She's thirty-two, a successful physical therapist who also paints. He's thirty-five, an environmental engineer and avid hiker. After eight years of marriage, Laura and Michael enjoy each other more than ever. They seem to have the perfect balance of independence and relatedness. Apart, she does yoga; he plays guitar. Together, they meditate, hike, and hang out with friends. They ski in Vermont and snorkel in the Bahamas. What more could they possibly want?

Possibly, they want a baby. But they don't know. And the question is driving them crazy.

"Why can't we decide?" asks Michael. "Are we neurotic? Selfish? Immature? Why don't we just chuck Laura's pills and let nature take its course? Maybe things were better in the old days when contraceptives weren't around. Sometimes I almost wish an 'accident' would take us off the hook."

"To make matters worse," says Laura, "we're not even consistent in our conflict. It isn't as if one of us wants a baby and the other doesn't. One minute I'll say to Michael, 'I'm just chicken. Let's throw away the pills,' and he'll say, 'But what about your work? Will you still be able to paint?' A few minutes later, Michael will say, 'I'm nuts about kids. I want to be a father.' Then I ask, 'But what about our relationship?'"

Michael wonders, "Will life still be exciting if the closest we get to Vermont is our pancake syrup? We think of our best friends who love being parents and who still practice law together. Then we think of my brother and his wife, who have a sick infant and a spoiled toddler. My sister-in-law wishes she'd never quit her executive job. One childfree friend sends us quotes about how children wreck your life. We've read books and articles about this decision, but we still don't know what to do."

Does this story strike a familiar chord? Are you and your partner, like Laura and Michael, caught up in an endless cycle of conflicting emotions and doubts? Do you spend too much time weighing pros and cons without moving forward? If so, take heart. Now you can find an answer. The baby decision need not drive you crazy. The question that tugs at you like a lead weight is actually a golden opportunity for you and your partner to grow as individuals and as a couple; to deepen your relationship; to *choose* the kind of life that will bring you both the most happiness. In fact, if you dig deeply enough, you'll find buried treasure at your feet. But you won't find this bonanza without a treasure map.

The Baby Decision is such a map. It will not only help you make a decision that's right for you but also show you how to use that decision as a springboard to greater fulfillment. It will guide you, step by step, to a decision you can live with happily.

"Why is this decision so difficult?" my clients and workshop attendees moan. Are we the wishy-washy-est people on the planet? "Wouldn't most normal, reasonable people have decided by now?"

I answer their question with a question of my own:

Do you want this job, which I am about to offer you?

Listen carefully:

If you accept it, you will have to do it for twenty years. Before you commit, you are not allowed to try it out or even meet your boss/coworker. Consequently, you may have no idea if you will like the job or the person. Nor will you know until you start it if you will love or hate it. During the three months of your apprenticeship, you will endure sleepless nights, twenty-four hour shifts, seven days a week. Sound good so far?

But wait. There's more. For this grueling job, you will not receive a salary. In fact, you have to pay tens of thousands of dollars to do it. Oh, and also there's no clause for quitting, at least not for the first eighteen years.

Are you grabbing the contract, pen in hand and pulling your partner over to the desk to sign up right away?

When, Dear Reader, you read this, are you still wondering why you and your partner can't make a decision? Do you have incurable indecisiveness? Or are you just being thoughtful and careful? This book will guide you to an answer that works for you.

You may be a little skeptical if you've read other books, posts, and articles on the topic. Perhaps they offered a little new information, but didn't get you unstuck. You and your partner may be long on talk because you're short on guidance. The available literature on the subject has focused primarily on weighing the pros and cons of parenting or measuring an individual's potential skills as a parent. Although these issues are useful and necessary, they add up to only two pieces of a larger puzzle. And because they overemphasize logic to the detriment of emotion, they're often less than helpful. This book, however, is much more comprehensive because it will fill in these five, important missing pieces:

1. How to discover secret resources for decision-making: feelings about children and life goals. Exercises designed especially for this book use fantasy, visual imagery, and other techniques to stimulate new insights.

2. How to make allies of emotion and logic. Often mistaken for enemies, emotion and logic form an amiable partnership in the best of all possible decisions. *The Baby Decision* offers steps to a rational choice based on emotional awareness.

3. How to use the new emotional awareness as a guidepost to growth. This book offers many examples of how people have grown from their decisions. It shows you how to reap similar benefits from your decision.

4. How to focus on potential happiness. I help you ask yourself, "Which choice offers me (and us) the most satisfaction?" I examine the ways that each lifestyle both helps and hinders personal and marital fulfillment.

5. How to overcome a dangerous blind spot. The "children are heaven" illusion has been replaced, in the swing of a pendulum, by a "children are hell" illusion. But who can base a wise decision on a foolish distortion? *The Baby Decision* splashes a bucket of cold reality over the new soap opera fantasy. It also challenges other illusions that prevent good decision-making.

Once you've learned how to tap into the *right* information, those seemingly fruitless discussions will yield a surprising number of insights. These insights will get you unstuck and moving toward a good decision.

Safety or Growth—It's Your Choice

The word "decide" comes from a Latin root meaning "to cut away from." Thus, decision-making, by its very nature, involves loss; we have to give up one or more options while at the same time grasping another. When we decide to have a child, we cut ourselves off from the freedom and other satisfactions of childfree living. Similarly, the decision to remain childfree means that we must give up the intimacy and joys of parenting. By *not* deciding, we hold onto the illusion that we can have it both ways—that we don't have to give up anything. Nor do we have to face the risk of discovering that we've made the wrong decision.

But we pay a price when we try to hang onto this illusion—emotional turmoil and feelings of frustration and ambivalence. And, in many instances, that price is too high. Our fears notwithstanding, when we face the issues of loss and risk squarely, we force ourselves to come to terms with our ambivalence and, in the process, we grow.

In *Toward a Psychology of Being,* the late humanistic psychologist Abraham Maslow distinguished between two kinds of motivation—growth motivation and deficiency motivation. When a person is motivated by deficiency or safety needs, he or she acts out of a desire to decrease anxiety. Any kind of change seems too risky, and therefore frightening, to undertake. On the other hand, when a person is motivated by growth needs, his or her actions reflect a desire for greater fulfillment. The risks seem less important than the possibility of improving one's life.

This distinction between growth and safety needs applies equally well to the decision-making process in general and to the baby decision in particular. There are, in fact, six possible baby decisions, three of which are growth decisions and three of which are safety decisions.

The three growth decisions are:

1. The decision to become a parent. You are taking the leap to make the best possible decision despite the lack of guarantees that you will be happy with the outcome. You have looked carefully, and despite doubt and fear, despite the attractions of remaining child-free, you are moving forward.

2. The decision to remain childfree. Like the decision to become a parent, you have found the courage to choose the life you think will be best, without guarantees. You are willing to fight against pronatalist pressure to live by your values.

3. The decision to postpone the decision but with definite goals for the postponement period and a target date for reevaluation. You are being clear-eyed and strategic. You will not let yourself drift endlessly in indecision. You set goals and plan a time to take stock. For example, "Between now and January 1st, we will see a financial planner, interview childfree and parenting friends about their lives and choices, and see doctors for basic fertility information. Once a month, we'll spend an hour on a Sunday night to take stock of our findings and feelings."

Why are these "growth decisions"? Because when you make them you:

- Take responsibility for yourself.
- Take a risk.
- Make a commitment.
- Learn something about yourself (and your partner).
- Have an opportunity to use all of the above, responsibility, risk-taking, commitment, and learning to develop and grow.

In contrast, the three safety decisions are:

1. The non-decision to have a baby (also known as the "non-accidental accident"). After perhaps five years of marriage with no previous "accidents," a couple struggling with the baby decision suddenly has an "accident." It may be unconscious (such as forget-ting to take the pill), or conscious ("Let's not bother with a condom tonight"); it may be a joint accident or the result of one partner's actions. However it happens, the result of such a non-decision (besides the baby) is that the couple is taken off the hook. They declare that nature or fate made the decision. They avoid having to answer to anybody—including themselves—for their "decision."

2. The non-decision to remain childfree. In this situation, a cou-ple tells themselves and others that they don't know whether they want children. Maybe later on, they say. So they simply drift with-out ever making a conscious commitment to the childfree lifestyle. And, in the process, they don't have to admit their desire to remain childfree or deal with disapproval from others or their own fear of regrets. They also miss the chance to be thoughtful and strategic in creating the childfree life that takes their specific needs and goals into account.

3. The non-decision to agonize. This is the antithesis of the growth decision to postpone. In the latter case, a couple postpones the decision for specified reasons and a finite period of time in order to meet specific goals. However, in this type of non-decision, a couple sets no goals; rather, they circle the issue frantically, full of doubt and confusion. Although they claim they would love nothing better than resolution, they actually get a payoff—in the form of unhealthy satisfaction generated by their painful soul-searching.

Although all three of the safety decisions appear to be emotionally cheaper in the short run, they are costlier in the long run. Non-decision-makers are bound to feel like victims rather than masters of their own fate. While they may avoid the momentary agony of making difficult choices, they are actually condemning themselves to chronic pain. By cling-ing to a safety decision, they miss an opportunity to take stock and use what they learn about themselves. We could even label safety decisions as "danger decisions" because they are detrimental to your development. If you make a non-decision, you won't have to deal with your pain directly, but you'll never really get rid of it, either.

In direct contrast, the three growth decisions allow you to get to know yourself and all your strengths and weaknesses. You may not like everything you find, but if you know what's there, at least you can make the best of it. With the help of this book you'll be able to make one of these three growth decisions—if you're willing to take the risks involved.

Hard as this decision may seem, it is undoubtedly one of the most important you'll make in your life. And it should not be made lightly, by default, or by blind adherence to custom. In fact, you're extremely lucky to be able to make a real decision about childbearing although in the midst of grappling with the issue you may feel less than fortunate. When your grandparents and great-grandparents had children, they didn't have to struggle with your dilemma. Men and women married and had children without ever making a conscious decision. It was, after all, the natural order of life, what their parents, grandparents, and great-grandparents had done. And many discovered, too late, that parenting was not as easy, natural, or rewarding as they had expected.

A talk show host once asked me whether it was a sign of sickness in our society that couples like Laura and Michael were questioning whether or not to have children. "Absolutely not," I replied. "It's very healthy for couples to decide carefully, rather than simply having children because 'that's what people do.'"

Certainly, not everyone is suited, by temperament, circumstance, or desire, to become a parent. And when couples have children without considering the issue carefully, they may find themselves trapped in a situation they did not anticipate and may not want. The result is a great deal of unhappiness for the parents, the child, and for society. Two happy, productive childfree people can contribute more to society than two unwilling parents and their unhappy child

John Stuart Mill said, "He who does anything because it is the custom makes no choice." Choice is the foundation of happiness and mental health. When we make a *conscious* decision about parenthood we can, if we so choose, embrace parenting wholeheartedly and joyfully, fully aware of all its responsibilities and ramifications. Similarly, if we *choose* to remain childfree, we can enjoy rich, productive lives without guilt or self-doubt. Only if we consider the childfree lifestyle a valid option can we be certain that a parenthood decision is a valid decision.

The decision-making process is both healthy and necessary, and there is no universal right decision. Whether you ultimately choose to become a parent or remain childfree depends entirely on the unique qualities of your personality and your relationship.

The Decision Maker's Bill of Rights

You are entitled to:

- Make a decision that is right for you and your partner.
- Take into consideration your needs, values, goals, and personality before making a decision.
- Base your decision on your potential happiness rather than a sense of obligation.
- Take time, if you need it, before making the decision.
- Be an active partner in the choice rather than acquiescing to your partner's demands.
- Make the decision that is right for you even if others disapprove.
- Put a stop to others' attempts to shame or intimidate you into making either choice.
- Be your own judge of your reasons for your choice: to be childfree without being accused of selfishness, immaturity, or neurosis; to be a parent without being accused of selfishness, immaturity, or neurosis.
- Be a parent regardless of your marital status, gender, or sexual orientation.
- Change your mind in the future, if you originally planned to have a child but now realize you don't want one; you once made a commitment to childfree living but now want to have a child.

adoption, pregnancy alternatives such a donor egg or surrogacy, or childfree living. Still other readers have no history or specific expectations of fertility problems, but because of their ages, they don't want to even consider trying for a baby without knowing something about the next steps if they have trouble. They may decide to try, but rule out strong drugs or invasive treatments. After knowing what's involved, they may want to go straight to adoption or childfree living and avoid the fertility roller-coaster altogether.

Are you undergoing fertility treatment or have you in the past? You can use this book, including Chapter 2, "Secret Doors" to clarify what appeals to you about parenthood, and in light of this, to consider which alternatives might meet your needs. For instance, if being a parent is more important to you than genetics or pregnancy, adoption could be a solution that puts an end to the stress of fertility treatment. If no alternative methods such as donor insemination or donor egg appeal to you, then the childfree choice might be an answer, even if right now, you cannot even imagine that could be a tolerable, much less satisfactory choice. While it is hard to consider the childfree choice after working so hard to have a child, it could wind up making sense later on. The bibliography includes readings that specifically address the needs of those who choose childfree after infertility, including my article, "Childfree Decision-Making" available at **www.resolve.org**. I also talk about this in the childfree section of this book.

If you are struggling with infertility, I also want to acknowledge that you may be frustrated as you read *The Baby Decision* to realize that some people who might be able to conceive or carry a pregnancy easily may choose to be childfree while your choices are more limited. Nevertheless, I have tried to structure the book in a way that may offer you healing, connection, and guidance. I hope this helps you move forward.

✦ CHAPTER 1 ✦
A BIRD'S-EYE VIEW

Even with a map in hand, exploring new territory can be frightening, especially since no map can illustrate every rock and pebble in your path. Therefore, it's helpful to scout out the territory first to get a bird's-eye view of what's to come. That's what this chapter is all about.

The questions in this chapter are those most frequently asked by couples when they first consider the baby question. And I've discovered that unless these issues are covered immediately, readers are too tense or worried to venture out. It is hard to make a decision if you don't know what to expect or how to proceed. This chapter, therefore, provides some basic and necessary guidelines: who should make the decision; how to get rid of a sense of panic; why a wrong decision won't ruin your life. After all, forewarned is forearmed. So use this chapter to gain some necessary perspective before delving into the decision-making process itself.

Is This a Woman's Decision?

"I don't want Walter to come to your workshop," Martha, a feminist client says to me. "I don't think I could discuss my feelings honestly."

"Sooner or later every *woman* faces the question of whether or not to have a baby" (emphasis mine)
—*Publisher's Weekly*

This is not a book for *women*. It is a book for people, male and female, single or coupled, gay or straight who are contemplating parenthood. A common problem for traditional male-female couples occurs when a woman assumes that she should have the biggest say in the baby decision.

Without realizing it, they may be holding onto the traditional assumption that mothering is more important than fathering—that women are necessarily more involved in parenting. And yet these women may be resentful when their partners don't assume their fair share of the child-care burdens. Shared investment in the decision paves the way for shared investment in parenting. On bad days, you don't want to hear, "This wasn't my idea." Lesbian and gay couples may run into similar conflicts if one partner is planning to be the primary parent but wants their mate to commit to sharing child care and housework.

Most single parents by choice don't decide in a vacuum either. They use trusted family or friends as sounding boards. These members of your "village" are not only useful in helping you talk through your decision, but also potential providers of physical and psychological support to you and your child. Offers to help may naturally follow if you include these people in your decision-making process. Of course, I'm not suggesting that you pretend to ask for decision-making help in hope of offers of support! (In this case, ask for help directly, and closer to the time of adoption or birth.) I am just trying to make the point that in general, it's best to include partners or other trusted helpers in your decision-making.

Even if a woman chooses to remain childfree and her partner goes along with her wish, a decision made independently still buys into the sexist notion that children "belong" to the female world in the same way that work "belongs" to the male world. In the past, when motherhood was a woman's primary source of identity and prestige, this assumption had some validity. Because most women stayed at home to care for their children while men worked, they *were* more involved in parenting. But now that women are also meeting career needs, they are becoming more aware of the difficulties of combining motherhood with a career and demanding their partner's involvement.

The importance of both members of the couple having a voice in the decision applies to gay couples, too. If one gay spouse is especially adamant about remaining childfree, the other partner, despite a willingness to grant the partner's wish, still needs to take stock of their personal decision and share that in a couple conversation. The person who would have preferred to have a child needs the other person's compassion and appreciation (see Chapter 6, "Tug-of-War".)

How to Get Your Hand Off the Panic Button

Because this issue often generates a lot of anxiety and tension, many couples make their decision about having a child prematurely simply because a decision—any decision—relieves their sense of panic. But hasty decisions are not always good decisions. The calmer you are, the better the chance that you will make the right choice. So give yourself time to read, relax, and daydream. The following guidelines may help.

1. Ask yourself why you're in such a hurry to decide. Do any of these statements strike a chord?

- You can't stand uncertainty about your future. Or you can't stand your own inner conflict. In either case, you feel desperate to decide quickly to end your discomfort.
- Based on your age, you're afraid that if you don't start trying immediately you may never get pregnant.
- Because panic is a catchable "disease," you have become infected with your friends' sense of urgency.
- You're leaning toward the childfree choice, and you're afraid that if you don't decide now, you'll change your mind and be sorry later.
- You're leaning toward parenthood, and you're afraid you'll have trouble getting pregnant. Even though you are not yet sure that a baby is the best choice, you won't relax until you get a positive slip from a lab.

- You know what you want. Your partner seems open to your choice but is wavering. You want to finalize the decision before your partner considers reversing it.

2. Jump off the "must-decide-today" treadmill. All these pressures stem from your feelings, not from the facts. It's not a biological time bomb but an emotional time bomb that is threatening to explode within you. Keep reminding yourself that you *don't have to decide now*. Even if you're in your late thirties, you can probably still have a baby.

3. Give yourself permission to be anxious. "Anxiety tells you that something important is about to happen," says Dr. Glenn Larson, a clinical psychologist in private practice in Nashville, TN. Of course you are anxious. You are making one of the most important decisions of your life. Anxiety indicates that you're taking the process seriously. In fact, moderate anxiety can be useful because it encourages you to work on the decision. It's only extreme anxiety that gets in the way, and you can reduce your anxiety level.

4. Turn your anxiety into excitement. Excitement is the flip side of anxiety. Instead of trying to escape it, try to get closer. Is there a part of you that is stirred by the baby question? A part of you that is eager to learn more about yourself and to put these bits of knowledge to work for you? A part that's curious to know what the final decision will be? Try to imagine how good you will feel when you have made the decision. Visualize the joy of having a child or living creatively without children.

5. Give yourself permission to be uncertain. In the name of no-nonsense decisiveness, a lot of nonsense is committed. You will have to live with the consequences of your decision for the rest of your life, so it's reasonable to take as much time as you need for decision-making. It's fine to make a quick decision about buying a car or taking a job. You can always decide just as quickly to sell or quit, but a baby decision can't be reversed. The amount of attention given a decision should be in proportion to the seriousness of its consequences.

6. Try to keep your sense of humor. A light touch is always helpful when you're facing a heavy question.

- Ed and Mary, who collect antique glass, joke about whether they'll be buying old lady's bottles or new baby's bottles next year.
- Cathy and Steve laugh at the idea of themselves rocking by the fire in their 60s and still debating whether they want a child.

Spending time with friends who are also tossing around the decision may help you lighten up.

7. Tell yourself that you will make a good decision. Shut off that raspy voice that says you are going to blow it and live with regret for the rest of your life. If you think through your decision carefully, you will be relatively satisfied with your choice. Rest assured that your intelligence, imagination, and courage will lead you to a good decision. And knowing that you will have some regrets – no matter what – may quiet the voice.

8. Don't compare yourself to other couples who decided quickly. They may have decided prematurely, or they may have made a poor decision. And even if they claim to have decided in a matter of days or even on one special night, if it's a good decision, they probably worked on it for weeks, months, or years. Perhaps they didn't have constant discussions, but in the backs of their minds, they had probably been considering the question for a long time.

Deciding Under Emergency Circumstances

In some cases, of course, a sense of panic is generated by more than emotional pressure. There are two circumstances in which a decision *is* a genuine emergency:

1. You have an unplanned pregnancy, and you have to decide whether to continue it.

2. You have an illness or a condition that is worsening, and your doctor tells you that with each month you wait: (a) your chance of conceiving lessens; (b) the probability increases of having surgery that would compromise your fertility; (c) the likelihood of serious

complications arising from a pregnancy increases; or (d) your health may be threatened by the delay in treatment.

If either of these situations applies to you, try to keep your wits about you. You'll make a wiser decision if you're calm. Even though you have to decide quickly, *you don't have to decide in the next five minutes.* Don't give in to the temptation to pick a decision, any decision, just to end the crisis. Taking a day or two could mean the difference between a desperate guess and wise choice.

You may not have several months, but you certainly do have a few days or maybe even a week or two to think things over. You (and your partner) may want to take time off from work to allow yourself time and energy for decision-making. As a preliminary step, try fighting off feelings of panic by meditating, deep breathing, running, swimming, or doing whatever exercise or activity helps you relax. Then, take the time to do the exercises in this book. They will help you uncover your deepest feelings about children. They'll also help you consider the compatibility of children with your other goals and values.

In the case of a medical problem:

- **Ask your physician to give you a full explanation of your condition, how it impinges on your childbearing potential, and the risks involved in delaying motherhood.**
- **Read lay literature on your condition. Take into consideration the source of the information.** Is it from a vetted website such as The Mayo Clinic or The American Society for Reproductive Medicine (ASRM)? Be wary of sources funded by pharmaceutical or medical device companies or blogs, which may include misinformation.
- **Get a second opinion.** Does the consultant also consider the decision an emergency? Are there other possibilities, contingencies, or treatments your doctor didn't mention that may make sense to try before undergoing the intervention recomended by your doctor?

Finally, whether your problem is an unplanned pregnancy or a medical condition, consider counseling to help you make your decision. If the first person you consult is not understanding and unbiased, seek out another counselor. (See Chapter 12, "Help!" and the Resources section in the Appendix for suggestions on finding help.)

How Long Is Too Long?

For some couples, however, haste isn't the problem. They've given themselves plenty of time to make a decision, but the right choice continues to elude them. If this problem sounds familiar, you may be wondering if it's possible to spend too much time on your decision. Ask yourself another question: "How do I feel?" Do you feel that you are using the time constructively, growing, and moving slowly but surely toward resolution? Can you and your partner tell each other, "Even if we don't know or don't agree, at least we're sharing something important with each other"? If your feelings are generally positive, don't worry. Quality of thinking, not speed, is what counts most in decision-making.

However, if you feel that you're caught on a treadmill, getting angrier and more frustrated, caught in a non-decision to agonize, then you're probably not using the time wisely or well. The same applies if you never talk about the decision and even find excuses not to talk at arranged times.

Will the Wrong Decision Ruin Your Life?

This question is often uppermost in many potential parents' minds. My answer: probably not, for two reasons:

1. How you make your decision and how you apply it to your life may be as important to your future happiness as the decision itself.

Let's look at two couples:

decision you make, a part of you will enjoy the outcome. And you can use the objections to help you steer clear of possible pitfalls.

Actually, no matter which decision you make, you'll probably have some regrets. But that isn't so terrible. Coming to accept the imperfection of life and making the best of it is a wonderful way to grow. It will help you cope with other issues that you're ambivalent about, too.

By now, you may be wondering why this decision requires so much care if a wrong choice won't ruin your life. Even though you can probably live a good life with or without children, it's definitely to your advantage to make an informed, thoughtful decision. Here's why:

- **It offers the opportunity to learn about yourself and your partner.** In order to answer the baby question successfully, you must also answer two other questions: "Who am I?" and if you have a partner, "Who are we?" And these answers can help you solve other problems.

- **It forces you to take responsibility for yourself.** By making a conscious decision, you take control of your life. Even though you risk failure or regret, you earn self-respect. You cannot help but take pride in assuming responsibility for yourself rather than drifting passively, waiting for an accident or your partner's preferences to take you off the hook.

- **It increases the probability that you will enjoy and make the most of your choice.** Working on a conscious choice forces you to consider carefully the possibilities offered by each lifestyle. This gives you a head start in taking advantage of your ultimate choice.

- **It provides an opportunity to build skills for future decision-making of all kinds.** Technological advances and changing societal mores mean that in the future you will have other big decisions. Making a good baby decision is good practice for future decisions.

Anxiety-Proof Yourself

If you are still anxious about the baby question, try this fantasy exercise before you delve any further into the decision-making process. Ask yourself: what is the worst thing that could happen in this situation? Pinpointing potential problems or disasters and recognizing your ability to cope with them is an effective way to reduce anxiety. And you can put the mental energy previously wasted worrying to more productive use.

1. Imagine that you and your partner decide to remain childfree. What's the worst thing that could result from this decision? How would you feel about it? What would you do about it?

> Susan and Mark tried this exercise. For both, the ultimate horror was the idea of facing a lonely old age full of sadness that they wouldn't live on through their grandchildren. They imagined they might be disappointed about missing parenthood, but realized they could find comfort in their artistic, athletic, and professional activities and in loving relationships with their nieces and nephews.

2. Imagine you decide to have a child. What's the worst thing that could happen? Try to picture it, as well as your reaction to it. What would you do about it?

> In this situation, Susan imagined that her career was ruined, filling her with anger and resentment at the baby and at Mark. Mark imagined that he and Susan wouldn't have any time together anymore and that their relationship would go downhill. They agreed that Susan's fantasy wouldn't happen because Mark would take equal responsibility for the baby if they had one. To deal with Mark's fears, they talked about ways in which their friends had managed to maintain good relationships while their children were young. These fantasies helped Mark and Susan feel a lot freer to explore both possibilities. Now, you try them.

STEP TWO

✦

Overcoming Obstacles

✦ CHAPTER 2 ✦
SECRET DOORS

How well do you know yourself? Are you in touch with the myriad emotions, beliefs, and attitudes that shape your personality, your life, and your choices?

All of us have an inner core—a reservoir of private dreams and goals—that has been building and changing since we were small children. But all too often, this inner core gets locked away in a back closet in our minds, in part, because our hectic lives don't permit leisurely introspection. In addition, many of us bury these thoughts and emotions because they are painful to acknowledge. We might be forced, if we took a good look at them, to accept unpleasant truths, give up cherished dreams, or work on unfinished business.

But how can we know what to choose if we don't know who we are? Because our inner life changes as we mature, we have to be able to separate old dreams from new ones, letting go of the parts of ourselves that are outdated or unrealistic. Otherwise, these unacknowledged emotions can hopelessly tangle our thinking process.

For example, Joan, a woman in her late twenties, couldn't seem to make a commitment to the childfree lifestyle and couldn't understand why. She didn't really like children, and she loved her work. She wanted, more than anything else, the time and freedom to pursue her career. On the surface, her decision seemed obvious, yet she felt conflicted in some way. With the help of self-exploration exercises, the reason came to light. Joan had been raised in a home that assumed that mothering was not an elective but a required course. When she was growing up, a girl's upbringing was synonymous with preparation for motherhood. Joan had learned her lesson so well that despite her total distaste for parenting and her husband's comfort with remaining childfree she could never quite bring herself to make a decision. Through careful thought and implementation of intentional exercises, she came to understand that this long-held image of exalted motherhood was holding her back. Even though she wanted to remain childfree, a part of her hung on to the old belief that she would someday find happiness in motherhood or that she couldn't be a complete woman or grownup if she didn't have a child. As soon as she held this flawed childhood belief up to the light, she was able to toss it and move on.

It's time for you to take the same journey that Joan did. You're going to open the door to your mind's hidden library. These exercises will help you draw out forgotten or hidden feelings and attitudes about yourself, your marriage, children, parenthood, and your life goals. You will be able to discard old beliefs that may be blocking you and track down and study the feelings and values that will shape your decision. With this knowledge, you can begin to lay the foundation for a satisfying life—a life that encompasses the goals and dreams that match your current self.

Inner Conflict

A. Chair Dialogue

When you're torn between conflicting desires—wanting a child and wanting to remain childfree—a conversation between these two parts of you can help you better understand the nature of your conflict. You may even discover that one desire is much stronger than the other.

To begin, place two chairs face to face, and label one "I want to be a parent" and the other "I want to be childfree." Sit in the parent chair, and tell the childfree part of you why you want a baby. Then, switch to the childfree chair, and tell the parent chair why you don't want one. Continue this dialogue, changing chairs whenever each side is ready to talk. To ensure total honesty, do this exercise alone; otherwise you might feel too inhibited to express all your feelings— both the positive *and* the negative.

To make this exercise as helpful as possible, don't let the voices be polite or intellectual. Be argumentative, even rude. You want to separate the two voices enough to be able to listen to and distinguish each voice from the other.

Here is an example of one young woman's dialogue. (PC = parent chair; CC = childfree chair)

PC: I think I would miss something if I never had a child.

CC: But I don't think I'm willing to make the sacrifices I'd have to make for a child.

PC: But wouldn't it be worth it for the pleasure of seeing a child grow and change?

CC: It looks to me like 90 percent pain for 10 percent pleasure. It isn't worth it.

PC: You're just selfish. Grow up.

CC: No! I'm looking out for what's best for both of us. My career as a systems analyst doesn't leave much time for a child. I don't want to give up my work, and I don't want to be overburdened, either. I don't think I would enjoy being a mother. I think Tom [her husband] and the baby would suffer as much as I would.

This woman was surprised at the strength of her childfree side. And as she continued the dialogue, her parent side became even weaker. Finally, in desperation, the parent side asked:

PC: I thought you and I were about even. How could you be so much stronger than I realized?

CC: Because you have never listened to me. Every time I tell you I don't want to be a mother, you ignore me.

PC: Why would I ignore you?

CC: Because Tom and my parents are dying for a baby. Because all my friends tell me what a good mother I'll make. You are more interested in pleasing others than you are in pleasing me.

Now, try the dialogue yourself. What happened?

- Was one side stronger than the other?
- Were you surprised by some of the feelings you expressed?
- Did you have different bodily sensations in the different chairs? Some people describe this observation as "a felt sense" of relief, fear, truth, or authenticity.
- Did you sound or feel different in the different chairs?
- Did you have trouble speaking for both sides? If so, this does not necessarily mean you have no opposing voice. It may mean you're afraid to face the other side, afraid of being persuaded by the other choice. Or you may not want to realize what you will lose with either choice.

Try this exercise again in a few days or weeks. You may discover that different sides are stronger on different days. Coming back to the exercise periodically is somewhat like using a compass—it helps chart your direction and keep you on course.

Moreover, this technique, based on Gestalt therapy, can be used in many other ways. For example:

- You can play yourself in one chair and take someone else's part—your partner, your mother, a friend—in the other chair.
- You can play two other people and leave yourself out entirely. For instance, put your mother in one chair and your father in the other, and have them discuss their hopes for grandchildren.

These two variations can help you understand why family and friends may be pressuring you. And that understanding may improve your ability to cope with the pressures.

- You can bring in another "actor." For instance, if you and your partner disagree on the issue, play each other's role to see if you're both really listening to each other's arguments. Or invite your partner to observe you playing both roles. Then, ask him or her if the portrayal was accurate. Then, reverse the process, watching and giving feedback to your partner.

Please don't try to sweep the thoughts of the weaker voice under the rug. That voice is a goldmine of information. It will give you all the clues you need to make the most of the other choice. Use that voice's objections and worries as guidelines for preparing for your choice and minimizing the sacrifices the choice requires.

Looking Back

The next exercise focuses on attitudes about children and parenthood that you learned in childhood. Even though you may not have been conscious of them lately, they may be tipping your decision-making scale.

A. Yucky Babies

Did you ever see the *Saturday Evening Post* cover by Norman Rockwell called "Home Duty"? It shows a boy wearing a suit and a frown as he pushes his baby sister in her carriage. Two friends in baseball uniforms smirk at him as they go off to play. The message: babies are a booby prize to avoid at all costs. If you're clever, you won't get stuck with baby care. And caring for babies is the opposite of having fun and an indignity to any red-blooded American male.

Even though there are no girls in the picture, the idea of babies as disgusting, and of obstacles to fun is one that women also relate to.

- **Do you remember thinking babies were "yucky"?** Where did you get that attitude? Were you repulsed by smelly diapers, spit-ups, and tears?
- **Did you have younger siblings?** How did you and your parents respond to those pregnancies and births? How did your sibling change your life? If you had more than one younger sibling, did you respond differently to each one? How did these experiences color your view of children?
- **Guys, were you ever called "sissy" for playing with a baby or a doll?** Who said this? How did you react?

- **Did you ever babysit for younger siblings or other children?**
  Was it fun or frustrating? Did you like children more or less as
  a result? Did you find some children more fun than others? Do
  you remember what you liked or disliked about them?
- **Do you still feel that babies are yucky?** If not, what made you
  change your mind?
- **Visualize returning to your childhood home.** Play with the dolls
  or stuffed animals you find there. Try to re-create the fantasies
  you had of growing up and becoming a parent, if any. If you
  or your parents still have some of these baby toys in an attic or
  closet, try to get your hands on them. Actually holding them
  may call forth some powerful memories and feelings.

Body Talk

A. Metamorphosis

Women, close your eyes and picture yourself:

- During early, middle, and late pregnancy
- During childbirth

Do these changes attract or repel you? Which, if any, attract?
Which, if any, repel?

- Does fear of childbirth pain affect your desire to get pregnant?
- Are you terrified by the possibility of gaining weight, feeling fat,
  or not being able to lose weight afterwards?
- Do you think pregnancy would make you feel sexier, less sexy,
  or the same? How do you think your partner would react to
  your changed body? Do you worry about whether he'd still be
  attracted to you?

If you won't be carrying a child, imagine these changes in your partner:

- How do you think you would react? Would you find her more attractive, less attractive, or the same? How do you think she would feel about her new body?
- How do both of you picture your sex life during pregnancy and postpartum?
- Do you feel positive about some body changes but negative about others? Which ones feel positive, and which negative?
- Many people who consider themselves sexually sophisticated, somehow feel embarrassed about pregnancy. Do you? Pregnant women sometimes complain, "Now the whole world knows I have a sex life. My private life has gone public." Would you feel this way, too?

B. Suckling

Women, imagine yourself nursing a baby.

- How does it feel?
- Is it erotic, as some women describe it?
- How does your husband react? How do you react to his reaction?

Now open your eyes and consider these questions: would you breastfeed if you had a baby? Why or why not?

Or imagine your partner nursing your baby. You're sitting beside them.

- How do you feel?
- Proud, turned on, jealous?
- Does she seem to be enjoying nursing? Why or why not?

Now open your eyes and consider these questions: would you want your partner to nurse if you had a child?

Both partners ask yourself some questions:

- Who do you know who has nursed or bottle fed? What comments have they made about their experiences? Has this made you more or less attracted to pregnancy or nursing?
- You are probably aware that there are medical reasons and social pressures urging you to nurse. Does this bother you?

C. Madonna

It's not always easy for a woman to separate a desire for the experience of pregnancy and birth from a desire for the experience of parenting for its own sake. These different wishes are like intertwined threads of two hard-to-distinguish colors. The exercises below will help you separate the two strands. Also, be aware that if parenting is more important to you than pregnancy or having a biological child, adoption might be satisfactory.

Imagine that you could get pregnant, give birth, nurse a baby, and receive lots of love, attention, and praise for doing so. Then, when you stopped nursing at say, six months, you could just hand the child over to someone else to raise for eighteen years. You could be a favorite friend, godmother, or auntie seeing the child when you wanted to but would be under no obligation. Sound good?

Taylor, like so many other women I've encountered, was in love with the idea of motherhood but would have hated the reality. A lover of novelty, she craved the pregnancy process but not the product. When she and her partner decided to be childfree, she was surprised by her sadness. What was up? She knew the decision made sense.

When she visited a friend who was nursing a three-month old, she burst into tears. She realized that she needed to let go of the physical experiences she would miss. Once she acknowledged this, she could get on with her childfree life.

In contrast, while finding this fantasy somewhat appealing, Sonya realized when she did this exercise, that she would not want to turn her child over to someone else when the physical experiences faded away. She wanted to be with the imagined child through every stage

ambiguous, but traceable to a woman's negative feelings about her pregnancy. *Such dreams are completely normal.* Don't interpret these as neurotic. Nor are they a tell-tale sign that you should not have a child. They simply show a healthy unconscious mind hard at work, adjusting to an uncomfortable body and making way for the baby.

Waking fantasies of baby-as-monster can also be healthy and helpful when applied to the baby decision.

Let your monster appear. What does it look like? What does it do to you? What do you do in return? How do you feel about it? Do you want to abandon it as Dr. Frankenstein abandoned his creation? Do you want to run screaming like a heroine in an old horror movie?

Is there anything cute or charming about the monster? Can you imagine how you might tame it?

The monster you imagine may symbolize your particular fears of parenthood. If you fear the baby would drain your energy, you might envision a vampire. If you're a passionate traveler, you might imagine a large-bellied creature chomping on your airplane tickets. A monster fantasy may also raise the age-old fear that we are somehow being punished for past "sins." The monster we give birth to in our dreams may have something to do with how we feel about the monstrous parts of ourselves.

Women seem to have more monster fantasies and take them more personally than men. A woman seems to think, "If a monster came out of my body that would make me a monster, too." Even a normal pregnancy is an invasion of the body that seems monstrous at times. A woman's organs are literally pushed out of place to make way for baby.

At the most basic level, monster fantasies are linked to the normal fear that the impending child will be less than perfect—disabled or deformed in some way. While such babies are entitled to the same dignity and esteem accorded to all human beings, society tends to stigmatize them. While compassion and inclusion of special-needs children is improving, we have a long way to go to provide the respect, caring, and services needed.

Of course you want a healthy child and are terrified of having one that is not. First of all, the statistical odds are in your favor. But you can ease the fear by doing everything possible to assure the birth of a healthy baby. Don't hesitate to take advantage of the various sophisticated medical procedures available. If you're thirty-five or older, have testing done to check for problems. If there are inherited diseases in your family history, seek genetic counseling. See Appendix 3, "Preparing for a Healthy Pregnancy," written by Kayla Sheets of Vibrant Gene, a genetic counselor in Boston.

E. The Wrong Sex

Phil wants a son with whom he can play football on Saturdays. Kathleen, a feminist, wants a daughter to raise as she wishes her mother had raised her.

Do you want a boy or a girl more than a *child?* What are your fantasies about that boy or girl? What would you do if your child turned out to be the "wrong" sex? Or suppose your longed-for son hates sports and wants to spend his Saturdays reading? Suppose the hoped-for feisty feminist in overalls begs for frilly dresses and dolls. Do you think you would be able to love and accept this child? Can you think about what you might enjoy about a child of the opposite sex?

Values

The following set of exercises is designed to help you identify some of the things you value most in life and to consider how those priorities relate to parenthood.

A. Epitaph

Whenever we think about birth, on some level we are also thinking about death. We may look to children as a way of assuring our immortality. Close your eyes and imagine the events immediately following your death:

- What would you like your tombstone to say? Your obituary?
- Who will mourn your death?
- What will you be remembered for?
- What product or contribution do you want to leave behind?

Do the exercise twice, once imagining that you had children, the second time imagining that you remained childfree.

How did the two fantasies differ? Did you prefer one scenario to the other? Why?

Even if you have a child, you still have a chance to contribute more than your genes to future generations. And if you never have a child, should you wish, you'll have many chances to enjoy and influence other people's children.

B. Surprise!

You have just discovered that you are pregnant (or that your partner is). It is unplanned.

- How do you react to the news? Do you feel both excitement and dread? Do you feel trapped?
- Will you have the baby or terminate the pregnancy? Why?
- Are you at all relieved that the "accident" made the decision for you?
- Are you ever tempted to have an "accident"? Why? Could this save you from having to make a conscious decision?

C. Knapsack

"What will I have to give up?" is one of the scariest questions that decision-makers ask.

Imagine that you are beginning the long journey that is parenthood. Take your baby and put her in your knapsack. Now imagine that she kicks a hole in the knapsack and other objects in the sack begin to fall out.

- What falls out?
- How do you react?
- Must you leave the objects behind or can you carry them with you, however awkwardly?
- If you leave them behind, will you be able to come back and get them later? Why or why not?

Scott saw the following slip away: freedom, peace and quiet, time for his band rehearsals and, worst of all, his wife Emily's happiness. He wanted to take the baby out of the pack and tuck everything else firmly back in.

Karen saw her independence, her solitude, and a piece of her career slip away. She tried to pick these things up by thinking about child-care arrangements, about her husband's cooperation, about what kind of work she could do during the quiet time when the child was in bed. A key question was whether her husband Rich would put in enough child-care time to allow her work time and quiet time.

Jack and Leila watched their expensive Bahamas vacations and their spotlessly clean home disappear. But they thought it was time for a change. Been there, done that. But they had never been parents. The fat pink leg sticking out was so cute that they realized they probably could adjust to camping vacations and toys in the living room.

If you, like Scott and Emily, feel that you're losing all the things you value, more or less permanently, and you don't find the replacement—a child—very appealing, you're getting some strong indications that parenthood is not for you. If, on the other hand, you're upset about these losses but are attracted to the creature who has dropped in, you can explore ways of rearranging or lightening the load. Remember, you don't have to pick up all the pieces immediately. You can retrieve some later, and you might discover that some aren't as important as you thought they were.

Katie Wilson, a Washington, D.C.-based health professional who decided to be childfree after attending my workshop, shared a brilliant insight about one of the benefits of being childfree: "You get to do some of the fun stuff earlier, almost like you're skipping a few grades. We have the freedom to do things that parents have to post-pone till they're empty nesters." Not only isn't Katie losing the good things in the knapsack; she and her husband are also adding to it.

D. Passed Up

This exercise helps you consider career sacrifices that parent-hood may demand.

Imagine that a colleague moves ahead of you in some way simply because you can't work as hard now that you're involved with your child. Perhaps he or she is promoted first even though you are more qualified. How would you feel about this? How would you react?

- Josh decided that having a child and assuming half the respon-sibility for its care was more important than being an all-star at work. His work and salary were already satisfactory, and he was ready for a family.
- Kristin couldn't stand the thought of falling behind on the career ladder. And fall she would if she became a mother because her husband wanted a child only if she agreed to take full responsibility for it.

Although parents of young children aren't necessarily confined to baby steps on the career ladder, they typically won't be able to take as many giant steps as their childfree colleagues. If you, like Kristin, can't tolerate the thought of pint-sized obstacles to your advance-ment, you're not likely to enjoy parenthood.

E. Moment of Truth

- Imagine that you are at a critical point in your career. Your gynecologist tells you that it's now or never for motherhood. You have a condition that will make pregnancy impossible by the end of this year. What would you do?
- For partners: What would you want her to do? Would you

encourage her to get pregnant now even though her career may suffer? (If you actually find yourself in such a situation, learn how to handle emergency decisions in Chapter 1, "A Bird's-Eye View.")

F. Bad News

How would you and your partner feel if you found out that there was an infertility problem? How would this change your thoughts about the future? Might you feel a little wistful or even angry?

- If you're leaning toward parenthood, would you consider infertility treatment or adoption?
- If you're leaning toward remaining childfree, do you think you'd regret the loss of this option, even though it's an option you'd probably never exercise?

G. Making Connections

Imagine that five years from now you lose your partner through death or divorce. If you were single again, would you rather be a parent or childfree?

Some single or widowed parents find their children a source of comfort, a means through which they can relate to the outside world. In the case of widowhood, the child can be a way of staying close to the lost partner. Others find single parenthood a burden that drains their financial resources and cuts into their social life, privacy, and quiet time.

Unless you're on the verge of being divorced or widowed, you should not base the baby decision on this possibility. You should assume that you and your partner will be together until proven otherwise. However, this exercise helps you with values clarification.

Timetables

A sensible baby decision requires a good sense of time. Wanting a baby now may be incompatible with starting a graduate program in September. Or combining career and motherhood may seem doable until you open your datebook and ask what would have to come out or be postponed if you had a child.

Here are some tools to give you a time frame for decision-making.

A. Countdown

How many hours a week do you spend on:

- Work
- Recreation and socializing with family and friends
- Hobbies
- Down-time: staring into space, petting the cat, or hanging out with your partner in front of the TV
- Relaxation, yoga, meditation
- Sports, exercise
- Political activity
- Religious or spiritual activities
- Time alone with your partner
- Sleep

How many hours a week do you think parenthood would require? How would your schedule change if you had a baby?

Your best source of information is probably some friends who have a one- or-two-year-old. Ask them for a breakdown of their week. If you are not sure whether or how much you will work if you have a child, you might want to check-in with friends who work full or part-time as well as one who is home full-time.

- Which activities might you cut out altogether?
- Would some activities be possible at home when your child is

asleep or playing? Might it be possible to bring the baby along to some activities?

- Can you think of substitute activities that would accommodate a child more easily? For instance, you can't swim with a baby on your back, but you can jog with a baby in a stroller.
- Are you willing to change your schedule?
- If the prospect of any change is repugnant, what appeals to you about parenthood enough to make you consider a baby?

As you plan, keep in mind that parents of young children sacrifice more weekend time than evening time. Of course, in the first few months, you will be too tired to use that evening time! You can pursue some of your favorite activities while a child is asleep, but on weekends and during the day, a child requires constant attention.

B. Life Cycle

In addition to the baby question, what else do you anticipate doing or having in your life? What would you like your life to be like, not just in the next few years, but through the whole cycle from now to midlife to retirement, aging? In five years, ten years, twenty years, forty years? What do you want to experience in addition to, or instead of parenting?

You might consider your current job, a career change, travel or living in another country, volunteer causes, sports or artistic pursuits. These activities may be something you did before you got bogged down with your career, something you've never done before, or something you do now, say hiking, that you would like to do more in the future.

Let's say you became a parent two years from now. If you had a child, how would your child's stages, e.g., infancy, pre-school, elementary school dovetail with your other goals and interests? For instance, if in five years you want to be focusing on parenting, then your three-year old's preschool stage would be a good fit. On the other hand, if you plan to do archeology in a third-world country, that might be a challenge for keeping your child safe.

How would a child's development coincide with the different stages

- Would you have to move in order to get more space, more playmates, a safer neighborhood, or better schools? Could you afford to move?
- Are there any parallels between the physical changes parenthood would require in your home and the psychological changes it would require in your life?
- Ed envisioned his house as terribly cramped after a baby's arrival. He and Marcia also felt a baby would cramp their lifestyle of eating out and traveling spontaneously.
- Randy and Carolyn, in contrast, have always viewed their unfurnished spare room as a future nursery. They enjoyed picturing that room filled with brightly colored furniture and toys and thought a baby would fill a void in their otherwise enjoyable existence.

It may be helpful, if you're a confirmed city dweller, to realize that parenthood doesn't necessarily mean being sentenced to suburbia. If you were to choose parenthood, perhaps you could convert an attic or den into a nursery. Or you might consider moving to a less glamorous neighborhood that offered more space for your money.

These individual exercises have given you a chance to take stock of your feelings about parenthood, to make the possibilities of parenthood or a childfree life less abstract and more real. For instance, if your throat went dry and your eyes filled when you thought about not having a child, that's a deeper response than you get from making a list of the pros and cons of parenthood.

Couples Exercises

Now that you've taken a good look at yourself, it's time to turn that same discerning eye toward your partner and your relationship. Do you have a clear understanding of one another's attitudes and feelings about this issue? Are you in total agreement, total disagreement, or somewhere in between? Have your discussions to date brought you closer together or driven you farther apart?

The next few exercises may start some meaningful conversations.

A. *Ring of Power*

Couples establish their own style of communicating and decision-making. Over the years, that style becomes a habit, and even when it's no longer effective, partners may not be willing or able to examine or change it. If you and your loved one are stymied about the baby question, perhaps it's time to take a good hard look at *your* style.

How do the two of you make other important decisions?

- Each person has equal weight; the couple decides together.
- Whoever feels more strongly about the issue makes the decision.
- One partner usually makes the decisions about salary and money; the other makes the decisions about house and family.
- One partner usually makes most of the decisions, and the other, while challenging the choices, eventually agrees.

Are you both still satisfied with your decision-making style? Will it work for this particular decision? If not, why? Asking the power question may be scary, but answering it may be necessary before you can go on to the baby question.

This is an important question for three reasons. The first is that you will want to make sure that both of you have your full say in the decision. The second is that if you or your partner is unhappy with the balance of power, that balance is something worth changing regardless of the choice you make. Sharing the power is an important ingredient in most good relationships. Third, it's important to talk about how you will share responsibilities and decisions if you decide to have a child. For instance, if one of you believes in discipline and the other is laissez-faire, how would you work this out? If a woman wants to be the major decision-maker in her child's life but her partner wants an equal voice, you would need to have a fair way of resolving this.

For most couples, power in general, and decision-making power in particular, is extremely resistant to change. It will be easier to work on this with a professional therapist than on your own.

B. "Are You the Person I Married?"

In view of all the uncertainty in modern life, most of us like to feel that we can count on our partners to honor their commitments. When we marry, we sincerely believe the promises we make to our beloved. But as we grow older and learn more about ourselves, we may change our minds. On minor issues, this generally isn't a problem, but on major issues, like the baby question, a sudden reversal can result in a major crisis. Partners are understandably furious when mates who agreed with them on the baby issue years ago change their minds. And they're quite likely to feel guilty if they're the ones whose mind changed.

Take a moment now to recall some of the talks you had before you got married. Did you and your partner discuss children? Did you agree or disagree? Have either of you changed your mind since then?

If there has been a change, try not to be too hard on yourself or your partner. Although you may be tempted to hurl accusations at one another, bear in mind that life decisions must reflect your situation and frame of mind *at that moment*. A decision made at age twenty-five simply may not be the right decision at thirty or thirty-five. Don't waste your time blaming each other. Sit down together and try to figure out how the change came about. Has either of you gotten to know yourself better, discovered your deep inner feelings about children, or come to see alternatives that seemed impossible years ago?

Also, keep in mind that there are varying shades of disagreement. A partner who agreed to have three children and now won't even consider one is obviously different from the partner who in the past made the same agreement but now asks, "What about having just one?" This is not as drastic a change as, "I want to be childfree."

Even if your partner's current position has changed drastically, don't panic. Try to get the whole story. Then you won't waste your breath trying to talk your partner out of something he or she is only tentatively bringing up. And even if your partner's new position is hard to take, you will have to give it a fighting chance as you work on your decision. (See Chapter 6, "Tug of War" for advice for negotiating.)

C. Fifty-Fifty

Even when couples work on the decision together, women often seem to feel more strongly about it. Maybe this is because a woman assumes that a baby will change her life more than her husband's. Even in egalitarian marriages in which the couple previously split chores fifty-fifty, the woman usually puts more time and energy into parenthood than her husband does. For instance, a mother more often winds up arranging for child care and tending to a sick child. Sociologist Arlie Hochschild called this "The Second Shift" in her book of that title originally published in 1989. Unfortunately, her most recent studies reported, in her 2012 book of the same title, that this is still the case. This can happen for many reasons, but here are two common ones: Before the baby, both men and women usually work full-time, but after the baby, the man, whose salary is often higher, works more hours and spends less time at home. Another reason this happens is that if you grew up in a home with a breadwinner father and a child-rearing mother, both of you may unconsciously slip into these traditional roles once you become parents.

Close your eyes and imagine how your workloads might change if you had a baby. Could one or both of you trim some time off your workweek? If one of you stayed home, how would that affect your relationship? If neither of you can gear down, how will you manage the new workload at home? Would one of you be more interested in having a child if your partner seemed more willing to actively participate in child care?

Don't make the mistake of saying, "We'll deal with this *after* the baby comes," because it's possible that the baby shouldn't come at all if your expectations of each other are in conflict. If you are confident you want to have a child together but your horns are locked, see a psychotherapist or counselor for help to make a plan you can live with.

D. Family Sculpture

Here, you and your partner will each have a turn at creating a "living" sculpture—your own portrayal of life as a childfree couple and as parents. It's your chance to be an artist, and the only "materials" you'll need are yourself, your partner, and a doll or a small rolled-up blanket. When it's your turn, place your loved one, yourself, and the doll anywhere you like in the room to express your view of your family. You can also bring in additional props to complete the sculpture if you wish.

- To depict the childfree choice, Pam placed herself on the sofa with her husband Dale in a relaxed, cuddly embrace. To depict the parenting lifestyle, she placed herself and Dale in separate chairs with their backs to each other, the doll naked and forlorn on the floor between them.
- To make his childfree sculpture, Stan pushed back all the furniture to create a feeling of emptiness. He placed himself and Gloria in the middle of the empty room, each slouching down. For the parenting sculpture, he brought Gloria to a neighbor child's brightly colored bedroom. Gloria, the doll, and he were all on the floor, grinning as they rolled a ball to each other.

Although you can fantasize the sculpture, actually arranging it is even more effective. Even if you and your partner seem to be headed in the same direction, your sculptures are bound to be different. Discussion of these differences may be helpful, especially if you can tell your partner how it felt to be part of all four sculptures.

You could also try to make an "indecision" sculpture. Divide a room in half by laying down a tape measure. Let each half of the room delineate one of the choices. Try placing one foot on each side of the line and notice any thoughts or feelings. What happens if you put both feet on the childfree side? If you put both on the child's side? Is there a side that feels more balanced?

These couple exercises will probably spark some interesting discussions. For instance, if your sculptures showed completely different guesses about what your relationship would be like as a childfree or parenting couple, tell each other about the experiences or knowledge that led to the sculpture. If your partner changed her mind, how do each of you feel about this? You might want to learn more about each choice and see if you can find a choice you both could live with. Or if this doesn't work, see a psychotherapist.

Checklist: Are You Ready for Parenthood?

- I am excited about bringing a child into my life, even if it sometimes scares me.
- I/we have a good support system of family and/or friends.
- Even if finances are difficult, we have a safe, adequate place to live. We have the ability to provide our child with basics such as food, clothing, and medical care.
- I can protect my child from harm by keeping him away from violent or abusive people, including family members.
- I am willing to seek medical care and counseling for my child when needed.
- I am in reasonably good health. If I have a chronic illness, it is well-managed with medicine and/or self-care.
- I am relatively happy and mentally healthy. I am not so anxious or depressed that I am unable to care for myself, work, and be in a relationship. I know how to control and deal with my anger without lashing out verbally or physically.
- I understand that even happy, healthy children have moments of irrationality, tantrums, rage or fear. In the first year of life I know that I will be faced with crying jags, wet and dirty diapers and interrupted sleep.
- I do not try to deny problems with a stiff upper lip or false cheeriness or unrealistic beliefs that I can make anything happen. I can acknowledge my own and other's suffering, and deal with these with caring and compassion. I could therefore be present with my child even during bad moods, which are part of life. I understand that respecting my child's moods is an important part of her self-esteem and learning to cope. Even

though correction, discipline and moral education are crucial, I have a sense that I can accept the child and correct the behavior. If I am in a relationship, I can accept and empathize with my partner's suffering.

- If I had a difficult or abusive childhood, I have had therapy that healed me enough to enjoy life more and feel more in control. My therapist and I both believe that I have healed enough to be able to enjoy parenting and do it well.
- I am capable of apologizing, giving sincere compliments, and negotiating.
- I do not assume that I can mold a child according to my desires and expectations. I am interested and curious in the personality and interests my child will turn out to have as her own person.
- I am comfortable with physical affection such as hugs and gentle touch.
- If I/ we are disappointed in our child or in parenthood, we know that some of this is normal and would seek support from family or friends as well as therapy.
- Even if my partner would have preferred to be childfree, he/ she finds enough that is attractive about parenting, in addition to pleasing me, that he/she is ready to make these sacrifices.
- I am not addicted to alcohol, drugs (including prescription drugs), sex, gambling, or spending. If these have been a problem in the past, I have been free of this for a few years and am under the care of a doctor, mental health professional and/or a twelve-step group I attend regularly.
- (If in a relationship): My partner and I enjoy each other's company most of the time. We are able to disagree and resolve conflicts. We do not experience uncontrollable anger, violence or days or weeks of silence. We are not isolated, but have friends or family or community groups we spend time with.

If there are items on the checklist that you can't answer yes, to, consider if there are ways to work on this problem before becoming a parent. If you and your partner disagree about whether any of the above issues are a problem, see a therapist or other professional such as a pastoral counselor to sort this out.

✦ CHAPTER 3 ✦
IN AND OUT OF THE PRESSURE COOKER

- Ilene, happily married and childfree, has a boss, an enthusiastic father of three, who can't understand why she doesn't want kids. He bombards her with family pictures.
- When Kenny and Nan told their best friend George that they were trying for pregnancy George tried to change their minds.
- Barry and Michelle, parents of a seven-year-old, feel that they're too busy to care for another child. But their parents keep telling them that Briana will grow up selfish, lonely and miserable unless they give her a brother or sister.
- Twenty-eight-year-old Diane is in her first year of a grueling MBA program. She barely has time to grab five hours of sleep or gobble a slice of pizza with her husband. She had to order her mother to stop sending her articles about fertility decline.

Family and friends. They sweet-talk us and soft-soap us. They are the pushy people in our lives, and they are SURE that we should or shouldn't become parents. We may be uncertain, but *they* are not. They believe they've been sent from heaven to save us from a wrong choice, but to us, their halos look strangely like horns.

All the people described above are emotionally healthy, independent adults. They don't care if somebody else thinks they should sell their home, apply for a new job, or save more money. So why are they so shaken by baby-related pressures? Because the pressures are internal as well as external.

Pressure from family and friends is hard to ignore because it acts like a magnet, bringing our own doubts and fears to the surface. Every time these key people voice an objection, we hear a corresponding echo: Will our lives be ruined? Will we lose our friends? Are we really being selfish? Will our parents forgive us for disappointing them?

Does this mean that you're doomed to suffer in silence, that you'll never feel "right" about your decision unless you banish the meddler from your life? Not at all. This chapter will show you what's behind their pressure tactics, how to handle well-meaning busybodies and manipulative meddlers, and how you can sometimes even turn such pressure to your own advantage.

A note of caution: If your parents were abusive, hurtful, or untrustworthy, the techniques below are unlikely to help. Avoiding such parents entirely or changing the subject if they bring up parenthood may be your best options. A few psychotherapy sessions or journal writing may help you cope with any comments they make on the subject. If you are out of contact with them, you certainly won't want to include them in your decision-making process.

You Can Go Home Again

You are in your twenties or thirties, you have a good job, a happy marriage, and a home of your own. You are your own boss, an adult who is ready, willing, and able to take responsibility for your life and make your own decisions. Or are you? Why, then, is it so difficult for you to imagine telling your parents that you've decided not to have a baby? Why are you tempted to avoid the discussion altogether, even to the point of visiting them less often? Why, if you're leaning toward the childfree choice, are you beginning to think that perhaps you are making a mistake, that you really won't be happy unless you have a child?

Although, in most cases, parents push for grandchildren, there are parents who take the opposite view. Some fear that their children will be unhappy as parents. Others don't want to be confronted with their own aging. And some mothers, especially if their own career aspirations were thwarted, take vicarious pleasure in their daughters' achievements and fear that a baby will ruin their daughter's career success. Also, parents who had you when they were young may be unaware of the feasibility of pregnancy or adoptive parenting in your late thirties or beyond.

It's entirely natural to want the approval and understanding of those you love and respect, particularly your parents. After all, you spent years trying to please them and basking in their praise. But, at a certain point, you have to separate from your parents and carve out your own identity as an independent adult whose decisions reflect your needs, not theirs. Murray Bowen, Georgetown University psychiatrist and a family therapy pioneer, called this process individuation, a way of coming to terms with one's parents, not by escaping, rebelling, or giving in to them, but by separating one's identity from theirs while maintaining a close relationship.

All of us want to relate to our parents as adults, but getting there can be difficult and threatening. It involves time, effort, and honest communication. It means that we have to accept responsibility for ourselves and give up the illusion that someone else will take care of us. And it means that our relationship with our parents will invariably change—and change, no matter how desirable, is always somewhat frightening. So, rather than risk such change, many people take the easy way out and handle parental pressure by giving in, running away, or rebelling. In fact, the decision itself can be a form of rebellion, as the following stories indicate.

- Alan's parents are dying to become grandparents, and his only sibling isn't married. But Alan is furious at his parents for a number of reasons, and even though he and his wife eventually plan to have children, he deliberately wants to postpone the pregnancy just to get back at them. He doesn't want to hear, "I told you so." Nor does he want his parents to claim responsibility for a decision he worked hard to make with his wife.
- Kathleen, a highly successful businesswoman who travels a lot, is angry because her parents keep telling her not to have a baby unless she quits her job. They predict that she'll lose her husband, neglect her child, or both. Although she and Brian are planning to be childfree she enjoys revenge fantasies of getting pregnant just to prove them wrong.

Fortunately, you are unlikely to give into thoughts like Alan's or Kathleen's, but noticing any similar thoughts can call your attention to unfinished business you will want to take care of. To spring the parental trap, you have to work toward genuine individuation by taking a trip back home, either literally or figuratively, and looking at your relationship with your parents as honestly as possible. Do you act like an adult when you're with them, or do you fall into old behavior patterns? When they raise doubts or criticize you, do you immediately get angry and start to yell as you did when you were an adolescent or do you turn into a subservient child? Can you discuss the matter in a calm, reasonable way? Have you stopped to consider what you want? Are you aware of the differences—and similarities— between you and your parents? It can be helpful to enlist aid from a therapist or friend. They may help you rehearse what to say and brainstorm responses to your parents' criticisms.

Consider following these steps toward individuation:

1. Talk to your parents about their lives, their relationship with each other, and *their* parents. Try to focus on emotions, not just facts. If Dad quit high school when his father died, how did he feel about it? Share some of your own feelings. This can be a wonderful way to venture beyond chitchat to the deeper feelings that often go unexpressed between parent and child.

2. Spend time with each parent separately ("Let's just the two of us go out for coffee"). Relate to each parent as a distinct individual, not just half of an indeterminate blob known as "my parents."

3. Try to recognize when a conversation seems to be a replay of old family scripts. Can you think of a time in your adulthood, when you were having what seemed to be a reasonable adult conversation, but then one parent said something that hit a sore spot? In that case, without even knowing it was coming, you may find yourself snapping and retorting like an angry teenager. Take the example of Todd and Christine:

> One evening Todd and Christine told his parents they didn't know if they would ever have children. Todd's mother asked: "How could you be so selfish?"

Todd pounded his fist on the dinner table and shouted: "You hypocrite! Don't you realize how selfish you are to insist on grandchildren?"

Todd fell into a time-worn pattern of answering his mother's accusation with an even stormier accusation. The end result of such a pattern is that nobody listens and nobody learns.

Hard as it is try to listen calmly and explain your thinking, make an effort to hold a conversation between the two adults you now are instead of between the parent and child you used to be.

If you're not ready to take these steps or if your parents are deceased, try the chair dialogue described in Chapter 2, "Secret Doors." Act out a conversation between you and your parents, playing yourself and each of your parents in turn. Even if they are still living, practicing these dialogues alone might give you enough insight and courage to risk an actual dialogue with your parents.

Before you start any serious discussions about the baby question, try to remember how you and your parents used to handle conflicts. What techniques did they use with you? Were they productive, counterproductive, or a mixture? What were your reactions and counter techniques? Use this information to avoid falling into destructive patterns that may have become habits over the years. Focus on the effective techniques, avoid the manipulative or ineffective ones, and watch for familiar manipulations on their part. Bear in mind, however, that you and your parents are different people now and that more open and authentic ways of relating may be possible. They too may have changed.

Defying parental expectations is not easy, but if you know what you're dealing with and what kind of changes you want to make, you can benefit from the experience. In fact, as the following story illustrates, these conversations can promote personal growth by giving you the chance to improve your relationship with your parents and overcome your need for their approval.

David and Marilyn almost had a baby they didn't want. "We were afraid of disappointing our parents," David said recently. "We had always been model children. After getting straight A's in high school and college, we went to medical school just as our parents had hoped. Until the baby decision, it was easy to do what they wanted because we had always wanted the same things. Without questioning our motivations, we agreed that Marilyn would go off the pill when we finished our residencies. But fortunately, she didn't get pregnant right away. Instead, she got headaches, and I had nightmares. We asked ourselves why and concluded that we didn't really want children. We had just wanted to please our parents. We decided it was time to start asking what would please us."

"It was scary to tell our parents about our decision," Marilyn added. "We were tempted to pretend we had a fertility problem. But that was the coward's way out. So we told them. All four of them were shocked and angry. They tried to make us feel guilty. It would have been very easy to just stop talking to them.

"But the weird thing is, we have better relationships with both sets of parents than ever before," said Marilyn. "We took on my parents one week and David's the next. We listened while they told us why they felt we should have children. And they listened while we explained why we don't want them. We were able to empathize with their disappointment about not having a grandchild. We still don't see eye-to-eye, but at least we're beginning to accept one another. I feel like a real grownup for the first time in my life."

If you're willing to take the risks David and Marilyn took, you may be surprised to discover that your parents are capable of making some changes, too. While disappointed in your decision, they may appreciate that your cared enough about them to discuss this important matter with them. Also, you may develop a new appreciation for your parents in the process. As you consider the responsibilities and sacrifices involved in parenting, you may come to realize just how tough the job is and how much credit they deserve for doing it, even if imperfectly! Once they get used to your decision and recognize that you are enjoying your childfree life, they may become more accepting.

The Family Tree

Family pressure doesn't necessarily have to be overt. Even if your parents are silent on the baby issue, you may still be influenced by family attitudes and values, often in ways you don't consciously recognize. According to Mel Roman, a noted family therapist and professor of psychiatry at Albert Einstein College of Medicine:

> We are all rooted to a vast underground network of family relationships, family patterns, family rules and roles . . . and we carry this network into any new family we form. We tend to overlook the power of the past in the choices we make and to underestimate the ease with which we fall into old patterns of behavior. But it is not desirable to be bound to the past in destructive ways. In examining the family context that we have inherited from our families . . . we can attempt to separate the aspects of our past that can be put aside as old business from the useful aspects that can become new business in our current families.

Such an examination is especially important in the context of the baby decision. For when we think about becoming parents, we can't help associating ourselves with our own parents, and long-buried resentments and feelings about parents, children, and family relationships may get in the way of your current decision-making.

An Unhappy Childhood

Some people are reluctant to become parents themselves because they have such negative feelings about their own parents and the way they were raised. "I only visit my parents out of duty," said one man considering fatherhood. "I can't stand the thought that my children would ever feel that way about me."

If you're worried that you're choosing the childfree choice

because your childhood soured you on family life, consider how and why you were unhappy and what you felt you missed. If your parents weren't affectionate, that doesn't necessarily mean you'll carry on the pattern with your own child. Perhaps your parents did indeed give you love in their fashion. Perhaps it simply wasn't enough for you, or perhaps you couldn't deal with the conditions, rejections, or put-downs that went along with it. Maybe someone else, an older sibling, a beloved teacher, a favorite aunt or neighbor gave you the love you missed from one or both parents. Whatever the circumstances, it's important to recognize:

- **The source of your ability to love.** Who made it possible for you to be affectionate with your partner or friends? Focus on that person or persons and build on those warm feelings. These may serve as a foundation for nurturing your child. Can you think of ways that you nurture your partner, cuddle with your niece, or mentor a younger person at work? Such awareness may increase your confidence. If you have trouble thinking about this, ask some people you trust if and how they have found you nurturing.
- **The possibility of parenting as a way of healing.** Although the act of providing your child with love and security won't heal your difficult childhood, it can be very comforting, especially if you have had a chance to work on your past with a caring professional. Just be prepared for some wistfulness as you realize, as Jen did, after patiently helping her child wipe up a spill, "My parents would yell and humiliate me when I made mistakes. They would never have treated me so kindly." Such moments are bittersweet. There is the bitterness of the recollection mixed with the sweetness of breaking the generational pattern for your child's benefit.

Obviously, a look back at your childhood is important, but you should not judge your ability to parent solely on the quality of your childhood or your relationship with your parents. Even if you hate your parents, that doesn't mean your children will hate you. You don't necessarily have to repeat their mistakes. If you enjoy parenting, respect your child, foster her independence, and avoid your parents' errors, your children will probably feel very differently about you. The point is that unless you assess the impact of your past on your present life, you won't have enough information to make a thoughtful and rational decision.

Take a few minutes to sit comfortably and ask yourself if there any ways that your decision may be influenced by your parents' behavior. Are there ways to free yourself from this? You may also want to think about how society, pregnancy, and parenting have changed for the better and worse since your parents raised you.

My Parents/Myself

People considering the baby question often fear that as soon as the baby is born, they'll turn into their parents, losing themselves and their independence. This is a more common fear for women, but men can have it, too. This fear may be based on observing a sibling or friend who was independent before the baby's birth but who has slipped into their parents' behavior or attitudes somehow.

Lois managed, with help, to recognize and break out of the trap. A management consultant with a good marriage and three children, she confessed that she was very smug about being superwoman. "I thought I was showing up my so-called incompetent mother," she said. "When she had me, Mom gave up teaching to change diapers. Not me! I continued teaching at the university and hired a housekeeper to change diapers. Mom never had any time to herself. Not me! I took one night a week as my special time all to myself. For months I thought I had all the answers, then suddenly I had to ask myself why I seemed to be on the verge of a nervous breakdown.

"In therapy I discovered that while the stage was different, the play was the same. My mother was a martyr at home; I divided my martyrdom between office and home. Mom put herself out to make the perfect dinner. I put myself out to make the perfect presentation. This was a sobering realization that made me look at both the strengths and the weaknesses that my mother and I share. It was only after acknowledging this that I was able to change my life. I cut down on my workload, stopped trying to entertain like Martha Stewart, and insisted that my husband and kids do housework."

Are you afraid of turning into your parents once you have a child? What did they do or fail to do that you would like to correct in raising your child? You can increase your chance of success by observing family or friends whose parenting styles you like, attending parenting classes, and asking your partner, friends, or therapist for support and feedback. The point is to make the best choice for you regardless of your parents' choices or parenting ability.

My Mother/My Wife

Some people are less concerned about losing their own identity than about losing their partner's attention. When they think about their husband or wife as a parent, they become terrified because they associate their partner with their own parents. If their parent was unhappy or struggled with raising them, they may worry that the same thing will happen to their partner. It is helpful to recognize and talk about this. Such conversations can make you feel more confident in your own future as a childrearing couple.

Lynn, a management consultant at a prestigious firm, terrified Fred when she announced her plans to take a year off to stay home with the baby. When they'd originally agreed to have a child, Lynn had intended to continue business as usual. Now three months pregnant, she is knitting a blanket while chatting happily about the year she's going to take off. Fred is terrified. Is this pregnant stranger an alien or still the Lynn he married?

Fred admitted he sometimes wished Lynn wasn't pregnant. He knew that his mother, a frustrated actress, had hated motherhood. She had poisoned his childhood with daily doses of "If it wasn't for you . . ." Now, he's confusing his wife with his mother. He's afraid, on some subconscious level, that Lynn will turn against him, blame him, as his mother did, for ruining her life.

The only way to overcome this kind of fear is by bringing it out into the open and discussing it. Lynn has to help Fred realize that her personality, her coping skills, and her career choice are very different from his mother's. Also, his fear can be put to good use, encouraging him to plan to prevent motherhood from being such a terrible burden for Lynn.

Too many people working on the baby decision forget to go home, to explore their own past, often because they're afraid to discover that in ways they neither understand nor control, they're still not quite grown. But, as you've seen, the baby decision can be a unique opportunity to work on individuation and develop a genuinely adult and authentic relationship with your parents. By examining some of these subtle doubts and fears, you can come to terms with your past and put aside old business. And by acknowledging the similarities between you and your parents, you can begin to appreciate the real differences.

Even if your parents have disappointed you by their response or lack of response, you know you made your best effort. You can let go of trying to win their approval and focus on your own decision.

Friends and Other Meddlers

In the past, only the childfree-choice raised eyebrows and elicited unwanted and even obnoxious comments about selfishness or immaturity. Some typical comments: "You're not a real grown-up until you have kids." "You'll change your minds." "There's more to life than beach vacations." Now, we've added a new prejudice to our repertoire. The fact is, no matter what you choose, you're bound to receive some flak. If you choose parenthood, some childfree friends will ask, "Why you are giving up your freedom for such a thankless job."

Ironically, depending on what crowd you're with at the time, you may hear the very same accusation followed by a slightly different rationale. As the following choruses indicate, identical prejudices can be twisted to fit the perspectives of either group.

Parent Chorus:	Childfree people are immature. They don't want to grow up and accept the parenting role.
Childfree Chorus:	Parents are immature. They just have children to please their parents or partner.
Parent Chorus:	Childfree people are irresponsible. They want all the pleasure but none of the burdens of adult life.
Childfree Chorus:	Parents are irresponsible. They just have kids because they feel like it. They don't stop to ask if they'll be good parents or if the earth has room for their offspring.
Parent Chorus:	Childfree people are narcissistic. Any mentally healthy adult would reproduce.
Childfree Chorus:	Parents are narcissistic. They force their kids to be extensions of themselves.
Parent Chorus:	Childfree people are selfish. They don't want to do anything for anybody else.
Childfree Chorus:	Parents are selfish. They only think about themselves and their kids. They don't care about wider issues.
Parent Chorus:	Childfree people are afraid to take risks. They're scared to let go of the status quo.
Childfree Chorus:	Parents are afraid to take risks. They become parents only because they can't resist other people's pressures.
Parent Chorus:	Childfree people will regret their decision later. Someday they'll wake up to realize they're all alone in the world.
Childfree Chorus:	Parents will regret their decision later. Someday they'll wake up to realize they sacrificed everything for kids who don't even visit them.

Ridiculous as this sounds, unless your family and friends are models of tact and understanding, you're bound to hear some of this. That's why it's important to learn assertive ways to deal with pressure before you've even made your decision. After all, how can you even think of jumping off the baby bandwagon if you think your loved ones will jump all over you? Will you be comfortable going to the gynecologist if your friends think you need a psychiatrist? Knowing how to respond assertively makes it clear that you are the final judge. But before we delve into the specific techniques, let's take a look at what's behind the flak.

The "Babies Are Wonderful" Crowd

Why does the selfish childfree stereotype persist despite research evidence and clinical experience to the contrary? Why do parents continue to pressure nonparents? Friends and family who are raising children may be smug or critical as they try to sell you on having a child. What is going on? How can they be so off-base? Why don't they get who you are and respect your sound decision? Here are a few reasons:

1. Ambivalence. Many parents, on a bad day, regret having children, especially as he or she leaves a warm bed at 3:00 A.M. to comfort, change, or feed a screaming baby. Remember, many pregnancies that weren't unplanned *were* unquestioned. The parent who would have chosen childlessness, had they believed it was an acceptable choice, may say, "You'll be sorry later" because he's sorry now and envies your freedom.

2. Ignorance. Many people aren't aware of the studies that indicate that the childfree are at least as happy and as emotionally stable as parents. Such reports tend to be tucked away in professional journals that don't reach the general public.

3. Failure to accept difference. People assume that what is good for them is good for their friends. A couple smitten with their cuddly cherub may not recognize that parenting offers little enchantment to friends whose weekends are devoted to backpacking and playing together in a jazz band.

Games Parents Play with Childfree People

In the grip of such feelings, people search for ways to vent them. But few are willing to be completely open and risk losing a friend, so they express their disapproval in less direct ways—by playing games. Psychologist Eric Berne in *Games People Play* defines a game as:

> . . . a social interaction which is in some ways dishonest and irresponsible. It is played for an ulterior motive. In many cases, neither the initiator nor the victim of the game is consciously aware of the payoff. Even though games serve a need, they are ultimately self-defeating. Honesty with oneself and others, though painful in the short run, leads down a longer path to fulfillment.

"You'll Be Sorry"

Lisa and Zack tell their friends that Zack has had a vasectomy. Jessie and Andy, parents of toddler twins, are shocked. "Won't you be sorry, later?" they ask.

The *purpose:* to "punish" the childfree person for the "sin" of freedom, for escaping 3:00 A.M. feedings and 3 million diaper changes.

The *payoff:* seeing the childfree person squirm and counterattack. For the player, the counterattack proves that the childfree person *is* neurotic about the issue. And that "proof" serves to soothe his or her own doubts.

The *price:* a phony, fruitless interchange in which neither person's feelings are revealed.

The *counter game:* an authentic dialogue in which the parents are free to state their own regrets and envy of the childfree couple's life and vice versa. The players can understand and respect each other's choices and remain close friends despite their different attitudes. They can even enjoy friends who have interesting lives that are different from theirs.

"Ha! Ha! We Knew It All Along"

Joanna and Brad had decided to remain childfree when they were 23 but changed their minds at 33. When they announced Joanna's pregnancy at a party the response was infuriating.

"Hah! The great childfree couple! You talked so much about your freedom, and now you've found out how empty it really is. We always knew you'd change your minds!"

The purpose: to deprive the formerly childfree couple of the right to change their minds, to express anger at someone who almost got away with "freedom" and to express relief that "you turned out to be like us, after all."

The price: the people who changed their minds feel angry and hurt. They are not being validated for a good childfree decision in the past nor the wisdom, at this point, of their decision to have a child. The bonds of friendship are weakened if not broken.

The counter game: an honest response to the change of heart and an expression of curiosity. "Congratulations! What made you change your mind?" The newly pregnant couple could then explain—but only if they want to—why the childfree choice was right in the past and why parenthood seems right for the future.

Remember that people who change their minds are *not* ex-fools who have finally embraced some absolute, universal truth that you have always subscribed to. Their earlier choice was right at the time, but they are different people now, and the change reflects these differences.

Another variation of this game occurs when parenting friends try to take some of the credit for their friends' new decision. "You listened to me at last. Because of my arguments, you have finally made the one true choice." In this situation, the players are wrestling for control.

"Do Me a Favor"

It's not easy to be the only childfree couple in a small town, as Kristin and Mike tell it. They're called upon to do whatever parents are "too busy" to do: raise money for the local hospital, run the church bazaar and, of course, babysit for free. It is assumed that such requests are a cure for their selfishness. These requests sometimes include the phrase "Since you have nothing better to do." And if they say no, that will be viewed as proof of selfishness. There you are accused, found guilty, and sentenced to community service without due process.

The purpose: to convey the message, "Since you don't have children, you're obviously not doing anything important."

The payoff: ensuring that the couple is as overburdened as they are so they won't have to feel jealous.

The price: Kristin and Mike feel so resentful that they don't do very well at the activities they're talked into. They're made to feel guilty about a perfectly good choice.

The counter game: Despite their fears of being accused of selfishness, Kristin and Mike have to start saying no to any favor they don't want to do. Accusations of selfishness can be countered with the assertiveness techniques described at the end of this chapter. The couple can insist that they are not gazing into space, margarita in hand. They are busy with activities of their own choosing according to their own values. They could also benefit from the support of other childfree people. (See Appendix 2 for Resources for Childfree Organizations.)

People who choose to remain childfree have to develop armor, particularly women. Because motherhood has always been sacrosanct in our society, we've developed a whole set of myths and assumptions about childbearing:

- Pregnancy is a woman's most fulfilling experience.
- You're not a real woman until you've had a child.
- Motherhood is a woman's destiny.

Even though feminism has countered these beliefs and choosing to be childfree is more acceptable now than in the past, these beliefs persist and still cause emotional pain. Spending time with childfree friends and parenting friends who respect your choice will help.

Consequently, childfree women are more maligned than child-free men. The childless woman is shirking her role: she's cold, selfish, immature, neurotic. The childless man, on the other hand, probably has something more important to do; he's devoting his energies to his career. So it's not surprising that women are more upset by med-dlers than their husbands are.

If you're hit by any of these accusations, recognize that sexism is an aspect of pronatalism, and point it out to the meddlers. If you're a childfree husband, listen empathetically to your wife's description of her frustrations. Offer her the support she needs to overcome them. Keep in mind that most people will judge her more harshly than they'll judge you, not that either of you should be judged.

The "Joys of Freedom" Crowd

Educating people about the childfree option is necessary and productive; pressuring couples to choose that option is not. Although the childfree still receive the most criticism, an increasingly large group of people is ready to point an accusing finger at you should you choose parenthood. And sometimes these are the very people who thought long and hard about both options! The problem is, they're not entirely comfortable with their choice.

- Eileen and Richard decided to have a child. During Eileen's pregnancy, their best friends announced their decision to remain childfree. These friends asked questions about parent-hood that made it sound as if Eileen and Richard had just been stricken by an incurable disease that would destroy their lives.
- After considering adoption, Joyce, a single woman, decided to remain childfree. When her best friend, Anita, also single, gleefully announced her pregnancy, Joyce offered Anita only a cool, subdued congratulations.

What is going on? Why such strong reactions from normally easy-going people? The answer is simple: self-doubt.

Psychologists use the term "cognitive dissonance" to describe the act of selling someone else our own choice because we're afraid *theirs* might be right. Seeing others revel in the pleasure of the opposite choice makes us question the wisdom of our own. To reassure ourselves, we feverishly throw ourselves into telling the other person that our choice is not only right for us, but for them, too.

Games Childfree People Play

Couples suffering from cognitive dissonance aren't always upfront with their attacks. Often, they play a game called "We Have More Fun Than You."

Although Keith and Sara have announced their plan to remain childfree, they are still uneasy about the choice. Their best friends have just had a baby, and they drop by for a visit one night at eight. There's a charcoal smell in the air, but no steak in sight. Judy and Ralph open the door to give an explanation that is repeatedly interrupted by the baby's screeches. While they debated what to do about Jennifer's colic, the casserole burned to a crisp. Dressed in their designer best, Keith and Sara observe that Judy's jeans and Ralph's shirt are decorated in spit-up and squash. Ignoring both their friends' appearance and the baby, they begin to describe their plans for the evening—a French restaurant, a Broadway musical, and a cast party.

The purpose: to make their friends even more painfully aware of the gap between their past luxury and their present drudgery.

The price: potential regret about alienating their friends.

The payoff: to cover up their anxiety about their decision.

The counter game: 1. To continue working on the decision until it's more solid. 2. To empathize with their friends' frustration. 3. To realize that Judy and Ralph's decision to parent may well be right for them. 4. To recognize that the difficulties of living with a newborn are temporary and that once life settles down for Judy and Ralph the gap between them and their friends will lessen. This screeching baby could turn out to be a feisty, charming three-year-old who would give Keith and Sara a chance to play with and nurture a child they don't have to raise.

"You're Just a Sheep"

In this game, childfree people claim superiority over parents by assuming that anyone who has carefully considered the baby decision would naturally decide against a baby. They believe, "We who don't have kids have total control of our lives. You, who are parents, have no control over yours."

The payoff: by feeling superior to parents, they mask their insecurity about the childfree choice.

The counter game: accept the wisdom of different strokes for different folks. When a nonparent feels insecure about his decision, that doesn't mean it's the wrong decision, just an unfinished one. After all, in a baby-peddling society, it's not surprising that those who refuse the purchase will sometimes feel uncertain.

The Conformity Syndrome

Sometimes nonparents accuse parents of giving in to society's expectations. In their opinion, childfree persons deserve a badge of courage for nonconformity. Although it's certainly true that in today's world, nonparents make the less traditional choice and deserve a great deal of support and respect for their decision, we cannot stereotype all parenthood decisions as conformist and childfree decisions as nonconformist. It's not that simple.

For example, sometimes what looks like conformity may really be a positive learning experience.

- In January, Brian and Amy consider parenthood. They're nervous and uncertain, and they make lists of reasons for not having children. In June, their best friends give birth to a child. The following January, Amy is pregnant. Other childfree friends accuse them of conforming.

Are they guilty or not? Guilty, if Brian and Amy didn't want a baby but followed in their friends' footsteps anyway. Not guilty, if they really wanted a baby but were scared to jump off the fence. Perhaps parent-hood seemed less scary once they noticed that their friends had not only survived but actually enjoyed parenthood. Maybe they had fun playing with their friends' baby. These experiences may simply have made it easier for them to do what they wanted to do in the first place.

Although they probably don't realize it, Brian and Amy benefited from two valuable psychological techniques: desensitization and role modeling. Desensitization is a process by which repeated small, safe doses of something scary reduces one's fear. Role modeling is the process of imitating the behavior of someone greatly admired. So what looked to their childfree friends like conformity on Brian and Amy's part was actually their own decision.

The fact is that every decision contains some elements of con-formity. Since there are going to be people criticizing both choices, the issue of conformity depends on the prevailing view of your partic-ular social circle. In a study of college students, Ohio State Professor Sharon Houseknecht found that those committed to the childfree choice had friends with similar commitments and/or friends who supported that choice. She concluded that the childfree choice could indeed be a conformist choice involving conformity to a small anti-parenthood social group rather than to the larger pronatalist society. ("Reference Group Support for Voluntary Childlessness: Evi-dence for Conformity," in *Journal of Marriage and the Family*, Vol. 39, May, 1977).

If you have a baby shortly after one of your friends does and the rest of your predominantly childfree crowd is shouting "conformist!" you could turn the tables on them and point out that you actually made the nonconformist choice in the view of most of the people you know. And if their doubts should get to you, check out the fol-lowing considerations. You're guilty of conformity if:

- You haven't thought through the decision on your own.
- You have a baby just because you always assumed you would.
- You don't want your family or friends to think less of you.
- You want people to stop hassling you.

You're the only one who has the right to decide whether your decision is genuine. If you're comfortable with it, ignore the pointing fingers and walk on.

Stilling the Angry Voices

Before we begin to examine some of the techniques you can use to take the heat off yourself without alienating your loved ones, take a moment to study:

"The Pressure Victim's Bill of Rights."

Keep in mind that you have, at all times, the following rights:

- The right to choose whether or not to discuss the decision with a particular person.
- The right to be heard if you do wish to explain your decision to chosen people.
- The right to cut the conversation short or change its direction.
- The right to point out and object to manipulative techniques.

Below you will find some techniques for resisting other people's pressures.

Dodging

This is a technique to use when you want to get a meddler off your back quickly. Simply agree with his or her viewpoint and don't add any fuel to the fire. You don't really have to agree; just acknowledge the possibility of some truth in what the person is saying. "You may be right about that. Perhaps it's true."

Light Retorts and Humor

When somebody's meddling is making you sick, laughter may be the best medicine.

Eva's mother told her that being childfree was wrong because motherhood is natural.

"Oh, yeah?" replied Eva. "So are rattlesnakes, malaria, and poison ivy!"

Bounce Back the "Shrink" Ball

If someone tries to push you onto the analyst's couch, bounce back with a response such as "What gives you the right to analyze me? How can you presume to know what is going on in my unconscious mind?"

Even people who have no trouble resisting amateur psycho-therapists can fall prey to real ones. And a friend or relative who happens to be a trained therapist can be very narrow-minded about the baby decision, especially *your* decision. You don't have to put up with slick pronouncements such as, "You don't want kids because your childhood was unhappy" or "You're only having kids because you want someone to control." Even a therapist whom you trust and whom you've asked for help should offer interpretations or advice tentatively. You have the right to ask your therapist to explain his or her opinion as well as the right to challenge it. Therapists are fallible human beings who are sometimes wrong about their clients. Talking about your disagreement may lead to a profound discussion relevant to your decision. And maybe your therapist will learn something from you.

Keep in mind that there are some therapists who believe that if you have "healed from your childhood," you will want to have children. They do not understand, and didn't learn in their professional training, that highly functioning, exceptionally talented, brave, and wise people choose childfree lives precisely because of healthy, creative activities they are involved in in their lives.

"Why Does It Matter to You?"

Shift the focus from yourself to the critic. Ask why the issue is so important to them. It will help if all of you see that their statements are based on their values, not on some absolute truth:

AMANDA: Is it true you're pregnant, Melissa? (Melissa smiles and nods.) I suppose I should say congratulations, but somehow I'm bothered. Have you really thought this thing through?

MELISSA: What is it about my being pregnant that bothers you?

AMANDA: Well, it's your career! How can you possibly continue to run the public relations department if you have a baby?

MELISSA: I see, you're afraid that having a baby means having to let go of a career.

Notice the phrase "you're afraid." Melissa has shifted the focus from herself to Amanda. She can now say, "You may feel that a baby means the end of a career, but I don't see it that way."

Let's look at another conversation:

ANDREW: You can't mean you'll never have a child! I'm really upset to hear you say that.

DAN: What is it about my being childfree that bothers you?

ANDREW: I'm afraid you'll regret it later when you're older.

DAN: I see. You believe that people without children end up being sorry.

ANDREW: I do.

DAN: You enjoy fatherhood so much; I can see how you would have regretted not having children. But I believe I would regret *having* them.

Don't burn your fingers on a hot potato question or statement. Throw it back to the cook! Remember, people who are comfortable with their choice have no reason to be uncomfortable with yours. And don't worry about hurting their feelings when you throw their remarks back at them. They haven't worried about hurting you. Don't insult or psychoanalyze them; just tell them how the pressure makes you feel and find out what feelings prompted the push. If you think they mean well, you can say, "I know you're trying to help, but I don't think you understand how my choice is different from yours."

Awareness

This may be used by itself or as a follow-up to the "Why does it matter to you?" technique. Ask the person how he or she came to believe that one choice was better than the other.

Explain

This technique is useful only when you care about the speaker, want her to understand, and believe that she'll make her best effort to do so.

An explanation should be:

- Short and sweet
- Non-defensive and specific
- I-focused—emphasizing what *you* feel and what *you* want; eliminating criticism of the other, especially saying, "You're conservative," "You're bigoted," etc.

Always keep in mind that *you're not obligated to explain yourself.* You're *choosing* to explain your reasons to this particular person and you can choose to stop midstream if the person launches an offensive. Here are some examples.

Richard talks to his parents about the childfree choice:

> "Because you're my parents, it's important to me that you understand. Kate and I think we'd be bad parents because we'd resent the children. We both travel a lot for

our political work and our jobs. We feel we'll contribute more to society by being enthusiastic workers than we ever could as reluctant parents."

Emily talks to Sarah about parenthood:

> "Sarah, I know you don't think I should have a baby, but because you're my best friend, I want to tell you why. At night when I meditate, I see myself holding and nursing a baby. I want a baby so much it hurts. Web designers are in demand, and I've looked into opportunities to freelance. Bob's going to gear down, too. I feel I can meet my need to be a mother and a person too."

After the explanation, be prepared for the other person's response. If he or she continues to attack, use the "Why does it matter to you?" technique. Don't let yourself or the meddler forget the issue of individuality. No decision is right for everyone. The two of you are different people, and it is hardly surprising that some of your choices are different. You might even discuss why each of you has made a different choice. Is it possible that these personality differences attracted you and your friend to each other in the first place?

Sometimes, a "meddler" can point out issues you hadn't really thought about and taking a deep breath and pondering their comments might actually be useful for your decision.

Samantha saw Taylor as so career-committed that she couldn't imagine her becoming a mother. Taylor listened carefully to Samantha and decided she'd better do some more soul-searching and establish herself in her career before making a final decision one way or the other.

Corey felt uneasy about her younger brother Dan's decision to have a vasectomy at age twenty-nine, after just one year of marriage.

> "Dan, do you really know what you're doing? I've seen the light in your eyes when you wrestle with Ethan [Corey's toddler]. Shouldn't you give yourself a few years?"

Dan had to agree he was in too much of a hurry. He was terrified of abusing a child as his father had abused him or getting his wife pregnant accidentally. A vasectomy offered a guaranteed end to a cycle of misery. But he did enjoy children, and he'd had an aunt and uncle who were very warm and loving toward him. Maybe another way to break the pattern would be to become a good father to his own child. He decided to postpone the procedure for a few more years to give himself and his wife more time to consider their plans.

It's important to discern the difference between inappropriate pressure and:

- Advice that is astute, open, friendly, and offered in a way that you can take or leave.
- Advice or thoughts from a person merely sharing his own values, rather than pushing them on you.

Devil's Advocate Technique

Turn the tables. Twist someone's argument to fit your own choice. For example, if someone says you're selfish to plan not to have children, tell him, "Well, that's all the more reason to stay child-free, isn't it? Because selfish people make lousy parents." The same argument works as well for labels such as immature, neurotic, and unhappy.

Refuse to Talk About It

This is a technique that pushes the listener away from you. Use it when:

1. You don't like or trust the person. You just want them to shut up.
2. You have tried to explain your decision and met with a deaf ear.

Simply say, "I don't care to discuss this," or more bluntly, "I'm not going to talk about this anymore." Or "You know, we've tried talking about this before, and we never get anywhere. It's time to kill the topic."

You Are Not Alone

Enlist someone else's help in coping with pressure. Ask your partner or a friend to play a supporting role, but don't let them take the lead. This is your act, and you will feel more prepared for the confrontation if you roleplay yourself.

You can also use a partner, a friend, a counselor, or a workshop group to roleplay ways to deal with pressure. This gives you a chance to hone your skills before you confront the person.

"Which Technique Should I Use?"

To choose the best assertiveness technique for a given pressure, you should consider:

- Your own personality. What's comfortable for you?
- The other person's personality. Which technique is most likely to succeed with this particular person?
- Your desired goal. Do you want this person to open up or shut up?
- Your relationship with the other person. How close is it? Do you want to make it more distant by dodging or silence, or closer by having a meaningful dialogue?
- How firm is your decision? Will pressure only get in the way or could it help test your commitment?
- Could this person help you with your decision? Has this person been a good listener or advisor in the past? If so, maybe you should listen to what they have to say even if it temporarily increases your doubt. Dealing with their comments may help you solidify your decision.

Is There an End in Sight for the Childfree?

As a final note of comfort, meddlers do give up and go home after a while. According to sociologist Jean Veevers in *Childless by Choice*:

> This social pressure seems to reach a peak for both husbands and wives during the third and fourth years of marriage—after sufficient time has passed for children to be "expected" but before the couple has learned to deal skillfully with (or avoid) their social detractors.

So if you do decide to remain childfree, there will be less pressure as time goes on, and you'll be more skilled at handling it.

However, there are some drawbacks to presenting family and friends with a *fait accompli*. For one thing, they just might have some helpful comments or insights. They might even surprise you and support your choice to be childfree. Or their questions may help convince you that it's the *right* choice. In fact, telling a few people about your leanings and finding out how well you handle their reactions may give you the confidence you need to make the childfree choice. Finally, dealing with the meddlers can be a useful way of gauging the stability and progress of your decision. The firmer your decision, the easier it will be to let others' comments roll off your back.

You can avoid some pressure by not bringing up the issue and only responding if someone brings it up. Before you have made the decision, choose only people you trust to be sounding boards. It will be easier to announce and defend your decision when you have given that decision some time to jell. You will withstand criticism or persuasion better when you are more confident.

✦ CHAPTER 4 ✦
POISON VIALS

Most of us like to think of ourselves as rational individuals, able to separate fact from fancy when we make a decision. And in most instances we can do just that. When a salesperson or real estate agent extols the virtues of a particular car or home, we take their inflated claims with a grain of salt, nodding politely while we mentally total up the pluses as well as the minuses. After all, we're too sophisticated to believe everything we're told

But, unfortunately, we may not be as sophisticated when it comes to the baby decision. Often, we tend to believe everything we're told about the virtues and/or horrors of parenthood, forgetting that we're being subjected to just as much salesmanship in this regard; we forget primarily because the salesperson is society at large.

Before the availability of contraception, people who were sexually active did not have a choice. Even after contraceptives became available people generally thought of them as controlling when, not if, they became parents. Parenthood was considered one of life's most fulfilling experiences, one that everyone should have at least if they were healthy, employed, and in a good relationship.

Today, many of us believe that giving birth is tantamount to fighting a war, a war that will deprive us of peace, tranquility, sleep, and personal satisfaction. In the wake of these two extreme views comes a whole flood of murky beliefs that we need to question. I call them "poison vials" because by polluting your mind they seriously hinder good decision-making. In this chapter, we're going to hold these beliefs up to the bright light of reality so you can make a rational decision.

Poison Vials About Parenthood

"Infancy lasts forever." People who are frightened by the end-less demands of a dependent infant tend to imagine a perpetual, child-rearing hell. In their view, once a baby always a baby. Actually when it comes to infants, what you see is not what you get, at least not for very long. Children get older, a little more independent, and sometimes easier. Few parents would even think about having a baby, if their child would stay an infant for his entire life.

"I know I would resent giving up my freedom, and that means I shouldn't become a parent." Every parent resents the loss of freedom at times. Who wouldn't prefer a trip to Europe to a trip to the pediatrician? Who wouldn't rather listen to pure Mozart than Mozart adulterated by a toddler's wails? Happy parents aren't people who feel no resent-ment. They're the ones who live with the resentment because, on their parenthood scale, the pleasures outweigh the suffering, and generally, they are also people who had already anticipated the resentment before becoming parents. They didn't make the choice while puffing on pipe-dreams of perfect parenthood. They knew there would be times when they would fume with resentment and other times they would be laughing, playing and cuddling. They also knew that as their children grew so would their freedom.

So the question to ask while working on the baby decision is not whether you would resent giving up your freedom. Of course you would. The question is, how much would you resent a child? If you value and want a child, you will be able to handle the resentment.

"I should only become a parent if I'm one hundred percent sure that's what I want." Children are never one hundred percent wanted because their parents are humans who, by definition, never want anything one hundred percent. We humans are ambivalent because we're aware of other possibilities, because we know we're giving up one thing to have another. Remember that "decide" means to "cut away from." Who doesn't have qualms about getting up in the middle of the night? Who wouldn't question the wisdom of an eighteen-year commitment, no returns, no refunds, no guarantees?

Don't expect total certainty. In fact, if you don't have *any* doubts about parenthood, that would be cause for concern because it might mean you have unrealistic expectations about the joys of parenthood and your ability to be the perfect parent.

Two important factors in preparing for parenthood are forming realistic expectations and accepting ambivalence. By recognizing and accepting your own conflict and sharing it with your partner, you will move toward a stronger relationship and a better family life.

"Everyone keeps telling us that kids are awful and that they'll ruin our lives." This assumption, which would have been an anathema in our parents' and grandparents' day, has become increasingly popular among certain groups of people, both parents and nonparents. What wonderful lives we would all be leading, they proclaim loudly, if these noisy, demanding, ungrateful kids weren't wreaking havoc on our lives and disrupting our sleep. The doomsayers view children as the dumping ground for all these frustrations. They tend to forget that childfree is not synonymous with problem-free. Time may be more available to the childfree, but it's still finite. Everyone has to make compromises, set priorities, and give up some pleasures for others.

Such people also fail to understand the nature of children. Like Henry Higgins, who wanted to know why women aren't like men, they want to know why a child can't be more like an adult. They view disobedience and misbehavior as a personal attack on their authority rather than the natural actions of someone who simply hasn't yet learned patience and control. One mother of two expressed it beautifully, "If there is just one thing I could tell your readers, it would be to think of children as smaller people, not as monsters or Martians." Although this woman's career as a mathematician has been hindered by her children, she has never forgotten that they are human beings, not inanimate objects or malicious creatures out to block her path.

Raising children is difficult, and certainly not everyone should do it, but a decision to remain childfree should never be made on the basis of this inaccurate assumption because it cheats *all* decision-makers by stunting the growth they're entitled to. Although this assumption is equally harmful to parents and nonparents, they suffer in different ways. When they fall prey to this assumption, nonparents stop too soon and parents go too far.

Sometimes, nonparents don't bother to analyze the positive implications of their choice. It isn't enough to know why parenthood is awful; you also have to know why the childfree choice can be so fulfilling. What would a child prevent you from doing? Making laws? Flying planes? Writing books? Whatever your mission or your goals, are you arranging your life so you can really devote yourself to those goals? Are you taking the risks and making the commitments that will make these activities as satisfying as possible? If you choose the childfree choice simply because you're convinced that kids are horrible brats, you probably won't be able to make the most of your life without them.

Parents and parents-to-be, on the other hand, get carried away with unnecessary anxiety. They worry excessively, expecting each new age/stage to bring disaster. They may wind up missing out on some of the fun of parenthood.

In the old days, parents of newborns complained, "Nobody ever told us it would be so hard." Now, some of my clients are surprised and relieved to discover that parenthood, while absolutely grueling at times, turns out, overall to be easier than they expected.

One young couple, ready to watch their marriage go down the tubes, was amazed to find themselves making love after putting the baby in his cradle. Expecting to hate the baby at 2:00 A.M., one father found rocking his daughter in the moonlight to be one of the high points of his day. Convinced that only insanity led her to take a three-months' leave from her high-powered corporate job, one new mother ended up taking off the rest of the year because she was having so much fun. Obviously there are many people who would not find these experiences pleasurable, but painting an entirely negative picture of parenthood simply makes it needlessly frightening for those who really would have fun with their children.

When someone's in the midst of a tale of parental woe, listen with a critical ear. Ask yourself whether this person is sincerely interested in warning you about the problems of parenthood. Is this person giving you a realistic view of parenthood in general or just a bitter slice of life today? In a calmer moment, you might ask, "Is there anything you like about being a parent? What do you like about your child?"

You might also ask yourself, "If I were in this parent's shoes, might I cope differently?"

If you spend time with other parents and children, you will get a broader view of not only the problems but also the joys. You will also note a variety of attitudes among parents. People who long to be parents and are reasonably optimistic and resilient have a lot more fun.

Poison Vials About the Childfree Choice

"I'm afraid I'll be sorry later, and that means I should have a child." You've made a careful, well-thought-out decision to remain childfree, but sometimes you worry that you will be sorry when you're fifty. Does this mean you should become a parent after all? No, it doesn't.

Everyone will regret his or her decision at some moments. Regrets over what might have been are an inevitable part of life. Therefore, the question to ask is, which decision will you regret least? (See the "Rocking Chair" exercise in Chapter 2, "Secret Doors.")

It is also worthwhile to consider how often you may feel such regrets and how they will compare with your positive feelings toward your life choice. If you've thought about these issues, chances are your regrets will probably be mild, and infrequent.

"I should remain childfree only if I have absolutely no desire for children." You can't expect an unequivocal choice. You just have to follow your overall leanings. You may have a strong desire for children but an even stronger desire to pursue your own goals without the responsibility of caring for a child.

Evan and Mia were fairly certain that the childfree choice was right for them, but occasionally "baby hunger" held them back from a definite commitment. Upon closer examination, they discovered that these pangs generally surfaced only on holidays when their young nieces and nephews were around. The rest of the time they rarely fantasized about babies; they were too engrossed in their careers, travel, and time with friends. They realized they had been socialized to believe that "holiday time is kid time." This realization helped them make a definite commitment. They redefined holidays

the parents whether they anticipate any problems, and if so, ask for advice on how to handle that problem.

3. Borrow the same child a few times. Keep in mind that a child may be more comfortable in his own home or may enjoy the novelty of yours. If the child comes to your house, ask his parents' advice on child-proofing.

4. Borrow children of different ages to get an idea of how you feel about infants versus toddlers versus elementary schoolers.

5. Don't borrow a child if your partner doesn't want to on that particular day. Or if you do and your partner doesn't, arrange to see the child alone.

6. Don't borrow a child when you're particularly upset about the baby issue. Your mood could affect the child's mood or interfere with your objectivity.

7. Don't assume that child-borrowing will completely resolve the parenthood dilemma. This experience is one of many that you can use in decision-making.

8. Don't assume you'll feel the same way about the borrowed child as you will about your own. In reality, your feelings about your own child will be much more intense. Because you'll be in love with your own child (even though you're afraid you won't be), you will have a higher tolerance for problems. You'll also have a larger repertoire of activities that you know your child enjoys.

9. After you return the child, take some time to debrief with your partner. Listen carefully. Don't try to talk your partner out of his or her positive or negative feelings because they differ from yours, and therefore threaten you.

10. Ask yourself these questions about child-borrowing:

Before you borrow a child:
- What do you expect to learn? Are your expectations realistic?
- Do you have a hidden agenda, such as the unexpressed hope that "If my partner can just see how awful kids really are, he'll give up the idea of parenthood," or "If she only sees how cute babies are, she'll be ready to go off the pill"?

After you borrow a child:
- What did you enjoy about the experience?
- What did you dislike?
- Did you take problems in stride or did you take them personally?
- How comfortable were you with physical closeness?
- Which age groups are most appealing? Why?
- Which age groups were least appealing? Why?
- Are you eager to borrow this child again? Why or why not?
- What does this experience tell you about your possible strengths and weaknesses as a parent? About your desire to be a parent?
- How did you as a couple relate to the child? Was there easy cooperation? Or was there competition over who could be the better parent? Was there any arm-twisting to involve a partner who really wanted to be elsewhere? Were there times you wanted to talk to your partner but the child got in the way? How did you handle that, and how did you feel about it?
- In what ways do you think you would respond differently to your own child?

"Changing my/our minds is a sign of weakness." Hogwash! I agree with Emerson that "a foolish consistency is the hobgoblin of little minds." Flexibility is a characteristic of happy people and exercising it can lead to a more fulfilling existence.

Jessie and Kyle were active members of the optional parenthood movement. At twenty-five, they had been certain they wanted to remain childfree and support zero population growth. At thirty-five Jessie gave birth to a son.

"It was hard to tell everyone we changed our minds," Jessie said. "We had been on talk shows, published articles, spoken at rallies. Would we be the laughingstock of the childfree world?"

"It didn't turn out that way," Jessie reported "Our friends were surprised, but they respected our choice."

"We don't regret our involvement in the optional parenthood movement," Kyle added. "In fact, we're still active members, supporting other people's right to remain childfree. And we know our decision really was our own, not something we fell into."

"We have to have two children if we have one." Grace is a victim of the all-or-nothing myth. "I think we could manage *one* child and two careers," she told me, "but I doubt we could manage two. We don't want a lonely, spoiled child. It wouldn't be fair. So I guess we won't have any."

Psychological research is punching holes in myths about only children. Only children turn out to be happier and more popular than the people with siblings. Rather than being spoiled, they are less competitive and more generous to their friends than children with siblings. (See Chapter 8, "Only Child—A Singular Solution.")

A Final Word About Poisons

Because these beliefs reflect our society's values and standards, it's hard to escape their influence. They are communicated to us in dozens of subtle ways: in the voices of friends and relatives, in the books we read, in the movies we watch. But if you maintain some perspective, you can minimize their power. Recognize that they are simply arbitrary and often misleading. They need not interfere with your decision.

partner arrange for quiet time? Remember that the issue of solitude is not solely a function of whether children are present or babysitters are available. The nature of your work is also important. If you are a mother of one quiet twelve-year-old and/or work full-time in quiet surroundings, you may enjoy more solitude than a childfree pediatrician or sales executive. Although it is possible to find private time as a parent, it's not easy, and if you require a great deal of solitude, consider that very carefully before having a child.

Although many people enjoy solitude, you may be someone who does not. This is worth thinking about while you are trying to make the parenthood decision.

Although solitude can be a peaceful vacation from our hectic, everyday lives, we often are afraid of quiet time alone. Many of us throw ourselves into an array of activities in a desperate attempt to avoid such self-exploration because we're afraid of the feelings—anger, jealousy, fear, helplessness, unworthiness, those monsters that lurk in the attic.

Discomfort with solitude can make it hard for you to carve out the reflective time that would facilitate your decision

However, we can't discover all of our positive strengths while we're bottling up our negative emotions. We have to be comfortable enough with ourselves to let all kinds of feelings come bubbling up during the quiet times. Therapy can help you deal with this and be able to enjoy more peace of mind.

Freedom

We tend to think about freedom as if it were money—accepting without question that more is better. But, like money, how it is used is often more important than how much there is. In fact, social psychologist Eric Fromm in *Escape from Freedom* claimed that many people would prefer the oppression of totalitarianism to the anxiety that comes with freedom: anxiety about making choices and taking responsibility for them. That's why so many couples who are anxious about the baby decision escape from their freedom of choice through an "accidental pregnancy" or what I call the "free drift."

There are other escape hatches as well. If you have a child because "everybody should become parents," or remain childfree because "nobody (except saints) should become parents," you're *not* exercising freedom of choice; instead, you're allowing absolutes to dictate your decision.

Freedom and commitment are interrelated, and both are necessary in a fulfilling life. As part of the decision-making process, consider not only whether you want to commit yourself to a child, but to whom else or what else you would like to commit.

Becoming a parent doesn't necessarily mean giving up freedom; it often simply means exchanging one kind for another. Some parents claim that the activities they had to give up were empty in comparison to the fullness of life with children, which they describe as the freedom to experience a wonderful new relationship. In contrast, the childfree choice will give you more freedom in the abstract sense, but it will be an empty sort of freedom unless you make that choice because your life is full of something else. Nonparents can exercise their freedom by choosing life goals more suited to them than parenting. It is OK not to know what your mission is yet, but it is important to ask the question. Also, remember that you have just as much right to be ordinary as anyone else. You don't have to make a big splash in the world to justify being childfree.

Intimacy

Whether you remain childfree or have a child, whether you are in a relationship or single, intimacy is an important part of life. You were not born in a vacuum, and you can't grow in one either. Although popular psychology in the 1970s asserted that one has to choose between personal growth and caring relationships, in reality, growth often occurs in the context of such relationships. A healthy loved one encourages and supports your growth. Moreover, if you are too scared to get close to others, you will also be too scared to grow. People grow in relation to others, or they don't grow at all. (See, for instance, *Women's Growth in Connection* by Janet Surrey and other contributors from Wellesley College's Stone Center in the Bibliography.)

Now that you have looked at personal factors of happiness, it's time to look at marital happiness.

Happiness and Marriage

Is there any truth to the increasingly popular claim that lullabies are death knells to a perfectly good marriage? I do not think so. I view this as a pendulum swing. We've gone from the old myth that children save bad marriages to the new myth that they ruin good ones. *If* your marriage is good; *if* you both want a child; *if* the child is planned; *if* you and your partner discuss the potential problems and stress both before *and* after the birth; *if* you make time for each other, then your relationship will not suffer. Of course, that's a lot of "if's." But there are plenty of "if's" in any marriage, whether children are present or not.

If you both long for a child, you may feel closer than ever after the baby's birth. Moreover, discovering how well you cooperate on late-night feedings, spelling each other during crying jags, supporting each other through blue periods, and coordinating child care can make you both realize how strong your relationship really is.

There is no doubt that the early years of parenthood are very stressful. Nor is there any doubt that people who are unwilling to endure those stresses would be happier and more productive if they remained childfree. But if you both want a child, you can feel more confident in the strength of your marriage.

However, if the strength of your marriage is based on the creation of your own little private world of two, a child would be a problem. In many relationships, one partner is dependent on the other, and he or she may feel very threatened by the prospect of a child. If either you or your mate is fairly dependent:

- **Don't have a child.** It would be a mistake for you as individuals and as a couple.
- **Try to work on the dependency issue.** Consider the following possibilities: (a) Individual counseling for the dependent part-

ner to help him or her recognize and overcome whatever is blocking growth. (b) Marital therapy to work on the changes required for the dependent partner to grow. The non-dependent, nurturing partner may have a "need to be needed." If so, he or she may need help adjusting to the partner's increasing independence.

You are the only one who can judge what effect a baby may have on your marriage. Some people argue that the skills called for in a good marriage are totally different from those in parent-child relationships. I disagree. Here are the skills that are essential to both:

- The ability to be physically affectionate.
- The ability to communicate, including intimate sharing, listening, and problem-solving.
- The ability to make a commitment despite the risks involved.
- The ability to accept the other's uniqueness rather than treating that person as an object or extension of yourself.
- The ability to be flexible, make compromises, and adapt to the other's need.
- The ability to give and to find pleasure in giving.

Marriage and parenthood differ not so much in skills required but in the choice of beneficiary.

What the Experts Say About Happiness

Research studies can't tell you whether or not you will be happier as a parent or a nonparent, but they can tell you a thing or two about the happiness of other parents and non-parents:

- Nonparents are at least as mentally healthy as parents.
- Childfree marriages are at least as happy as marriages that produce children.

- People are most dissatisfied with their marriages during the years they're raising children. Marriages are most successful prior to the birth of the first child and after the youngest leaves home, and they are most troubled when there are very young children in the home.
- Even though married people with young children are less happy and more stressed than married, childfree persons, the differences are not considered statistically significant. Married people with young children are much happier than single people and much more similar in their happiness to childfree couples than they are to single persons.
- Despite the stress children put on marriage, one nationwide study reported that many more parents felt that their children had brought them closer together rather than pulling them apart.
- Marriages are happier when a couple has successfully controlled fertility; that is, a couple who either has no children or no more than the number they wanted. Couples who conceive accidentally are not nearly as happy. (The references for this research can be found in the Bibliography under the names Angus Campbell and Harold Feldman in the Relationships section.)

For a summary of several recent studies on the topic of happiness and parenting status, see *All Joy and No Fun* by Jennifer Senior. See also "Parenthood and Happiness: It's More Complicated Than You Think" by Kim Parker (full references are in the "Relationships" section of the Bibliography).

Although there are many different ways to interpret these studies one clear statement can be made: No couple should have a child unless both really want one. There is no justification for claims that children are essential for happy lives or happy marriages. A person deciding to remain childfree is *not* condemning himself or herself to a lower quality of life, a bad marriage, or poor mental health.

Research is not a crystal ball. However, it *is* useful for:

- Shaking up old assumptions like "marriages with children are happier."

- Justifying a new lifestyle: "See, childfree people are mentally healthy after all."
- Suggesting new angles that you may not have considered. "Maybe social pressures have influenced us more than we realized."

But research should *never* be taken as gospel simply because no scientist is infallible, least of all the social scientist. All data are influenced by the questions scientists choose to ask and by the way they ask them. Moreover, both researchers and their respondents are influenced by current social myths. So when you read a study, consider these guidelines:

1. Who did the study? How might the researcher's professional affiliations or personal beliefs affect both the questions and the answers?

2. How did the author come to his or her conclusions?

3. Do the parents and the childfree couples fall into the same socioeconomic group so that meaningful comparisons can be made?

4. How do the researchers define "childfree"? Many studies are difficult to interpret because they lump together childfree persons who are merely delaying parenthood, would-be parents who are infertile, and couples who definitely plan to remain childfree.

5. How does this study apply to me and my partner? In what ways are we like the people in the study? How are we different?

Get more information. You may be able to contact the researcher through his or her university to get a link to the original article or research report or references to books or journal articles. Even if you don't have a strong social science background, you may be able to get more out of the original journal article than you could in a summary found in a newspaper article or pamphlet.

If you and your partner have a good relationship and you're both positive about having children, don't let the research discourage you. Because you value children, you'll be able to deal with the stress. And if you don't want children, take heart in the fact that most studies indicate you'll be at least as happy as parents are, if not happier.

✦

Making the Decision

✦ CHAPTER 6 ✦
TUG-OF-WAR, OR WHAT TO DO WHEN COUPLES CONFLICT

> In the healthy confrontation neither person loses sight of the fact that each is seeking to express the truth and find a meaningful way to live. In a true confrontation, the persons always remain persons. And because there is awareness and knowledge and sensitivity, the argument, the face-to-face struggle, follows its natural course and opens new pathways of relatedness.
>
> —Clark Moustakas, *Creative Life*

Probably the hardest decisions of all are the ones made by couples in which one person wants a child and the other does not. Although many marital conflicts can be resolved through compromise, there is no such thing as half a baby.

Even couples who are in the habit of listening to each other may turn a deaf ear during baby conversations. It's hard to accept someone else's needs if they clash so brutally with your own. You may find yourself saying or hearing, "How could you do this to me?" or "If you really loved me, you would do what I ask."

In his book, *I and Thou*, existentialist theologian Martin Buber describes two kinds of relationships, the I-thou relationship and the I-it relationship. In the former, a person talks with respect and listens with understanding. In the latter, a person relates to the other as he would to an inanimate object—ignoring the other person's needs while pushing to get his own way. While a good marriage is, by definition, an I-thou relationship, a marriage full of I-it interaction tends to result in unhappiness, if not divorce.

But even happily married couples can slide unknowingly into an I-it relationship when considering the baby dilemma. This can happen for two reasons. First, most couples aren't accustomed to such major conflict since people generally marry someone whose needs coincide or at least do not conflict with theirs. But the baby decision can divide otherwise compatible couples. When they said "I do" to marriage, they may have also said "I do" or "I don't" to children, only to change their minds a few years later. Second, the stakes are high either way, and accepting your partner's choice may seem like an invitation to disaster. People feel much too strongly about the decision to be able to compromise. Even in an excellent relationship, your partner may suddenly seem like an ominous barrier between you and your goal. This may feel extremely lonely, especially if you are used to feeling close.

What generally happens when a couple disagrees? There are four possible outcomes:

1. They postpone the decision until agreement is reached at a later date.

2. The ambivalent partner agrees to the choice of the partner who feels more strongly.

3. One partner twists the other's arm.

4. The partner who feels more strongly about the issue resorts to devious tactics to push for his or her choice. This is similar to arm-twisting, but the methods used may be subtler.

Obviously, the first possibility has the least potential for harming the relationship, as long as the postponement period is mutually agreed upon and as long as the couple set a definite date for re-evaluation. Postponement gives both partners a chance to think over the issue privately and in a less tense atmosphere. Often, they are more willing to negotiate and compromise the second time around. Remembering their earlier battle can motivate both to find a better way this time.

The second solution can be a good one if the ambivalent partner is genuinely ambivalent and can swing either way. In such a case, he or she generally would be able to find either choice satisfying. However, ambivalence sometimes may mean that one partner simply

- Recognize that your preference is simply that—a preference, and that neither your choice nor your partner's is right or wrong in any absolute sense.

First Aid for Battling Couples

By now, I hope you and your partner are ready to discuss the issue of having a baby openly and honestly. But before you do, it might be a good idea for both of you to ask yourselves the following questions. You may come up with some insights that will lead to a faster solution and, at the very least, you'll both have a clearer sense of *all* the issues involved.

- How unhappy would you be if you agreed to your partner's choice? Could you be happy with either decision? Are you feeling stuck even though you think that accepting your partner's choice would probably work?
- Are you totally opposed to your partner's choice or just ambivalent? After doing the exercises in this book and discussing issues with your partner, can you think of any advantages of doing what he or she wants?
- Do you object to your partner's decision itself or rather to the feeling of being pushed? If it's the latter, then ask your partner for a pressure-free moratorium period to give you a chance to make your own decision.
- Is the disagreement unconditional, or are you simply battling about specific conditions such as:

  a. when to have a baby;
  b. how much money can be saved first;
  c. whether you can afford a child on one salary or even two;
  d. whether career issues have to be resolved or career training has to be completed;
  e. incompatible childrearing approaches;
  f. natural pregnancy versus adoption;

    g. the division of labor that would occur after parenthood;

    h. the need for more time before deciding;

    i. a fear of risk-taking;

    j. unresolved ambivalence;

    k. whether to have one child or two?

- Is it possible that you are somewhat in agreement with your partner but stalling in order to bargain for something else? Do you fear that you can't get what you want from your partner if you address the other issue directly?
- Were you originally drawn to your partner because of the very same nurturing qualities that now attract him to parenthood? Or were you attracted by your partner's desire for independence and solitude, qualities that now propel her toward the childfree choice? If so, what would you, your partner, and your marriage lose in terms of those qualities if *your* choice were selected? What pleasure and meaning might you find in honoring your partner's wishes even though this wasn't your first choice?

A useful question is "How could I make my choice easier or more attractive to you?"

Working It Out

Here is how one couple negotiated a compromise. Bettina definitely wanted a baby. Hal was not only uncertain about fathering but also unwilling to talk about it. One day the couple managed to knock down the barrier.

BETTINA: Why do you always change the subject whenever I ask you about having a baby?

HAL: Because I just don't see how it would work out.

BETTINA: Why shouldn't it work out? Don't you want to have children as much as I do?

HAL: Well, I don't know. I guess I want a baby, but I don't think it makes any sense to have one. Look, you complain as it is about my working so hard and not being around much nights and weekends. You want me to take more responsibility than I do. If we had a baby, wouldn't you be even more resentful? You'd have even more work, and I just wouldn't be able to be much help.

BETTINA: Wouldn't be able to or wouldn't be willing to? Lots of men are taking half the load of housework and child care and still managing to get ahead at work.

HAL: But those men are sacrificing their career success. They're just not going to go as far because of their family. That's fine for some men, but it's not fine for me. I'm not willing to slip behind just to have a family. I do think I could offer a child a lot of love and caring. But I can't see myself taking the time to do all the day-to-day diapering and doctor's appointments.

BETTINA: Well, I want to have a baby, but I sure don't want to have to do all the work. I know what you're getting at. You want to have your cake and eat it, too. You're saying to yourself, "Oh, good old Bettina, I know what I'll do. I'll say I don't want a baby even though I do. Poor thing is so desperate to get pregnant she'll agree to anything. I'll get her to say she'll take all the responsibility for the baby." You get the pleasure of fatherhood while I get all the miseries.

HAL: Bettina, maybe I *am* doing that. I don't know. I'm certainly not doing it on purpose. I do want a child but not if it's going to mean sacrificing my career. I don't *feel* like I'm playing a game. I'm really in a quandary. I do want a child, probably as much as you do. I just don't know how we can work it out.

BETTINA: I'm willing to do more than you. I always have, even though I've never liked the situation. But I refuse to be Cinderella. What are we going to do about it?

HAL: For one thing, let's not force ourselves to decide right this minute. If I hit you with an ultimatum like "the baby's all yours or else we're not having it," I know that's not fair. If I agree to have a baby and promise to do more than I really will, I'll be unfair to both of us.

BETTINA: So how can we work this out? Let's see. What if you agree to think about, say, spending Saturdays being responsible for the child? Maybe one day off would be enough for me.

HAL: That is something to think about. Maybe if we didn't have a baby for another two or three years, I might even *want* to gear down a little. I've seen Bill and Harry do that at work. They used to burn the midnight oil a lot more than they do now. They seem to spend more time with their families than they used to. And maybe if I get another promotion or two, we'd be able to afford some help. That would take a lot of the burden off you, and it would take pressure off me.

BETTINA: That sounds OK—I guess. I can't help resenting the sexism in getting yourself out of the housework by paying somebody else to do it. But it does sound like a possible way of having a kid without ruining our lives.

HAL: Yeah, it really seems more workable now. Do you feel better about all this?

BETTINA: I'm still upset, and it's far from resolved, but I do feel more optimistic. I feel better now that you're finally willing to listen and to think about compromises.

HAL: And I feel better, knowing that you're not out to take my career away from me. Why has it taken so long to have this talk?

If you've discussed these issues and you still don't seem to be making any headway, think about these alternatives:

2. How will you handle the decision about having a child if you remarry? Can you be sure a solution will be any easier the second time around?

3. Have you considered the pros and cons of single parenthood? (See Chapter 9, "Alternative Parenting")

4. Do you have realistic expectations about parenthood? Do you think parenthood is so wonderful that it might be worth risking the end of a good marriage?

5. Are you really prepared to leave you partner over this conflict, or are you threatening your partner in hopes of getting what you want? Consider the possibility that your partner may feel so angry and hurt by such declarations that it may take weeks or months to get over this, time that could have gone into planning together in a way that would deepen your relationship.

Try to be realistic about the loss of your partner: it might include emotional turmoil, conflict, loneliness, missing your partner, and the expenses of legal fees and maintaining two households. Even if there is a part of you thinking or saying, "Good riddance!" there is likely another part that still loves and values your partner. That part might wail later on, "What have I done?" Unless your relationship was already on the rocks and you were already considering divorce, leaving could turn out to be even harder than accepting your partner's choice. This situation calls for therapy. I recommend that each of you have a least one individual session with a therapist to clarify your feelings. It's impossible to do this in a couples' session because your partner's presence will inhibit you from fully expressing your feelings and exploring your options. Next, it makes sense to see a couples' therapist to help you either work on the baby conflict or to help you separate with a minimum of animosity.

Even if divorce is the right decision, take care with this transition. Even if you initiated the divorce, and especially if you didn't, you will still need some time to grieve the relationship. There will be things you will miss about your partner and your shared life together. You will need to accomplish this task, no matter how relieved you are that you will be remaining childfree or how much you are looking forward to becoming a parent. Whether you have therapy or get support from family and friends, you will need some transition time. Don't neglect self-care, such as eating, sleeping, and exercise. Ask for help when you need it.

Taking the time for this transition will prepare you for seeking a new relationship and/or parenthood.

It may be appealing to think about how you will become a parent in your new life situation. Perhaps you are considering adoption on your own as a single parent or with a new partner. Keep in mind, however, that adoption agencies will want to ascertain that you have healed enough from your marriage to be fully ready to focus on the adoption process and on nurturing your child, and they will usually want you to have been married for at least two, if not three years before you are eligible to adopt. If you are considering pregnancy, should you need a high-tech, stressful fertility treatment such as in-vitro fertilization, your program will require a psychological evaluation, and you may face disappointment if the program's psychological screening evaluation professional thinks you need more time healing to be ready for the roller coaster of hope and disappointment as well as the medical and logistical stresses.

Of course, if you are thinking of leaving your partner in order to remain childfree, you will not have the same time pressures as the people who are divorcing in order to meet their needs to parent. Nevertheless, you will experience financial losses and emotional losses that may inhibit your starting a new relationship or pursuing the activities you preferred over parenting.

None of this is to say that leaving your partner to become a parent is impossible or that it might not be a good solution. These notes are simply to help you think your decision through carefully. Your resilience will help you weather the storms, and this decision may work out well for you. Obviously, these are tough considerations.

The Second Time Around

Simon and Judy's marriage seemed to be made in heaven—the first year, that is. This is his second marriage, her first. At their first anniversary dinner, Judy made a toast: "May we have a little one to celebrate by our second anniversary."

Simon choked on his shrimp cocktail. When he stopped coughing, he looked at Judy as if Dr. Jekyll had suddenly turned into Ms. Hyde. "But, Judy! Why spoil all this? Do you have any idea what a kid would do to our marriage?"

For the moment, joyous thoughts of their marriage were overshadowed by gloomy visions of divorce. Simon knew more about divorce than he wanted to. His previous twelve-year marriage had ended in divorce. And when Simon moved out he didn't just leave a wife. Simon already had an eight-year-old daughter and a twelve-year-old son with his first wife.

Although Simon loves his children, he never chose to have them. His ex-wife's first pregnancy was an accident. He had enjoyed having a son, even though the marriage was stressful. Then against his better judgment, he agreed to have a second child "so Josh won't be lonely."

Simon and Judy talked about the baby decision before they decided to marry—well, they half-talked about it. Both had been aware of Judy's interest in children, and both had mentally filed this under L for "later." The question was just too scary. After all the emotional trauma they had gone through to be together, surely they wouldn't let a teeny tiny baby issue keep them apart? They didn't want to lose each other.

They managed to get back into the anniversary spirit, and postpone discussion about the conflict. They felt uneasy about the topic, but felt their relationship was strong. They were committed to working it through.

If you want to be a parent and you marry someone who already has children from a previous marriage, you can expect the tug-of-war to be more intense for the following reasons:

1. **Differential willingness to sacrifice.** The ABP (Already Been a Parent) has experienced both the joys and stresses of parenthood, and the idea of starting all over again can be quite daunting. For the NBP (Never Been a Parent), on the other hand, the pleasure of having a baby would appear to outweigh the sacrifices involved during the early years. The trade-off seems worth it. But the ABP has already experienced those pleasures firsthand, and in his or her eyes the sacrifices involved in parenting, at least a second time, with today's possibly lower energy level may outweigh the joys.

2. **Economic considerations.** Many ABPs have to make child-support payments, and the idea of new bills may be quite frightening. If the budget is stretching to care for two existing children, perhaps it will burst with a third. The specter of one more college tuition can be terrifying.

3. **The unfairness issue**. If you are longing for a baby, you'll resent that his ex-wife got to have kids, but you may not. And even if you do have a child, you may have to live frugally because of child support. There may be stress about the time your husband spends with his older children at your home or elsewhere.

Separate Faces – An Exercise for the ABP

Are you blurring your ex-wife and your present wife into one image of Wife-As-Mother? Try to imagine your ex-wife's face. Now imagine your wife's face. Picture a solid white line between them, separating them in your mind. Now try to figure out how much of the unpleasantness of your fatherhood experience stemmed from the unpleasantness of your first marriage? How would parenthood be different with your present wife? Are you making an unfair assumption that all women mother in the same way your ex-wife did? You chose your second wife because you thought you would be happier with her. Is it possible that you would enjoy parenting with her more than you did the first time? What characteristics does she have that might make her a better mother? Are they the same characteristics that make her a lovable partner, i.e., affection, patience, an ability to communicate?

enjoyed traveling, or spent years hanging out with friends, you're less likely to chomp at the bit if you have to stay home with a newborn. And despite the persistence of the stereotype, most older couples have little trouble adjusting to being tied down even though they are used to so much freedom.

- **You probably have more patience and tolerance** to bring to parenthood now than you would have had when you were younger.
- **You are likely to be more financially secure than when you were younger** and, therefore, more likely to be able to hold on to your standard of living and to hire household help and babysitters.
- **If either of you wants to cut back to part-time employment or take a year off, it's easier if you're both established professionally.** And of course, your increased nest egg facilitates such cutbacks.
- **Because you're older, you may be better at combining career and parenthood.** In *Passages*, Gail Sheehy thought that older women seemed to have a better chance of integrating career and motherhood.

Disadvantages of Delayed Parenthood

- **The medical risks for both mother and baby are higher.** There is also a higher risk for genetic defects.
- **Some older parents find that they don't have enough physical energy to keep up with their kids.** It may be harder to play ball with them or take them on camping or hiking trips.
- **Although life expectancies are increasing, with many people having long, healthy older years, there is some chance your child might lose you to death before he's reached adulthood.**
- **You may never get to see your grandchildren, especially if your child herself delays parenthood.**
- **You may have to face the problems of retirement and empty nest at the same time.**
- **If you take several years off from work, you may have trouble going back.** You may run into ageism.

- **If you're thirty-eight when you give birth, then you'll be fifty-six by the time the child is grown.** You may wind up envying your friends who had their children at twenty, emptied their nest at forty, and have more energy to play with their grandchildren.
- **If you have fertility problems, they may get worse as you get older.**

The Medical Story

Although the chances of fertility problems, miscarriage, and birth defects increase with age, your chances of having a healthy baby are probably still reasonably good. If you're healthy, eat well, exercise, and have good prenatal care, your chances of having a healthy baby may be *better* than those of a younger woman whose health is below par. Of course, you will want to talk to your gynecologist, urologist, and other treating specialists for information specific to you.

It is possible to test for some genetic defects during the pregnancy. If the baby would have serious problems, you might consider terminating the pregnancy. This is obviously a difficult choice, but knowing it is possible may be important to you, especially if you are over thiry-five. Even if you do not terminate the pregnancy, you might want to have the information in advance so that you and your medical team can be prepared. (For detailed information about this concern, see genetic counselor Kayla Sheets' "Preparing for and Screening for a Healthy Baby" in the appendix.)

Motherhood Over 35 Is Not for Everybody

For many women, motherhood before thirty is preferable; those women who want to have it all, but not at the same time, may want to put their energies into parenting first and focus on work in their later years. This can be a good choice for a woman already in her mid-twenties who hasn't made a career commitment yet. By the time she decides what she wants to do and establishes herself in that

3. Old wives' tales continue, but you can challenge them and sort this out for yourselves.

According to Margaret Mead in *Margaret Meade, Some Personal Views*, (Rhoda Metraux, ed.) the one-child family is the family of the future. She predicted that women would marry and have one child relatively late in life in order to be mature enough to integrate motherhood and career. She thought that if women had more than one child, the demands of work roles and parenting roles would be too great. Having one child could make for a balanced life without undue stress.

If you are a two-career couple, having an only child may be the perfect way to have your cake and eat it, too. You can reap all the rewards of parenthood without being overwhelmed by too many burdens.

Advantages of an Only Child

- **You spend fewer years raising young children, so you're less tied down.** You also don't have to spend as many years worrying about child care or as many dollars paying for it.
- **You can involve the child in your work and your social life.** It's not so hard to take one school-aged child to a friend's house, to a meeting, or even to some workplaces.
- **You have more time and attention to give one child.** It's hard enough to juggle one child and a career, but when you have two children, what little "quality time" you do have has to be juggled between both. Parents of only children treasure their one-to-one time with their child. Fathers and mothers may take turns having special, intimate reading times or special trips.
- **Even if you're a full-time, at-home mother, a one-child family may turn out to be the most satisfying.** You have the time to paint, dance, do volunteer work, or pursue other activities you like. Or you might want to revel in motherhood, making natural baby food, starting a play group, and picnicking in the

backyard. There are mothers who love these activities with one child but who would not enjoy them as much with two. They would feel frustrated having to divide their attention between two children.

- **Two children are noisier than one.** If you must have a house that rivals a monastery, then you shouldn't have a child. But if you want a relative balance of child and quiet, you might be more satisfied with just one child.

One child means less distraction. You won't have two children competing for your attention. You have to referee a lot of fights. Also there are no guarantees that siblings would actually enjoy each other's company. Even if they do get along, they may have very different interests that make it hard to plan joint family activities. One child makes planning easier.

Disadvantages to Having an Only Child

- **Some only children demand a lot of attention because they lack companionship.** You can solve this problem by helping your child make arrangements to be with her friends, but this doesn't always work. Winter snowstorms and summer vacations may deprive your child of companionship, while other children have siblings as built-in companions. However, don't let this problem hold you back from having an only child. Most parents of only children prefer the hassle of making social arrangements for one child to the far greater hassles of raising two children. Play dates are popular with all families so typically they are not hard to arrange.
- **Other only children don't demand attention, but they get it anyway.** As one described it: "I think about my folks as Mama and Papa bird—each perched on one of my shoulders." As the parent of an only child, you do have to be careful not to smother or overprotect the child, or make him the repository of all *your* dreams and hopes. All children need independence, need to

make their own decisions and dream their own dreams. If you give your only child these gifts, rest assured he will thrive.

Deciding to Have a Second Child

Couples who make the first baby decision carefully often become careless about a second (or third). They assume that since one child has been fun, two children will be twice the fun. Although you can't be sure that your pleasure will be doubled, you can assume that your workload will at least feel as if it has been tripled. According to some parents, one plus one equals 200 percent more stress. So think twice before you decide on two, and read the preceding section to make sure you're not falling prey to only-child myths.

The only *good* reason for a second child is a strong desire for one. And even then, you have to ask yourself:

- Can we afford another child financially and psychologically?
- Can the world's population accept another contribution from this family?
- Are we willing to be *much* more tied down than we already are?
- What do we want from the next child that our first child can't give us? Are our expectations likely to be met by a second child?

As you work on your second baby decision, make sure you're not considering another child for any of the following reasons:

- Your first child is becoming too grown up and independent, and you want someone you can cuddle and hang onto.
- You need a change in your life, a new meaning.
- You're tired of being pressured to have another child, and it seems easier to give in.
- You believe the myths about only children. You think you have to give Sean a little sister.
- You want a child of the opposite sex.

If this last reason hits home, consider why it is so important to you. If you're the mother of a boy, do you want a girl so she can become the kind of woman you always wanted to be? If you're the father of a girl, do you feel a son will somehow validate your masculinity? There are many hidden agendas involved in a desire for a child of the opposite sex. If you would simply enjoy a child of the opposite sex, is there an already existing boy or girl with whom you could develop a special relationship instead? For instance, if you love little girls' dresses, could you shop for your niece? If you want a boy, could you coach a boys' sports team?

And what will you do if the child turns out to be the "wrong" sex? Try again? And again? There must be a better way!

Considering a Third Child

Jocelyn is a happily married mother of three-year-old twins and has a part-time job as a mental health professional. She and her husband Matt, who is very involved in the children's care, live in a comfortable house outside Boston. They have been talking about a third child with a mixture of attraction and fear. What if a new baby wasn't as easy as the twins? Can their income stretch enough? Might they be overwhelmed? At the same time, Matt, who comes from a large family, has fond memories of growing up. Jocelyn, even though blessed with an easy, uneventful twin pregnancy, longs for a chance to have just one newborn with whom to cherish a quiet intimacy.

Jocelyn and her husband Matt are lucky. They earn good incomes; their children are relatively easy. Both of their mothers live nearby, and her mother-in-law is the children's nanny. While they may be the envy of cash-strapped couples who can't even imagine the costs of child care and college tuition for a third child, the decision is still scary.

Parents of three children comment that the addition of the third child means that a larger proportion of family time will be spent at home than when there were only two children. You might want to think about how much you like hanging out at home while considering a third child. Does this vision seem ideal to you, or might it give you trepidations of cabin fever?

The "Don't Confuse Me with the Facts" Game

Let's take a look at what can happen if you don't make your second child decision carefully.

Alina and Jake have started trying for a second pregnancy, without anticipating any potential problems. They have always cherished dreams of a family of four in a big white house in the country. Their reality is very different: not four children but one, a toddler named Chrissy, and not a large house in the country, but a small apartment in the city. There isn't enough money for more children or more space. Jake is a paraprofessional counselor with high job satisfaction but low pay. Alina is home with Chrissy full-time. The couple vaguely considers finances but dismisses the question with platitudes such as, "Where there's a will, there's a way." That's a great slogan but it doesn't change their bank balance.

The purpose of the game: to avoid looking at the realities that would lead to a decision to forgo or at least delay child number two.

The payoff: getting child number two.

The price: Jake and Alina are going to be pinched tighter than ever before. And they'll feel like kicking themselves for their impracticality. They may even find that Alina has to work, instead of raising Chrissy full-time, a goal the couple has felt strongly about. She might have to bring two children to day care instead of being home with one.

The counter game: Alina and Jake should sit down and go over their budget. They should ask themselves how and when another child might fit in. They might:

- Seriously question why it's so important to have another child, and ask themselves how they might otherwise fill the need. For instance, if they want companions for Chrissy, she and Alina might join a play group. Or Alina could become a day care mother.

- Consider ways to boost their income. Jake could look for a higher paying job. Alina might consider supplementing their income with freelance or part-time work.

By being willing to talk about the issue, this couple won't just fall into a sea of second child distress. They will either make their peace with being a one-child family, or they will address the above issues before having a child. By being proactive, they will enjoy their family life regardless of the choice they make.

The moral of this story: be honest and realistic about your ability to cope with a second child both financially and emotionally. If you can, that's great. But if you can't, find a way to have a good life with the child you already have. Take the time to grieve the fantasized second child you will never know. You may want to write a letter or have a good-bye ritual.

Read about and seek out other one-child families. Now that we have exploded the myths, you can be confident that you will enjoy your family life. It will certainly help that this family form is becoming more common, due to finances, later parenthood and infertility, and more couples choosing to stop at one for better work/family balance.

If you are going to have another child, plan ahead for the financial, psychological, and emotional changes for everyone in the household. Take a refresher adoption or childbirth class, preferably with your partner if you have one. Expect the first several weeks to be chaotic, and ask for the help you need from each other, family and friends. Find out from friends, your pediatrician and reading how to prepare your first child for a sibling. Ask your librarian for picture books on the topic, such as *No One Asked Me if I Wanted a Baby Sister* by Martha Alexander.

✦ CHAPTER 9 ✦
ALTERNATIVE PARENTING

Gay Parenting

The legalization of gay marriage, in addition to being a cause for great celebration in and of itself, also bodes well for wider acceptance of gay parenthood. An important shift in the world at large has been to see that gays have wanted to marry not to destroy marriage but to respect it by participating in it and committing to the same sort of loving, long-term committed relationships that straight people have enjoyed. It is a logical extension of this concept that gay people who choose to have children are likewise honoring and respecting the wider meaning of family.

Despite the advances of gay rights, including marriage, homophobia has not yet been erased, and concerns about hostility or disapproval of gay parenting may give you pause. My gay clients often say something similar to Liz, a thirty-seven-year-old who is considering adopting a Guatemalan child with her partner: "I managed to survive coming out despite prejudice and the snail's pace at which my family accepted me. But now Elli and I wonder, what discrimination might our child have to face, without the adult coping skills and support groups that helped us?"

Kevin McGarry, who adopted a daughter with his partner, offers inspiration in his book, *Fatherhood for Gay Men:* ". . . we concluded that we could not let the bigotry of others determine the shape of our family and lives. There remains a lot of hatred for gay people, but we realized that if we let the hatred stop us from adopting, then the hate would have won, and that was unacceptable to us."

In *The Lesbian and Gay Parenting Handbook*, April Martin also offers encouraging thoughts on the acceptance of gay families:

People's worst fears—that our children will be harmed by teasing, shaming or social ostracism for coming from a gay family—do not seem to be coming to pass. On the contrary, the pride we feel in our families gives our children the tools to deal with prejudice. As in any family that contains a member of an oppressed minority, our children learn to understand the problems of ignorance and bias. Depending on where they live and who they are, they make decisions about whom to tell and whom not to tell. In general, our children only rarely encounter any significant homophobic treatment. In instances when they do, they are prepared to handle it.

Martin also points out that how gay parents talk to others can lead to respect: "When we speak about our families without hesitation, with a cheerful, confident attitude that presumes we will be respected and liked, we make it almost impossible for other people to respond negatively."

It is also important to recognize that some LGBT persons don't care to marry even if they are in a committed relationship nor do they consider parenthood attractive. They say that these institutions, generally embraced by straight society, are confining and detract from the freedom and alternative ways of living that being gay has afforded.

Some lesbians find that becoming mothers brings them closer to their mothers. Casandra McIntyre writes about this in her essay "Two Ubermoms Are Better Than One," in *Confessions of the Other Mother.*

That Amy and I each gave birth made us feel more like a legitimate family to our respective parents. . . . It was something that made sense to both our moms. And it gave each of them a role in our lives that they were comfortable with: grandmother.

An important consideration for family continuity is to formally adopt your child if she is biologically related to your partner but not to you. (see Bibliography and Resources.)

What's on your mind as you think about becoming a parent? Did you and your partner talk about a family when you first met, or is this something that has come up more recently? If you both are interested in parenting, then you can get right down to the logistics: pregnancy if you are lesbians, surrogacy or co-parenting with a friend if you are a gay couple, or adoption. You will find guidance in the checklist below as well as the Bibliography and Resources in this book.

If, however, one of you wants a child and the other does not, or if one of you is very certain and the other has a lot of questions, give yourselves time to sort this out. You can do the exercise in Chapter 2, "Secret Doors." You should do them individually so you won't be unduly influenced by your partner's responses. If after time and reflection, you find you are disagreeing on whether to have a child follow some of the suggestions in Chapter 6, "Tug-of-War."

Checklist for Gay Couples Who May Become Parents

- Whom can we count on for support?
- Whom can we talk to in our social circle?
- What are the pros and cons of this decision for each of us as individuals, and for us as a couple?
- How can we find out how gay parents deal with schools and communities to promote both understanding and our child's and family's wellbeing?
- Are we disagreeing about whether or when to have a child? How can we resolve this through conversations or counseling?
- Do we prefer pregnancy or adoption? If we are a male couple, do we want to consider a surrogate pregnancy with a donated egg? Have we considered a co-parenting pregnancy with a female friend?
- If we are a female couple, have we decided which of us will carry the child?

- Do we both want to be biological parents? If so, do we want more than one child? If so, how do we determine who goes first? Is one of us more eager than the other to be a biological parent?
- If we are lesbians who both hope to experience pregnancy, do we want the older person to go first because she might be less fertile later, or do we want the younger or more fertile person to go first? (if we have this medical knowledge)? Based on age, health, career development, and other family obligations such as a frail parent, who should go first?

If you are gay but don't have a partner, you may find the Single Parenting section of this book useful as well.

Single Parenting

Did you assume that by the time your reached your current age that you would be married and have a child? You are not alone. Many women who have chosen to have a child on their own have done so when they realized that "It's now or never for motherhood." They realized that their biological clock might run out before they found an ideal partner to be their child's parent. Although they typically have had a rougher time than two-parent families, most are glad they made the choice.

In this context, the phrase "Single Mothers by Choice," for almost everyone I've worked with in this circumstance is inaccurate; it would be more accurate to say "Single Mothers by Second Choice." This phrase would more appropriately recognize the efforts they have made to find a partner even though it doesn't fully recognize the current power and joy of the families created.

When I was clinical director of RESOLVE, one of my duties was managing a national telephone hotline for women with fertility problems. I frequently heard an anxious voice over the line. "Please can you help me? I don't know if I have a fertility problem, but I'm single and want to do donor insemination. I have been curtly turned away by one practice that does D.I. in my small city. Can you refer me to someone who will work with me?" It was clear to me that these women felt as desperate and distressed as our fertility patients. Since this problem didn't meet the mandate of our organization, I was not able to offer help as a RESOLVE employee other than to suggest other donor insemination referrals. The national organization, Single Mothers by Choice did not yet exist. Seeing a great need, I knew I needed to help.

I began leading adult education workshops on single motherhood, did some research on supportive doctors, and set up a monthly support group, Boston Single Mothers by Choice, to have monthly potluck dinners and share resources for decisions, pregnancy, and adoption, and parenting. I'm happy to say the group still exists, and members who have already raised their children sometimes mentor younger women in the decision-making process.

I was disappointed that most of my mental health colleagues were not enthusiastic about my efforts. "What you will find are women who are highly anxious, moody, and describe their lives as empty. They are looking to a child to care for their needs and will not be able to nurture their children."

In the thirty-three years that I have worked with hundreds of single mothers, I have found the women described above to be a tiny minority. I have met courageous, successful, pro-active women who have the maturity, the finances, and the motivation to devote themselves to a child and be excellent mothers. These women may not be in ongoing, committed relationships, but they have healthy, emotionally close relationships with family and friends. I am so grateful to have worked with these women in Boston and learned from them some of what you will learn in this book.

I am also glad to say that my colleagues, after observing so many healthy single women and their babies thrive now sometimes bring up the idea even before their clients do! And of course, some mental health professionals themselves are single mothers by choice and serve as role models.

Now let's look at ways to help you figure out if you, too, would like to be a single parent. Let's start by taking stock of your current thoughts.

List of Possible Decisions for
Single People Considering Parenthood

1. I want to be a single parent although I hope later on to meet a partner who can help me raise my child.

2. I want to be a single parent and put relationships on the back burner

3. I'm between twenty-nine and thirty-five, so I'd like to see if I can meet a partner. If I can't I'll consider doing this on my own down the road. (You may find peace of mind by having this option.)

4. I've decided to pursue parenthood. I need to decide among pregnancy, surrogacy, and adoption.

Another Possibility/ The Reframe

Have you ever considered that having a baby or finding a partner might not be your best response to your "What Next? Is this all there is?" question.

Some people are choosing to make life more meaningful not by having a baby, but by focusing less, if at all, on finding a partner, and focusing more on what a single, passionate life could yield in meaningful work, friendship, and whole-hearted commitments. In Kate Bolick's *Spinster: Making a Life of One's Own* and Rebecca Traister's *All the Single Ladies,* you will find fascinating reading and interesting role models.

If you choose single parenthood, some of the issues you will deal with will include handling dating and relationships while pursuing parenthood or after you have a child, and helping your child deal with identity issues, e.g., "Do I have a daddy?"

Another issue that comes up in single parenting is that there may be a need to dilute the intensity of the parent-child bond that could contribute to separation anxiety on the part of the parent and child, including when beginning school or new activities or when the nest empties.

Will My Child Feel Weird and Alone?

Many parents worry about this possibility. Single or LGBT parents or those who adopted, used donors, or surrogacy also are concerned about whether their child will stand out, be ridiculed, or otherwise be mistreated. Familiarity with and respect for non-traditional families varies according to the population make-up, school districts designations, and the religious and political beliefs of your neighbors, congregants, and community. When you add to the mix children of divorce and children from other countries and practicing other religions, you may be pleasantly surprised at just how diverse your child's circles turn out to be. And of course, all children benefit from being exposed to so many families and possibilities, including childfree families of two. (See the Bibliography and Resources to find advice from professionals and parents from alternative families on communicating with neighbors, teachers, and others.)

You may also want to participate in support or meet-up groups of families similar to yours. Such groups may include groups of people considering parenthood, parenting groups, or groups of single mothers that combine the two, with separate groups for "thinkers," "tryers" and mothers, followed by a potluck where everyone interacts.

One good thing about single parenthood is that your child will know he or she was loved and wanted. You made a conscious choice and went to great effort to bring this child into your life.

When people say, "It's hard enough to raise a child with a partner. Isn't it going to be tough for you?" give them the benefit of the doubt. They're wishing you could parent with a partner (and maybe you actually will down the road), but they're not thinking realistically about your choices. Elle told her older sister, "I'd rather be a forty-two-year-old single mother than be childless. I'm forty-two anyway, and I'd rather be fulfilled than disgruntled."

Some people worry that if they "tie themselves down with a kid" they will never find a partner. In fact, some people wind up with the Great American dream in reverse order, finding a partner who falls in love with their child as well as them. Many women who have attended my workshops tell me that it is suddenly easier to look for a partner when they know that they can have a child on her own. You can kiss desperation goodbye when tonight's date isn't your only ticket to motherhood. You no longer have to wonder if he will commit fast enough to beat your biological clock.

You now get to replace desperation with curiosity. Am I attracted to him? Do I feel good when I'm with him? Is he fun? Do I want to see him again? You may also find that a new partner is attracted to you partly because of your decision. He could admire your courage and value your nurturing abilities.

Some single friends, in addition to being happy for you, may be eager to coach you through childbirth, encourage you through an adoption process, or be involved in your family life. In some single mothers-by-choice support groups, women who rule out motherhood for themselves connect with another woman who has a child so that they can have a special relationship with a particular child and provide respite for the mother. Everybody wins. (See "Para Dads and Para Moms" by Pepper Schwartz, in the Single Parent section of the Bibliography.)

You may find that siblings and friends in more traditional families are enormously excited for you, even if they worry about some of the problems you may face in terms of discrimination or overwork. If they have enjoyed being parents themselves, they can be glad that you will enjoy childrearing, too. They may have a strong sense of what you'll miss if you never have a child, and they may also find inspiration in your courage to have a child under tougher circumstances.

In addition to single men and women and LGBT persons, other people may be judged negatively by some people including fertility doctors, adoption workers, or other professionals. If you are low-income, have a medical problem that could make pregnancy or parenting harder, are an unmarried couple, or are over forty, it is absolutely crucial to find professionals who treat you with respect. It is worth asking around: friends, doctors, clergy, or counselors you trust, or adoption and fertility referral organizations, or online groups. The extra research will pay off in your comfort-level when you work with people who want to help you become a parent. Their support doesn't necessarily mean they won't have questions and guidance for you. In fact, their expertise may well be useful, but because they are supportive, you'll know their questions and suggestions are intended to help rather than hinder your choice. These professionals may also be able to refer you to support groups, classes, or websites.

Thank goodness for options. Today single people can get pregnant or adopt. In this section, we won't be talking about people who became single parents through divorce or death. We'll be talking about women and men who consciously choose to become parents on their own, without a partner.

Why Be a Single Parent?

There are a number of reasons for choosing single parenthood. Some people simply don't want a partner even though they do want a child. Others would prefer to be married but haven't found the right person yet. Single parenthood, for many, is a better alternative than marrying the wrong person just to have a child before the biological alarm goes off.

The typical single mother by choice is a college-educated career woman in her late thirties to mid-forties who is divorced or never married. At this point on her fertility continuum, having a child is more important to her than having a partner. She knows that she may find a life mate at forty-seven or fifty, but she can't wait that long for a child. She may have wanted a child for a long time but "delayed her gratification" until finishing her education or getting established in her career. But when the "right" time came, Mr. Right hadn't yet shown up.

Joys of Single Parenthood

- **An intimate relationship with a child.** Discovering the pleasure of sharing, caring, and commitment with another human being. Some singles feel their lives are lonely and meaningless, devoid of human connections. A child can provide meaning and stability in one's life. However, this should be a benefit, *not* a motivation for choosing single parenthood. If you have a child because you're lonely or unhappy, both of you may suffer.

- **The satisfaction of doing things your way.** Partners often disagree about child-rearing tactics, and power struggles are common. As a single parent, you can call the shots and make all the decisions.
- **In the case of adoption, the joy of providing a good home to a child who needs one.** Just be clear that you are doing more than a good deed. "I need this child as much as she needs me," adoptive parents tell me.
- **A new self-respect for having the courage to make a choice that's right for you even though others may disapprove.**
- **A sense of pride in being able to manage parenthood without a partner.**
- **A sense of interdependence.** You may never have realized how loving and caring your family and friends were until you needed their help in caring for your sick child or relieving you for an afternoon. They may even anticipate your needs better than you do. And even if some of these people disappoint you in their follow-through, you may be pleasantly surprised by others who step in.

Difficulties of Single Parenthood

- **You may feel isolated at times as a one-parent family in a two-parent world.** And you may feel overburdened both psychologically and financially.
- **Your social life and your life as a parent may clash.** Your child may resent your partner, your partner may resent your child, and you may resent their resentment! Dating becomes more difficult since time is less available and child care arrangements have to be made.
- **You're soloing in a job that's tough even for two.** Can you handle the frustration, the isolation? Remember that if you are resourceful and resilient, you may parent better than many couples!
- **You may encounter prejudice from unexpected quarters,**

such as family and friends whom you thought would be supportive. Such disapproval can be hard to handle especially if you weren't prepared for it. And even if you expected it, living with it may be more difficult than you thought it would.

It's Your Choice

Despite these difficulties, there is one important compensation: you've chosen to be a single parent voluntarily and consciously. In contrast, those who become single parents by default—through divorce or death—have no choice in the matter. You are proactively *adding* a child to create your family. In the case of widowed and divorced parents, fate has *subtracted* a co-parent. You prepared in advance to handle single parenting. The divorced or widowed parent, on the other hand, expected to share the responsibility and may be ill-prepared to go it alone. Another consideration, if you're intimidated by the potential burden is that many mothers who are married might as well be single for all the help they get from their husbands.

Mikki Morrisette, single mother of two and author of *Choosing Single Motherhood: The Thinking Woman's Guide,* ends her book with two paragraphs that can, along with the checklist below, contribute to your self-evaluation:

> It is never my intention to encourage women to take this step lightly. While I believe everyone can, I recognize that many should not. Yes, there are issues of finances, fatherlessness, biological identity, energy, and ability to offer basic, quality parenting skills: open communication, authoritative discipline, respect, and effective stress management. But what it boils down to is whether each one of us has the heart to raise a child.
>
> To be a responsible parent, quite simply, requires the capacity to love. If your heart is open, and you have the good judgment required to be responsive to someone else's needs, as well as the capacity to set limits,

then you have the ingredients needed to build a Choice Home {the author's term for a family created by a single mother by choice} filled with the simple, connect-the-dot moments that every child needs.

Considerations for Potential Single Parents

1. What is your financial situation? Can you reasonably support a child? If you want to work part-time after the child's birth or after you adopt, will you be able to afford to? If you want to continue working full-time, what sort of child care can you get, and how comfortable will you be with it? Are you willing to cut down on travel, movies, dinners out? Can you live on a tighter budget? Remember, the money you've been spending on yourself will have to be spread to cover two. Your willingness or unwillingness may serve as values clarification for how much a baby matters to you.

2. What is your social situation? If you are in a relationship, do you want your partner to be the biological and/or psychological parent? Is s/he willing? If so, how will this affect your relationship? Are you harboring unrealistic hopes that parenting together will lead to a permanent commitment? And if a man serves as biological father or as the major father figure, how would your partner react? How will a child affect your relationships with your friends—male and female?

3. What is your family situation? Will your parents, siblings, and other relatives be supportive or critical? How will a child affect your relations with them, both negatively and positively? If these people are conservative, will they accept the child once they get to know him? It's important to distinguish between hostile criticism and sincere concern for your welfare. Are they expressing narrow-minded or rigid attitudes, or are they asking important, useful questions that may not have occurred to you? And if they are just narrow-minded, can you live with the hostility or perhaps even outright rejection of you and the child? Can your child live with it as well? Keep in mind, that many people who originally discouraged you may fall in love with your child, and realize that you made a good decision after all.

4. What is your support system? If you have a baby, who would coach you through childbirth? Who would help you when you got home from the hospital? Who would you visit on Sunday afternoons? Where would you and the child spend Christmas or Passover? Would you be able to call someone and say, "This kid is driving me crazy. Do you have time to talk?" or "Could you come over and stay with Emma while I go out for a while?" With whom will you share the bad moments (terrible twos, high fevers) and the good (first tooth, a blue ribbon at the science fair)? You may not need a partner's support, but you will need somebody's. That somebody can include lovers, friends of both sexes, family members, and paid help. No happy, single parent truly parents alone. If she lacks a co-star, she'll need a whole cast of supporting actors instead. You may not be able to anticipate or predict who all these people will be, but you should have some people in mind and check out their availability.

5. Can you establish a comfortable balance of independence and interdependence? Are you independent enough to raise a child on your own? Can you also allow yourself some healthy dependence, asking others for help when you need it?

6. Are you choosing single parenthood for any of the following *wrong* reasons:

- Do you believe that a child will cure your loneliness? He or she may, for a few years, but older children generally spend more time with their peers than with their parents. And then they leave home.
- Do you like being in control and believe you can control a child better than an adult? Would it be easier for you to be intimate with a child than with an adult? Again, these are problems to be worked out in therapy, *not* through your child. If you become a parent for either of these reasons, you could wind up becoming intrusive, tyrannical, or overprotective. You and your child would both suffer.

7. What resources are available in your community? Are there single-parent support groups that offer emotional support as well as practical assistance with housing, jobs, and child care co-ops? It's really great to share joys and frustrations with others in your situation. Are there any single mothers around with whom you might want to live? Find out if there is any co-housing or other communal housing that includes parents and children, both married and single. If you know other single parents, ask them about their experiences, both pro and con. If you can, spend some time with them to see what their lives are like. Compare the similarities and differences between their situations and reactions and yours. Might it make sense to move to a more accommodating community, for instance Oregon or Vermont with a slower pace or a lot of support? Don't forget the online communities and listservs that can overcome isolation.

8. How will you go about getting or having a child? You have three basic options:

- A biological pregnancy
- Donor insemination
- Adoption.

Let's consider some of the advantages and disadvantages of each.

Pregnancy Through Intercourse

Women who decide to conceive through intercourse, rather than via donor insemination, have two alternatives: to choose a man with whom they have a committed relationship or a man they know casually. In either case, a woman has to decide whether to be honest about her objectives. Some women are having unprotected sex without telling their sex partner about their interest in a baby. They reason that if their lover knew they were trying to get pregnant he might refuse to cooperate, end the relationship, or try to get custody at some later point. Therefore, by not telling, things will be less complicated. However, when a single woman is trying to get pregnant and not doing clinic insemination, the relationship is complicated and there's no getting around that fact.

First, consider what might happen if the man involved is a longtime lover whom you don't want to lose. What will you do when you get pregnant? Pretend it was an accident? Confess?

Suppose the potential father is a new lover. You might argue that sex is taking place between two consenting adults. But just because a man has consented to intercourse doesn't mean he has consented to fatherhood. You are taking the liberty of making a parenthood decision for the two of you. Some women counter by saying, "Well, men have always used us for sex, leaving us with unwanted babies in the process. Why can't we use them for babies that we *do* want?"

I believe that men and women are both entitled to make decisions about procreation. Even if you are willing to take complete financial and psychological responsibility for the child, I don't think a man should be put in the position of unintended fatherhood. There are many conscientious men who wouldn't like the idea that a child they fathered is being raised by somebody else and that they are not caring for her or him.

Perhaps you think that what he doesn't know won't hurt him, and you may be right. But it *will* hurt you and your baby. A good parent-child relationship, in my opinion, is based on honesty. When you use a lover as if he were a non-anonymous sperm bank, you are falling into the kind of I-it relationship we discussed in Chapter 6, "Tug-of-War."

Another problem is that at some point your child will ask you about his or her father. You will either have to pretend you don't know or admit that the father has never been told. Obviously either of these responses could cause anguish for both you and the child, not to mention the father, should you or the child contact him later.

However, legal morasses may, unfortunately, prevent you from being open with your lover even if you are so inclined. According to attorneys specializing in family law, if a man knows he's your baby's father, he can sue you for visitation rights and/or for custody even if you're not married and he previously signed an agreement waiving paternal rights and you previously signed an agreement not to demand child support. Even if you don't tell him the baby is his, if he suspects it is, he can file a paternity suit. If the appropriate blood tests, etc., establish him to be the father, he can sue for visitation rights and/or custody.

At any rate, if you are considering motherhood via a sex partner, *it is essential to consult an attorney specializing in family law.* The attorney will need to know family laws in more than one state if your partner lives elsewhere. With the proper information, personal and legal conversations, you can make an informed decision.

Donor Insemination

This procedure has an advantage in that the anonymity of the father is guaranteed and all parental rights are legally terminated. For this reason, women who want to ensure that the father will never try to see the child, become involved in his or her life, or sue for custody often choose this method. Other women are drawn to artificial insemination because it does not risk inadvertent coercion, or relationship confusion with the men in their life. If you are interested in artificial insemination, contact a women's health clinic, a hospital obstetrics and gynecology clinic, or a private doctor.

There is an option called the "Yes" donor. These donors, like permanently anonymous donors, release parental rights at the time of donation but express a willingness to be contacted when their donor offspring reaches the age of eighteen. He may or may not agree to contact but is potentially open to the possibility. The advantage of a "Yes" donor is that there is the potential for some contact when the child is grown. However, there is no guarantee that the Yes donor will actually agree to the contact, and the child and mother could wind up disappointed. This outcome, or having a potentially unpleasant experience if there is a meeting, needs to be weighed against the advantage of the child's potential satisfaction with meeting their donor. Similar to adoption searches, the child may feel a desire to find "the missing puzzle piece" as a part of coming of age. If you are planning to use donor insemination, your fertility clinic and sperm bank can provide you with more information.

Women who are understandably uncomfortable with the idea of an anonymous donor—"too impersonal," "too clinical," "like science fiction"—give more consideration to pregnancy with a man they know. This can occur with the man being screened at a fertility clinic and donating sperm, which are injected into the woman's uterus at the clinic.

For some women, who prefer to bypass doctor's offices, it is possible to inseminate themselves at home with their donor's semen. If you want to do this, be sure to consult with a medical professional, e.g., a nurse or midwife at a community or alternative clinic. You will want to make sure that your donor has been fully screened for medical history and infections that could affect you and your baby. You will also benefit from the professional's advice on timing of inseminations in light of your menstrual cycle.

Most women prefer to do their inseminations at a doctor's office or clinic. There they have medical expertise, sterile conditions, and the neutrality of a clinical setting.

A few considerations: however the woman gets pregnant, it is important for the man to be screened for family and personal medical history and sexually transmitted diseases. If the woman is over thirty-five, it is useful to do some basic fertility testing for ovulation and hormone levels.

If you get pregnant by a man you know, there are legal and psychological considerations. Even if the man assures you he has no intention of parenting the child, he could change his mind and sue for visitation and custody. Even if you promise him never to ask for financial support, he could still be ordered to pay if you or a court demanded this. You can spell out your wishes in letters drawn up by lawyers, but these agreements are not always legally binding. If you are going to make such arrangements, it is wise to seek psychological counseling and legal advice. Be sure your attorney has experience with donor insemination and family law. S/he will know the laws in your state and any pending legislation.

Choosing a Biological Father

It is important to like and trust the man with whom you are considering having a child. If he is more in love with you, than you are with him, beware. He may be saying yes to win you over at the same time that you are viewing him merely as a friend helping you out.

It is important to talk about your and the biological father's expectations. Does he want occasional or frequent visits with you and/or the child? What happens if life circumstances make him decide in the future that your child is the most important person in his life? What happens if you and the child are used to spending time with him and he marries or moves away, or decides he is no longer interested in the two of you?

Using anonymous donors for insemination is obviously less emotionally loaded than conceiving a child through intercourse. If you are ex-lovers, you and he may unwittingly regress to previous relationship patterns and expectations. If you are currently lovers and the man agrees to help you conceive but is uncertain whether to become a father or commit to you, there are myriad opportunities for misunderstandings, shifting expectations. The accompanying stress could put a damper on the pregnancy.

I know these questions can be daunting, and many men and women work out very satisfactory arrangements. I am simply offering points for consideration and conversation.

Adoption

It's easier for single persons to adopt today than it was in the past. The policy began to change when agencies realized that a single parent was better than no parent at all for hard-to-place special needs or older children. Then they began to see how successful single adoptions could be. Now single men and women regardless of sexual orientation and gay couples adopt infants domestically, internationally and through foster care/special needs.

Under some circumstances, single people offer some advantages over two-parent adoptions. Children whose birth parents or previous foster parents quarreled constantly sometimes do better with just one parent, for instance. And a child who was abused by his father may adjust better to living with a single mother than he would to a mother-father combination. One loving happy parent is certainly better than two unhappy ones. And a single parent's attention is not constantly divided between a partner and a child, so the child gets a lot of needed attention (see Chapter 11, "Adoption.")

✦ CHAPTER 10 ✦
SOLVING FERTILITY PROBLEMS

Because the websites **resolve.org**, **resolvenewengland.org**, **creatingafamily.org** and the patient blog of **asrm.org** (American Society of Reproductive Medicine) are goldmines of information on the causes and treatments for infertility and what to expect in a fertility workup for men and women, I am going to focus on the psychological aspects of coping and decision-making.

Early Stage

Wondering if you might have a problem? Infertility is defined as the inability to conceive or to carry to term in a twelve-month period if you are under thirty-five, and in a six-month period if you are over thirty-five. Because you will be eager to get pregnant and give birth once you've made the decision, you may jump to the conclusion that you have a fertility problem when you really just need a few more cycles for the egg and sperm to come together and for the embryo to implant. At this stage, you may want to talk to your OB-GYN about enhancing your fertility through ovulation monitoring, and the possibility of some hormonal blood tests. A man might consider having a semen analysis since it is non-invasive and might alert you to male-factor problems. Check and see if your insurance will cover these tests before you have waited the number of months required to be considered to have a fertility problem.

You may find it helpful to talk to a few friends, or see a therapist for support.

Pregnancy Loss

I prefer the phrase "pregnancy loss" to "miscarriage" because it acknowledges that your family has lost a potential child. This is not a minor event. After deciding to have a child, finding out that you're pregnant makes it look as if you're on a fast track to parenthood. Unfortunately, that path isn't always smooth. You may have barely had the time to celebrate when cramps and a flow of blood send you crashing into despair. Although one-time losses are devastating, they are typically followed by successful pregnancies.

Self-Care after Pregnancy Loss

Although for many people the emotional pain of loss and anxiety about future pregnancy is foremost on you mind, let's start with your medical needs.

Take care of yourself, and ask family and friends to do so as well.

If you have had an ectopic (tubal pregnancy that had to be surgically removed), if you had a D and C (dilation and curettage, scraping of the uterine lining) and/or have lost blood, follow your medical team's instructions for healing. Don't go back to work before you have been medically cleared and you are psychologically ready. Get lots of rest. Ask for lots of TLC from your partner, family and friends. This is not a time to tough it out.

Understand that your feelings are normal.

Some typical reactions include:

- Anger, sadness, and disappointment.
- Worry that you or your partner did something to cause the loss (this is rarely the case).
- Shame, embarrassment, or a sense of failure.

Prepare yourself for hurtful, if well-intentioned, comments:

- "Don't worry. You'll be pregnant in no time."
- "It wasn't meant to be."
- "At least you know you can get pregnant."

Your reality is that no matter how quickly you might get pregnant and no matter how many future children you might have the potential child you have just lost will never come again. If you went through infertility before getting pregnant, if this was a painstakingly high-tech conception, or if you have had previous losses, you know your next positive pregnancy would not end your worries or guarantee a birth.

Overcome isolation by talking to a trustworthy friend or family member. Choose someone who will honor your confidentiality. Other possibilities are a fertility counselor or support group referred by RESOLVE or other hospital or community resources. (see the Resources Appendix 2.) A hospital social worker can be a good referral source. A benefit of telling others is that you may learn that several friends and relatives, now happy parents, also suffered a loss. They are more common than we realize because people rarely talk about them.

What do you need for comfort? A massage from your spouse? Some TLC from a friend or parent? A weekend away someplace beautiful with your partner? A day home from work to cry and write in your journal followed by a friend delivering cookies and tea? You are not coddling yourself. You are taking care of the business of mourning your loss and healing your body so you can move on.

Logistics

Find out how soon you can start trying again and if there are any steps you need to take to prepare your body. If you were able to save any tissue that could be analyzed, you may get some information, but this is often not the case. Usually your medical team will not do any genetic testing unless you have a concerning family history since first losses are frequently followed by a successful pregnancy. (see Appendix 3 if you have genetic concerns.)

Evaluation and Diagnosis

Once you have reached the six or twelve-month mark based on your age, it makes sense to see a Reproductive Endocrinologist and begin a fertility workup.

Things to Keep in Mind

1. Having a workup doesn't mean you have a serious problem. It just means you're gathering information.

2. Having a workup is not a commitment to taking fertility drugs or undergoing another fertility treatment. The workup will enable your doctor to let you know of treatment possibilities, possibilities that you don't have to act on. There are conservative, less invasive, more natural ways to proceed. You can accept or reject each possibility. You can also use RESOLVE, chat groups, and a second opinion reproductive endocrinologist to help you evaluate treatments you are considering.

3. It is important to work with a Reproductive Endocrinologist, a fully trained and licensed gynecologist who has done a number of years of training focused exclusively on fertility. Keep in mind that a brilliant, world-famous lecturer and medical school professor, someone you are comfortable with and trust (and would prefer to stay with) has to keep up with training, literature, and conducting or reading research in all aspects of obstetrics and gynecology. You can return to this doctor once you are pregnant. One of the biggest regrets I hear from infertility patients is not starting with a Reproductive Endocrinologist in the earliest years of treatment when they were younger and the treatment might have been successful sooner.

The Middle Stage

You may be embarking on fertility drugs, intrauterine inseminations with your partner's or donor's sperm at your doctor's office, surgery for endometriosis or uterine fibroids or in-vitro fertilizations. While still hopeful in some ways, you may find these treatments exhausting, time-consuming, and if insurance doesn't cover, extremely expensive. Be sure to check with your fertility clinic, **resolve. org** and **creatingafamily.org** to see if there are any lower-cost options.

At this point, you will need lots of emotional support. You may not feel comfortable or trusting enough to tell many/any family and friends. However, you need to talk to someone other than each other. This is a great time to contact RESOLVE if you haven't already and attend a RESOLVE women's or couple's group. Doing short-term work, just a few sessions, with a therapist specializing in fertility issues can release a lot of stress and improve your communication with your partner and/or anyone else in your support system. Stress management techniques such as meditation, yoga, and exercise can help you better tolerate the stress treatment and each sharply divided month: two weeks of trying, followed by two weeks of waiting anxiously to see if treatment worked.

Although the public has long assumed that stress causes infertility (hence the old wives' tales of wine and candlelight dinners), frequently the truth is the reverse: the frustration of not getting pregnant, the fear of not getting to be a parent, and the biochemical changes of hormonal treatment cause stress in mentally healthy people whose lives have the ordinary amount of stress.

See Ali Domar's *Conquering Infertility* for good stress management advice. Whether or not stress management techniques increase your odds of pregnancy, they do decrease depression and anxiety, increasing your sense of wellbeing as an individual and as a couple. They prepare you mind and body to tolerate the stress of treatment and the uncertainty of outcomes. Consider taking a yoga or meditation class or exercising with your partner. Acupuncture may relieve stress and depression and may positively affect your hormones.

If you haven't already, you will probably also benefit from websites and blogs for those trying to conceive. Dawn Davenport's Facebook group **creatingafamily.org** is an especially good one; she moderates it with wisdom, knowledge, and compassion. Keep in mind that if you are participating in chat groups, you can find yourself emotionally derailed by devastating unusual stories of bad luck/poor medical treatment or by disgruntled, not-so-emotionally stable people who will discourage your hopes. Just remember that when someone tells a horrible story, they may be grieving a new diagnosis or a pregnancy loss that just happened, and they could wind up parenting happily in the future.

Coping with a Pregnancy after Infertility or a Miscarriage

"Congratulations! You're pregnant," says your medical team. "Congratulations," exclaim your family and friends. Now you can put infertility behind you and enjoy the pregnancy.

Enjoy the pregnancy? You listen. You smile. You try to get into the spirit, but you can't. You're on a different planet. In addition to the sinking feeling in your chest, you're plagued by a sense of unreality. You may be asking yourself, "What is everybody so excited about? The lab probably made a mistake. And even if they didn't, I'll probably lose the pregnancy. I find it impossible to believe I'll actually be holding a live baby in my arms in nine months."

Your partner may be as scared as you, as much in disbelief. On the other hand, if he or she has crossed over the river of belief and is cheering along with the medical team and family and friends, you may not know what to make of him or her. On the one hand, you may hope your partner will boost your confidence, but on the other, you may feel lonely if you're the only one who isn't cheering yet.

If you've worked for a long time with a fertility specialist or team that you know and trust, you may be terrified to switch to an obstetrician. Ask your fertility team for OB referrals to practitioners they personally know. This will make it easier to go to your first appointment. It is totally normal to secretly doubt that you are really pregnant despite all medical facts, despite your symptoms. Take your partner or a friend with you to your prenatal visits, at least the first few. Don't be shy about having a list of questions. Consider interviewing more than one doctor or practice. Ask friends and doctors you trust for referrals.

Bill of Rights for Women Pregnant after Infertility

You have the right to:

- be anxious without being told you're neurotic, depressed, or pessimistic. It is the normal reaction of a mentally healthy woman in your circumstances to be afraid. You need support and compassion, not cheerleading.
- work with a medical team that understands how precious this pregnancy is to you, who will allow you to come in for extra visits or call frequently if you have concerns. Many practices and clinics offer compassion as well as medical competence. Switch if you need to.
- take your time before telling most people— the end of the first trimester is typical, but if you previously lost a baby at twelve weeks, you might wait until your middle trimester. Ideally, you will feel more trusting in the pregnancy when the fetus is moving and kicking.
- take your time before signing up for childbirth classes, or furnishing the nursery, even if others are urging you forward.
- receive the support you need from family, friends, counselors, and support group members.

Your best resources may be friends or women online who can tell you about their experiences. You will typically feel some hope when you realize that these women were as scared and disbelieving as you but wound up with a child. Even if your most frightened voice says, "Yeah, they eventually got lucky, but how do I know it will happen to us?" you may be able to feel somewhat more hopeful.

Also, talk to your medical team about their plans for monitoring your pregnancy. Are your hormone levels increasing as they should? Will you need any medical treatment to increase the chances that the pregnancy will continue? Are there suggestions for prenatal care?

Aline Zoldbrod, the author of *Men, Women and Infertility: Intervention and Treatment Strategies,* recommends a mantra, "So far, so good," for each day that you are still pregnant.

This situation is so difficult and so confusing because medical realities and your loved ones' assumptions that you are on your way to parenthood may be at odds with your feelings. Professional help can provide relief. I recommend seeing a psychotherapist when you first get the results and making follow-up appointments throughout the pregnancy. You and your partner may want to come together for the first visit and then toward the end of the final trimester when your worries about childbirth and about the baby's health peak. You will probably want some individual sessions as well for extra support and perhaps a chance to speak more freely than you can when your partner is there. The mid-trimester tends to be the easiest because you are can see and feel the pregnancy and you are most likely to be physically comfortable

When I see clients who are pregnant after infertility, I use guided imagery for relaxation and, for those who wish, for visualizing yourselves as a happy family a few months after the birth. I include affirmations in each session. I record the session right on their smartphones so that they can listen as often as they like. Perhaps your therapist can do this for you, too, or if she lacks this expertise, can refer you to a hypnotherapy/guided meditation expert.

Later Stage: Thinking About Stopping Treatment

A time will come when you (and your partner) become more tired than ever of treatment, and less optimistic that the treatment will work. Sometime, when you and your partner are just beginning to consider stopping, your medical team, family or friends may be bringing up the possibility of moving on. If you have been working with your own gametes (eggs and sperm), you may be considering ending the current treatment and turning to donor egg or donor sperm. If there are uterine issues that may be contributing to fertility or to pregnancy losses, you may be considering surrogacy.

If you have ruled out these alternatives because you are not comfortable with them for psychological or ethical reasons or the medical risks involved, or if you have been told that these treatments are unlikely to work, you may be thinking of stopping altogether. In this case you may be considering adoption or remaining childfree.

But how do you know when to say "Enough is Enough!" when there may be a new treatment your team has just told you about, or they are proposing a new protocol that might improve your chances?

First of all, you may be able to reduce your stress in decision-making if you realize that you don't have to decide to stop *and* choose an alternative simultaneously. You may need and benefit from some time off from treatment for your bodies and minds to recover. Walking in nature and lounging over brunch and the newspaper, for instance, may refresh you mind for new insights.

Compassion is key in being able to say, "Enough is enough. My body and I [or my partner and partner's body] have had about all we/they can take! We start cycles feeling hopeful, but these hopes are dashed every time. It is time to end this suffering." "We like ourselves too much to continue," said one couple who went on to adopt their two children.

Another aspect of compassion, is that when the time comes that continuing to try is harder and less promising than it used to be, that you don't let the compulsion to succeed at pregnancy override your need for relief and need to get on with your life.

When we talk about resolve to keep going no matter what, we often associate this with the Puritan ethic. But actually, the Puritans had compassion for their own suffering. They said, "Enough is Enough—enough of religious persecution in England, time to move on to a place where we can practice our religion in peace." They were looking for religious freedom. When you say enough is enough you are looking for freedom from medical intervention and from riding the monthly roller coaster of uncertainty.

Here are some of the actions to help you decide when to stop.

Couple Actions

Have a conversation about stopping. Tell each other how you feel about recent treatment. Are you optimistic, or feeling exhausted and burned out? Is it possible that one of you has been ready to stop while the other wants to continue? You may have already talked about this, but I have met couples who did more treatment than either wanted because they thought that the other wanted to keep going.

Do either of you have in mind the number of cycles you are still willing to do, or the number of months after which you would like to stop if you're not pregnant? It may bring you a sense of relief to even think about stopping.

Consider a sabbatical. Maybe you aren't ready to stop, but you might benefit from a break, sometimes referred to as a "vacation from trying." This could be a month or two with no doctor visits, no ovulation monitoring and no treatment, a month that you will not have to ride the rollercoaster (two weeks of hope and trying, two weeks of waiting with an unbearable mix of hope and dread resulting in the woman's getting her period).

During this time, many people literally take a vacation, often going to a favorite spot they enjoyed earlier in their relationship. This is a chance to connect with happy memories of falling in love at a time when you weren't trying to have a baby. You might even enjoy lovemaking in these circumstances. You may connect with what you like and love about your partner, things that pre-dated infertility and that you will enjoy about each other when you are parents (or have made your peace with being childfree).

Although you may be terrified that your sabbatical month might be the only month that a successful conception might happen, postponing treatment a month or two down the road is unlikely to decrease your chances of success.

Medical Actions

Call your medical team and ask for a longer meeting to discuss your treatment plan including the possibility of stopping soon. Be sure to bring a partner or a friend, obviously your partner if you have one, since you are making the decision together. Your companion can write down the team's answers to questions you ask, and might record the conversation.

- Your team could be trying to encourage you with new techniques to try if they think you are eager to continue. If they know that you are thinking of stopping, you can take stock of what makes sense if you will only do one or two more cycles.
- Get a second opinion to see if there are other things you haven't tried yet, or anything has been overlooked. A fresh eye can be useful even if your team is well-regarded. Don't worry that your regular specialist will be insulted. Most won't, and as a matter of course, they also give second opinions to their colleague's patients.
- Make sure your second opinion consultant knows you are leaning toward stopping. You want to focus on what, if anything, it makes sense to continue doing or to do differently if you decide to go forward a little longer. Even if this person recommends continuing a treatment you're already doing, s/he may have a suggestion for doing it differently, for instance, using a different medication or different dosage of a current medication.

Now that we have dealt with the medical issues, let's take a look at the psychological ones.

Psychological Actions to Help You Consider Stopping

Now that the preliminaries are established, it's time to do some inner work.

Values Clarification

1. Is having a child and getting on with parenting becoming more important than how the child arrives in your home, or than whether the child is genetically connected to you?

2. How much is treatment costing you financially, mentally, and physically? Do you feel too exhausted or reluctant to go to medical appointments?

3. Would you cheer or would you groan if you found out that new treatments were available for you condition?

4. Do you have a deadline in mind for stopping? E.g., January 1st, your birthday, in six months.

5. On a scale of 1 to 10, how confident are you that treatment is going to work?

6. On a scale of 1 to 10, how willing are you to submit your body (or watch your partner's body being submitted) to the next treatment?

7. Consider a tentative deadline for stopping that you could extend if you chose to. This might be easier than setting it in stone.

8. Each of you can do a chair dialogue between the part of you that wants to keep going no matter what until you finally succeed at pregnancy and the part of you that wants to get on with your life as a parent by some other means (or even make your peace with being childfree).

Through **resolve.org** or your own social connections, talk to other people about how they made the decision to stop.

Grief Work as Preparation to Stop Trying

There is a Zen proverb, "The way to control a bull is to give it a big pasture." I use this proverb in every talk I give on grief, because I believe that infertility grief is a kind of freedom from struggle. Imagine that in trying not to feel your grief, you are hanging onto a bull's horns, getting dragged all over a muddy pasture while those horns are bloodying your hands. Then imagine hopping over the fence and just watching the bull run and charge, bringing an end to your suffering.

I believe that dealing with grief in this country, where we are ordered to "stuff it down" tosses us right into the bull pen. The task at hand is to allow yourself to let go of all the anger and sadness that you have been trying not to feel about not having a baby or about pregnancy losses.

But Merle, you may ask, *how can you insult me? I've been crying and raging for years.* Unfortunately, it seems we can let out about 90 percent of our grief and get only 10 percent of the relief we need.

I am going to give you some ideas that may make your grief more tangible so that you can get more relief. Rather than thinking about these losses in the abstract, you are about to use sensory detail to connect emotionally to these losses.

Some advice: Don't do these in public. You will be more comfortable in the privacy of your home. If you have a psychotherapist, you can do these with her/him. Or you might want to start seeing someone for short-term grief work.

1. What month and year did you started trying for pregnancy? If that had worked, how old would that child be now? For instance, if you have been through five years of infertility, you might have a four-year-old and a one-year-old.

2. Make a list of all the family, friends, neighbors and co-workers who have had children since your start date. This is your validation for how many times you have watched others get their dream of parenting, while still waiting for your own dream to come true.

3. Imagine a child of each sex, perhaps three years apart. What do they look like? What characteristics do they share with you or your partner? Looking at your own baby pictures may help with this.

4. Collect any baby objects you have in your home, an heirloom baby spoon, your niece's teddy bear, the rattle you bought at an art fair. Spend some time holding these objects. You might bring them to a therapy session to show your therapist.

You may find it helps to take a day off from work, or to clear regular activities on a quiet Sunday. Most people say they are surprised that, despite their sadness, it was easier to let these feelings out than to be struggling to keep them in a pressure cooker. Be sure to talk to an understanding person to process this experience.

Many people who are trying to say, "enough is enough," are pleased to discover that after grieving, it is easier to make this decision and also decisions about alternatives.

✦ CHAPTER 11 ✦
ADOPTION

Although first-time parents usually turn to adoption only after ruling out pregnancy, it has many attractions:

- The chance to provide a loving home to a child whose life might have otherwise been much harder. If you have concerns about population growth, you may feel that adoption of an existing child is better for the planet.
- The chance to be free from the medical and psychological stresses of fertility treatment.
- In the case of those with genetic concerns or whose physical or medical problems would mean risk to the mother and to the child, if pregnancy was chosen, the relief to not have to endure a high-risk pregnancy.
- If you have had a number of miscarriages, you can avoid putting yourselves at risk for another.
- If you are in an educational program, work situation or caring for another child or family member who needs a great deal of care, the possibility of bedrest or having activities restricted is bypassed by adoption.
- The chance to know that your child has already been born healthy (even though some problems don't show up until later.)

In some cases, you are given the chance to choose your baby's sex, for instance in international adoption, where the placement happens after a child is born. With a domestic adoption of an unborn baby, the child's sex may be known from prenatal tests. Keep in mind that agencies are more likely to work on sex preferences if you have had a miscarriage, stillbirth, or child who died around birth, and would prefer a child of the opposite sex.

Adoption does also have some disadvantages, however:

- The costs. If you live in a state that pays for fertility treatment, even if you want to move on to adoption, you may stick with the fertility path because it is less expensive.
- The scrutiny. No one likes the idea of having to prove to a stranger that they will make a good parent, when cruel, emotionally clueless or abusive people weren't subjected to an evaluation. Be aware that states and children's service organizations have a legal and ethical obligation to get enough information about you in order to conclude that the child will be safe and cared for.

So why adopt? There are a number of reasons for using adoption to create your family:

- One or both of you are infertile.
- You have one or two biological children and want another child, but you don't want to contribute to the world population problem. You also want the satisfaction of providing a good home to a child who really needs one. Or maybe you aren't a parent yet and find the population/environmental concerns compelling, as well as getting matched to an existing child.
- You're a gay couple who has ruled out pregnancy for medical or personal reasons.
- You have one or more biological children and have tried again but with no luck.
- You are a single woman who wants to become a mother. For various reasons, you prefer this option to pregnancy.
- You're a single man who wants to become a father without the complications of creating a pregnancy for co-parenting.
- All of these reasons are good ones, and acceptable to adoption agencies.

Guidelines for Considering Adoption

1. Do some reality testing. Have you been too caught up in romantic notions to ask and answer realistic questions? Are you fully prepared for the sacrifices as well as the gains?

2. Talk to successful adoptive parents. Discuss the problems they have faced, and find out how they have coped as well as their joys and satisfactions. Is your level of patience and tolerance equal to theirs? Could you cope with the problems they have had? Although it's unlikely that your problems would be the same, you will get food for thought for decision-making.

3. Face disappointment about infertility. If you're adopting because of fertility problems, make sure you don't leave any unfinished business behind. You have to mourn the biological child you will (probably) never have before you can welcome an adopted child into your life. Otherwise, you may consider the child a substitute at best, and you won't be able to give him the first-rate love he deserves.

4. Consider the rest of the family. If you have biological offspring, have you considered their needs as well as your own? If they are old enough, discuss the possibility of adoption with them, after consulting a psychotherapist or adoption worker.

5. Be realistic about potential problems. If you adopt a mentally, emotionally, or physically-impaired child, are you still planning to work? Will your agency let you work after the child comes to live with you? You may find it even harder to juggle career and child than if you had a biological child.

Common Forms of Adoption

- **Domestic adoption, in which your adoption agency places a child whose birthmother worked through your agency.**
- **Domestic adoption in which a local agency in your state (if required) works with an out-of-state agency, law practice, or children's home.** This is common if most women with accidental pregnancies in your state keep their babies or terminate

the pregnancy. For instance, it is more common for women in the South, West, and rural areas to consider adoption the best solution. This choice may be based on religious or personal beliefs or a clear-eyed understanding that they are not in a life situation to raise a child.

- **Independent domestic adoption in which you locate, through networking, advertising, or a law practice, a birthmother interested in relinquishing her child to you.** If the child is in another state, you will need a lawyer in your state and another in the other state to coordinate logistics and be sure you follow the requirements of the Interstate Compact regarding adoption across state lines.

In all these types of domestic adoption, you often receive a placement shortly after the baby's birth.

- **International adoption, in which your local, in-state agency either has its own relationships with foreign agencies or orphanages, or connects you with an out-of-state agency that arranges the foreign adoption.** Depending on the country, you may or may not travel to the child's country of origin. In some situations, you will go the country twice, once to meet your child/choose a placement, and then a few months later when all paperwork and legal steps are completed. Sometimes you are asked to spend a few weeks in the country.
- **Foreign independent adoption, in which you make direct contact with a lawyer, orphanage or adoption agency in that country.** If you follow this option, you will work with a lawyer who knows the laws of your state and with a lawyer in the country of origin.
- **If you're considering adopting a child of another race or culture, be sure you take full advantage of all the information available to you for decision-making and support.** Your adoption agency, multicultural organizations, and the website Creating a Family, **www.creatingafamily.org**, are excellent resources for information, coping techniques and support.

The adoption books and resources in the appendix will offer you questions to ask in evaluating all of these choices.

It can also be helpful to talk to adoptive families who have worked with the agencies or lawyers you are considering using. You can also check with your state's Office for Children to see if there have been any problems with the programs that you are considering.

Open Adoption

If you are doing domestic adoption, another consideration you need to weigh is whether you and/or the birth mother and birth father are interested in meeting or talking by phone or videoconferencing. The advantage of this "open adoption," is that the adoptive parents may feel that they have conscientiously placed the child with you as opposed to just handing a baby to an agency. This gives them a chance to feel that they are making a responsible plan for the child. The advantage for you is that you will (if you're like most parents who do this, even though the idea may have terrified you when you first heard about it) feel more empowered to raise your child, having a sense of the birth parents choosing you. In fact, many adoptive parents of two, whose first adoption was "closed" and whose second was "open," wish their first child had the knowledge that the two sets of parents spoke to each other.

Your adoption agency or consultant can help you decide whether or not you want to do this. (See *The Open Adoption Experience* by Lois Melina and Sharon Kaplan to learn more, including some variations on this practice.)

Special Needs Adoption

Another adoption option is to an adopt an older child (often six or older) or a child who is hard to place due to emotional problems or, sadly, their identity as a person of color. Such adoptions, whether through state offices for children or private agencies are often less expensive for a number of reasons. Children with physical, emotional or cognitive disabilities are also considered special needs. In the case of children of color, there are not enough families of color to place them all in matching homes. Older children and those with disabilities are harder to place because most parents-to-be are hoping to start out with a healthy young infant. For potential parents who are considering a special needs child, adoption may be less expensive because there are few, if any, costs involved in finding a child, and you will not have to provide medical or other expenses of birth mothers. The special needs children are readily available through public and private agencies. To learn more about special needs adoption, see the resources section or go to **creatingafamily.org.**

Legal Risk Adoptions

These are children for whom you become foster parents with the hope that the child will later be available to adopt. These children are in situations in which Children's Services organizations are giving parents who have been neglectful or abusive a chance, through supervised visits and counseling, to regain custody of the child. They are called "legal risk" because of the possibility that you may have to relinquish the child. This risk may be considered "low," "moderate," or "high," depending on the Department of Social Service's estimate of the risk of your not getting to keep your child.

Although this method could match you with a wonderful child you would eventually adopt, there are no guarantees. If you are currently childless and have been through the devastation of infertility or pregnancy loss, this option would likely be a poor choice for you. How much more grief could you stand? Of course, legal risk adoption carries emotional risk as well, both for you and the child if the placement isn't permanent.

In general, special needs and legal risk adoptions work best for families where one parent is home full-time with a blend of biological and adoptive or foster children. In many of these families, the other parent may work from home or be in the home a great deal. These families enjoy centering their lives around their children. These are couples or individuals who have devoted their lives to children who need a lot of attention. But if you work full-time and are hoping to start out fresh with a newborn, a special needs adoption is not likely to be your best match.

Transracial or Multi-Cultural Adoption

Your adoption worker, independent adoption consultant, and parents who have done such adoptions are great resources. If you are Caucasian and you were raised or now live in a multiracial/multicultural neighborhood, or if your own family is a blend of backgrounds, races, and cultures, you may be confident about such adoptions. You may even find such adoptions more interesting, more challenging in a good way, than adopting a child who looks like you. Adam Pertman, in *Adoption Nation*, writes about how many Americans are becoming more inclusive to people from other races, and cultures as international and transracial adoption have become more common. Nevertheless, our country still has a long way to go to become non-racist and more accepting of people from other countries and cultures. Your adoption worker can help you sort out what makes sense for you. The website, **creatingafamily.org**, offers advice and a bibliography on this topic. Reading books on international and transracial adoption listed in the bibliography can help you picture yourself in such families. Adoption agencies and cultural organizations offer education, support, and family activities that help parents and children adapt to their new family.

An Overview of the Adoption Process

Home study is a misnomer. Most meetings take place at the agency site, and an adoption worker doesn't usually come to your home until she/the agency has already decided to pass you, and let you know that ahead of time. You will not be deprived of a child because of a dust bunny or a cobweb! The worker is meeting the needs of the state and perhaps also the adoption agency or country your child is coming from to insure that your house and neighborhood are safe and that your home is de-cluttered.

A typical schedule of your involvement with the agency looks something like this:

1. An informational meeting at the agency where you are not being scrutinized and the agency may not even know your name. You are not committing yet to working with the agency, and typically people visit a few agencies to decide which one they feel more comfortable with. People who have already adopted through the agency may briefly tell their stories. This may help you feel more hopeful. If you are a couple, your first meeting will be with both of you. You will get an overview of the home study process. If you decide to pursue adoption, you will fill out the agency's paperwork, have a background check, and submit evidence of your health and financial security. You do not need to be well off. You just need to show that you can support your child.

2. An individual meeting with you, regardless of whether you are single or a couple. You will talk about your interest in adoption and your upbringing. The worker will tell you more about adoption than you learned in your introductory informational meeting.

3. If you have a partner, there will be a couples meeting. The adoption worker will want to get a sense of your relationship and your interest in adoption. You will discuss how you came to the decision to adopt. If you have been through infertility, or are adopting due to a medical problem that precludes pregnancy, the worker will want to get a sense of how you are coming to terms with disappointment and loss. She wants to make sure you have processed this loss so that you will be able to enjoy the adopted child for who he or she actually is, and not a substitute for the biological child you are not going to have.

4. A group meeting or class where you will learn more about adoption, meet other adoption workers besides your own, and be introduced to other individuals and couples involved in the process.

5. Follow-up meetings to answer your questions and learn more about adoptive parenting.

6. The home visit.

After the home study is complete, there are typically once-a-month optional meetings to help you cope with waiting for your placement and offer further education and support.

It's normal to be apprehensive about the home study. You may be afraid you won't be approved and will wind up childless. You may be furious that strangers can require you to participate in the process, when terrible people who can reproduce answer to nobody. Fortunately, home studies today are usually more focused on preparing you for adoption, helping you to consider whether adoption is for you.

Please remember that reading the above information can't provide you a sense of the warm, joyful feelings adoptive parents feel when they first bring their child home, or the satisfaction of raising the child.

To get a fuller picture and to see the full scope of the home study and other logistics as necessary steps to adopting a child, talk to adoptive parents, read books, and explore the resources in the Appendix. I especially recommend the website **creatingafamily.org** and Lois Melina's *Raising Adopted Children*. Although Melina's book focuses on post-adoptive parenting, my decision-making clients have found it a useful tool for imagining themselves as adoptive parents.

Simultaneous Trying

You may consider pursuing pregnancy and adoption simultaneously, particularly if you are in your late thirties or early forties and are afraid 1. neither option may work, and you want to hedge your bets to wind up with at least one child, or 2. you are facing fertility limits/biological clock for pregnancy and age cutoffs of adoption agencies.

Suppose you want both the adoptive placement and the pregnancy. Some agencies will allow this; others will not. The best circumstances would be if you are at the tail end of fertility trying and your medical team is not encouraging, AND your agency is willing to work with you under these circumstances. They will not want to work with you if you have every reason to assume you will get pregnant on your own; for instance, if you haven't yet started a fertility workup, or are newly diagnosed with a fairly treatable problem. While most adoption agencies don't want to work with you if you are still trying for pregnancy, some are willing to do so if they know that you are making one or two last efforts at high-tech treatments that have failed so far. Their willingness will depend on their sense that you are psychologically ready to adopt. This means that even though you still have some hopes of pregnancy, you have grieved your fantasied biological child intensely enough that you would fully welcome and be ready to love your adopted child.

If you have been going through fertility treatment for months or years, especially if you are in your late thirties and forties, adoption may start to look attractive. Although you think you are capable of loving and welcoming an adopted child, at this point, you are not yet ready to stop treatment. You may want to start the adoption process, so that you know at least one path will lead to parenthood. If you would like to have two children, you may feel that you would want your adoptive placement even if you had a successful pregnancy (see Chapter 10, "Solving Fertility Problems").

The advantage of double pursuit is that you have two ways to become parents. This may take some of the pressure off your disappointing treatments. It might even make it easier to decide to stop treatment. You may also want to pursue both paths if your adoption agency or others involved in your adoption—for instance, a foreign country—have age limits such as forty, which you are approaching.

The disadvantages of simultaneous pursuit of adoption and pregnancy include emotional, physical, and financial exhaustion, the difficulty of working full-time while balancing two "part-time jobs," and couple conflict if one of you is more eager for this plan than the other. Also, you might get more out of your adoption agency meetings if you have stopped medical pursuits and can focus more fully on adoption. There is also the possibility of disappointment if your agency won't give you a placement if you're pregnant (see below).

Before we talk about how to manage simultaneous pursuits, I want to acknowledge that you may believe that agency rules are unfair. After all the unfairness you have already been through with infertility, it seems as if you should be rewarded by having adoption be a lot easier.

Although it's hard when you're frustrated about having to adopt and you've already waited months or years while pursuing pregnancy or trying unsuccessfully to carry to term, take a minute to briefly consider adoption from the point of view of the adoption agency and its mandate to serve your birth mother and your baby's needs. The agency's goal is to place babies as soon as possible. If you have accepted a placement and tell the agency, before the child comes home to you, that you don't want the match because you are pregnant, you are lengthening the time that your "almost-adopted" child must wait before reaching her permanent home. Even if the agency has a long list of other applicants, they have lost time working with you and have a lot of paperwork and phone calls before this child can go home to other anxiously waiting parents. The worker is naturally disappointed for the child and also faced with extra work. Looking at this from the agency's concerns about placing each child as quickly as possible, you may feel a little less disgruntled.

You should also consider the possibility that if the agency takes your name off the list and you then miscarry, you could end up with neither child. A grim prospect! It's also important not to burn bridges with your agency, since you might want to apply there in the future for a second child.

Ground Rules for Pursuing Adoption and Pregnancy Simultaneously

1. Choose an agency you can be honest with. Ask around or have a friend call the agency anonymously. Lying is stressful, and your home study will be a richer experience, a more focused preparation for adoptive parenthood if you're not hiding your medical efforts.

2. If you are a couple, make sure both of you are willing to pursue both options simultaneously *and* that if you got pregnant, you would both want to continue the adoption or both want to drop out. You should avoid at all costs the unpleasant discovery, if you haven't talked about it, that one of you is heartbreakingly bonded with your potential or already matched child while the other wants to release the placement. Even if you never hold that child in your arms, you will feel enormous heartbreak. Women often liken the experience to a pregnancy loss when they lose a specific, hoped-for, and anticipated child.

3. Carve out the time and energy you need to pursue both paths and still manage to work. Both adoption and medical visits are time- and energy-draining, emotionally demanding processes. Don't volunteer for new projects at work. Scale back social plans and family and community activities.

4. Arrange your adoption visits several days apart from doctor's appointments so that when you are at the agency you can wholeheartedly focus on adoption. While this isn't always possible, do your best, and be willing to reschedule to avoid confusion and conflict, i.e., going to an adoption meeting the same day you learned that a few eggs fertilized. Even if you are psychologically ready to adopt, of course your mind will turn to the possibility of pregnancy when you get such news.

To find out more about adoption, see the Bibliography. For adoption referral, see the Resources section.

✦ CHAPTER 12 ✦
HELP!

The big moment has arrived. You've done all the exercises; you've thought about all the issues; you've talked to your partner, your family, and your friends. Both you and your partner are pretty sure you know what you want, but you're still scared. Why? Because when you make a change, any change, some last-minute panic is perfectly normal. So don't assume that your sudden paralysis means that you've made the wrong decision. You probably haven't.

Try going back to Chapter 2, "Secret Doors," to do a new "Chair Dialogue," "Rocking Chair," or "Diary" exercise. Doing these exercises again may reveal some unfinished business, which once addressed, will make the decision clear. If you jotted down some notes the first time you did the exercises, reading them may show you that you are farther along toward the decision than you realized.

You can "try on" the decision for a week or two. Just imagine, along with your partner, that you have already decided to be childfree or have a child. How does that feel? What excites you? What scares you? What actions might you take to move forward such as going on childfree websites or making an appointment with a gynecologist. Are you and your partner feeling excited, feeling that the decision fits? The decision will probably feel more solid over the two-week experiment. If not, read on below if you're leaning toward parenthood, or see Chapter 13, "Embracing the Childfree Life" if you are leaning in the childfree direction.

1. Before you throw away your contraceptives or schedule a vasectomy, read over the guidelines that follow. If after you've finished, you are still convinced that your choice is right, accept those lingering doubts as par for the course, and act on the decision. However, if your doubts intensify, that could be a sign that you haven't done enough work on the decision. If so, give yourself some more time and consider seeking some professional help.

2. Think child, *not* children. Baby decisions should be made one at a time. Nature may give you twins, but you ought to at least decide on one pregnancy at a time! You don't have to commit to two children before you have even experienced one. When you are ready to consider a second baby decision, your experience as a parent will make that decision much easier.

3. If you are both certain that you want to have a baby, but you're afraid—of a change in the status quo, of the responsibility—try to overcome your paralysis.

a. Try a chair dialogue (Chapter 2, "Secret Doors") by yourself or with your partner, and talk out some of your fears. Role-play some of the scenarios that seem frightening. Are you afraid your husband won't find you attractive during pregnancy? Are you worried your wife will become too wrapped up in the baby? Are you nervous about handling a newborn? By acting out your fears, you may be able to conquer them, especially with your partner's support. It can also be useful to role-play in reverse, acting out each other's fears to get some insight into one another. If you step into your partner's shoes, and vice versa, you'll both be in a better position to support and help each other if and when real problems come up.

b. Realize that some of your fears cannot be overcome beforehand. If the baby decision is right for you, you'll adjust. Parents who claim that their children ruined their lives are, for the most part, people who should never have had children. They may have started parenthood with an unplanned pregnancy. They are unlikely to have made the kind of thorough, thoughtful choice that you are making.

c. Remember that waiting may only make things worse. If you know you want a child, but haven't been able to say "tonight's the night" for six months, it may be time to take the leap. Remember the first time you stood on a diving board, frozen with fear? The longer you stood and stared at the water, the harder it became to take the plunge.

d. Consider switching to a riskier contraceptive. By using sponges or condoms, you will move toward pregnancy less abruptly than if you went straight from the pill or patch to nothing. Or, use contraceptives occasionally, but not every time you make love. This is a good way to test the strength of your choice. If you're absolutely panicked about having sex with less protection or no protection, consider going back to safer contraceptives. If starting to get pregnant panics you, give your decision more time to jell. Re-reading parts of this book or talking with each other or trusted friends may help.

e. Realize that you may not get pregnant immediately. Unfortunately, many couples, anxious about the decision, expect to conceive immediately, perhaps hoping that pregnancy will magically dissolve their ambivalence. And when they don't conceive right away, they panic. Give yourself time and assume that you will soon conceive.

4. If you still have serious doubts, reconsider the possibility of remaining childfree. If you're childfree and you change your mind, you do have three options: a pregnancy if it's not too late; adoption; or substitute gratifications such as special friendships, volunteer, and professional work with children. But if you have a child despite your doubts, the options are limited. So if your doubts are more intense than the normal last-minute panic, give the childfree choice some more attention.

Seeking Professional Help

Finding this decision painful doesn't mean you need therapy. When you examine your past, it's not unusual to find some painful memories. When you consider your possible future as a parent or nonparent, it's not unusual to feel sad about the road not taken. A childfree man contemplating a vasectomy may mourn the son he'll never teach to ski. A woman who's trying to get pregnant may mourn the freedom she is relinquishing. Don't be afraid of your pain. It is part of making a good decision. Only if it becomes intolerable is it a reason for seeking professional help.

Yet, if any of the following situations apply to you, seeing a counselor may be a good idea.

1. You're frustrated because you've spent six months or more on the decision, and you haven't made progress.

2. You and your partner are poles apart. One of you says "Now!" and the other says "Never!" Before calling a counselor, reread Chapter 6, "Tug-of-War." If you're still at loggerheads, then you probably need professional help. The chapter may help you make a list of issues to bring to the therapist.

3. You're too "stuck" to do the exercises. If you draw a blank when you close your eyes, your unconscious mind is clamped shut. Trying working on them with a therapist.

4. You've done the exercises, and you are disturbed by what you're discovering. You may be threatened by the choice you're leaning toward, or perhaps you're coming to the unnerving realization that you have a lot of emotional problems to resolve. Talk to your partner and friends first. If this doesn't help, maybe a professional will.

5. You and your partner can't converse on the subject long enough to find out whether or not you disagree. Perhaps your partner refuses to discuss the issue. Or maybe one or both of you are disappearing into long silences or making accusations rather than speaking openly. Perhaps you plan times to talk but wind up doing "more urgent things" and never manage to sit down together.

6. You're leaning toward parenthood, but one of you was abused as a child. Perhaps you or partner worry that if you become a parent, you will fall into the same abusive pattern with your child. Or perhaps you have an emotional problem that makes you doubt your ability to be a good parent. Spending some time working with a professional can help you figure out whether you have healed enough to feel comfortable parenting.

Choosing the Right Kind of Help

The Baby Decision Workshop

A special workshop focusing solely on the baby decision may be conducted by a psychotherapist, counselor, or teacher. It may be a one-shot deal for a day or a weekend, or it may meet one evening a week for several weeks. The workshop serves several purposes:

- It gives you an overview of what's involved in making a baby decision.
- It offers you tools in the form of exercises and activities that help you get a handle on the problem.
- It allows you to share your confusion and your solutions with others, getting and giving feedback and support.
- It shows you how others are dealing with the baby decision. Listening to other people's struggles can help you sort out your own, especially if their values, needs, and interests are similar to yours.
- If other students speak of the attractions of a choice you find unappealing, you may get some new perspectives that make you more open to that possibility.
- It offers you and your partner an opportunity to talk in a non-threatening atmosphere.
- Reacting negatively and viscerally to someone's statement may show how strongly you are committed to the other choice.

You can usually attend without your partner if he or she won't come. Some groups are for women only, but most are open to all men and women, single and coupled, LGBT and straight. If a workshop is full and there isn't another one scheduled for some time, ask the workshop leader (if he or she is a therapist) whether you and your partner could set up a few counseling sessions.

A good workshop will have the following characteristics:

- A workshop leader who accepts the validity of both choices.
- A balanced format consisting of presentations, informal discussions, and values-clarification exercises such as the ones in this book.
- A group large enough to bring in a number of viewpoints but not so large that you'll feel too shy to talk. Six to twelve is ideal, in my experience.

If you are unsure about whether a workshop is right for you, or if you would just like to find out more in advance, don't hesitate to call the leader and ask some questions such as:

- What is your professional training?
- Are you open to both choices?
- What decision did you make? (If the leader is defensive, angry, or uncomfortable about answering this, you don't want to be in the workshop.)

The leader's decision needn't reflect the choice you think you're leaning toward. And if he or she is any good, that won't even be an issue. All you need is someone who will support and accept the choice you do make because it's the right one for you. You want to make sure the therapist is even-handed about the topic and is able to talk about it without sounding upset. If the therapist sounds upset, the decision may be loaded for them. The decision could be unresolved for them, or they could be living with a decision imposed by a partner.

You can also ask the instructor to send you a course outline and if available, some course evaluations if these are not posted online.

Individual Therapy

While a baby decision workshop is educational in focus, individual therapy will apply the concepts and techniques in a way that uniquely addresses your personal needs and emotions. It is a time, place, and relationship completely focused on you.

You can set up a specified number of individual sessions, four to six for example, to work solely on the baby decision. Or you can keep the number of sessions open-ended to explore not only the baby decision but related personal growth issues. This is up to you and your therapist and depends on your decision-making deadline and your goals. But you don't have to sign your life or your wallet away. You can see a therapist for just a few goal-oriented sessions.

Individual therapy is appropriate if:

- You've attended a workshop and want to explore your decision or your conflicts about it more fully than you could in a group.
- You are already familiar with the issues and are busy exploring them but want some expert help in sorting them out.
- You're disturbed by what you're learning about yourself or concerned about your ability to be a good parent.
- You want to remain childfree, but you're overwhelmed by guilt about disappointing your partner or your parents or are having difficulty withstanding the pressure from the meddlers in your life.

Couples Counseling

If you and your partner are in serious conflict over the baby decision, marital counseling may be appropriate. But resolving mutual conflict isn't the only reason to seek such help. You may just want an objective third party to help you explore the issue together. Since it takes two to decide (or should), joint counseling sessions can be very useful.

Here are some special tips about couples counseling.

- To save time and money, prepare in advance. Do the exercises in this book before your first session. That way you will already have pinpointed your trouble spots and can get right to work on them.
- Tell the therapist you want short-term, decision-focused therapy. You may want to plan for a specific number of weekly

sessions. When you are starting this process, it's often useful to attend weekly for a few weeks to get the momentum going. Then, it may work well and save money and travel time to meet every other week, using exercises in this book between sessions. The extra time between sessions gives you a chance to reflect on these exercises.

- Feel free to visit or interview by phone more than one therapist before making your choice.
- Paying for therapy: your health insurance may cover if your therapist is licensed for insurance payments. If you don't have insurance, a mental health center, family service agency, or hospital psychiatric clinic may have a sliding scale. If you are in a Health Maintenance Organization, or Preferred Provider Organization, make sure that the therapist has expertise in baby decision-making. Some people decide to pay out-of-pocket for a one-time consultation or a few sessions with an expert. If they want more follow-up, they can work with an in-network therapist using suggestions from the expert.

What to Look for in a Therapist

Choose a therapist whom you like and can talk to easily. He or she needn't specialize in the baby decision although it is helpful if the therapist has worked with children and families and, even if childfree, is familiar with the joys and sorrows of family life. However, your own feelings are the most important barometer. Feeling comfortable with the therapist is more important than specific degrees or number of years of experience. It is preferable to see someone who is licensed as a social worker, psychologist, family counselor, psychiatric nurse, or psychiatrist. You will want to find out about insurance coverage and fees.

If you can't decide between a workshop and counseling, remember that a workshop goes wider and therapy goes deeper. A workshop covers a lot of issues but not as intensively. In counseling, you'll delve into the specific issues that are most germane to *your* baby decision.

And with a growth-oriented therapist, you'll discuss the implications your choice has for your personal and marital growth.

How to Find Help

Although it is easy to feel alone when struggling with decision, there is a lot of help available. See Appendix 2 for some organizations that might refer you to a therapist. You might also search online for the nearest Planned Parenthood or Family Service Agency. Also visit **resolve.org** even if you don't have a fertility problem. A RESOLVE chapter can refer you to local therapists with expertise in the transition to parenthood.

- **University departments of family studies, education, psychology, or social work are possibilities for both service and referrals.**
- **Try word-of-mouth.** If you have friends who have been to a workshop or tried baby decision counseling, ask them whether and how it helped. Therapists your friends have found helpful in non-baby-related personal or marital counseling might be able to see you or refer you to someone else.
- **Try searching therapist-finder websites such as PsychologyToday.com or GoodTherapy.org.**

The baby decision is a life choice, not a sickness. Having trouble with it doesn't necessarily mean that you need outside help, and seeking such help definitely doesn't indicate weakness, neurosis, or failure. It means that you're being thorough.

✦

Acting on Your Decision

✦ CHAPTER 13 ✦
EMBRACING YOUR CHILDFREE LIFE

You've finally made the big decision, and you're going to commit yourself to a childfree lifestyle. In this chapter, you'll learn how to maximize the benefits available to you.

Congratulations on your momentous decision. You worked hard and courageously. You read the book, did the exercises, reflected, and worked with your partner. Or if you are single, you worked with a friend to think and talk it through. You may have gone to psychotherapy or a workshop. Take a minute to breathe deeply. Congratulate yourself and each other for arriving at a momentous decision.

Note to readers if childfree wasn't your first choice

If childfree was not your first choice, you may need a break before reading this chapter. If you are deciding to be childfree after disappointing infertility treatment, I encourage you to visit **resolve.org** and read the "Childfree Decision Making fact sheet." It includes essays from people who are now comfortable with being childfree post-infertility. The packet also includes my article on guidelines for childfree decision-making, including encouraging information on how your suffering will be alleviated without your becoming parents.

Once you read this material and talk about it together, it will be easier to return to this chapter and use it for planning a good life.

If you are agreeing to be childfree because it is clear that your partner would be unable to raise a child with you, you too may need a break before you can enjoy this chapter.

Regardless of how you arrived at the childfree choice, if it wasn't your first choice, you may benefit from re-reading Chapter 6, "Tug-of-War."

I strongly recommend some short-term couples therapy. A wise, compassionate expert can help you navigate your emotions and keep your relationship strong. From this vantage point, you will be able to start planning for your future.

As you read this, you or a partner may have cold feet. "Am I ready to say I'll/we'll be childfree?"

For now, let's assume this is normal ambivalence and the normally expected first few days of embracing a decision. Keep in mind that people who decided to try for a child are also feeling some doubt.

Remember that "decide" means "to cut away from" and that you may be letting go or even grieving some of the potential satisfactions of parenthood. Give yourself a little more time to get used to your choice.

Living with the Childfree Choice

Although parents also can be criticized for their choice, due to the pronatalism rampant in our society, announcing your decision can be stressful. So before we discuss the satisfactions of living childfree and how to benefit fully from your choice, I offer you these guidelines.

1. Get off the hot seat. You don't have to justify your decision to *anyone* (except yourself and your partner), unless you *choose* to do so.

2. Peel off the selfishness label, and tear it to shreds. Your choice makes you no more selfish than a parent who fulfills personal needs by having a child. Keep in mind that some people who envy your freedom and ability to take care of yourself may use the label. They may be clueless about the difference between healthy self-care and selfishness.

3. Spring the perfection trap. Non-parents sometimes feel so guilty about their choice that they try to compensate by becoming super achievers in other areas of their life. They feel that if they're not going to have kids, they have to do something spectacular instead. But liberation from unwanted parenthood should not translate into enslavement to unreasonable demands. You don't have to struggle to be exceptionally productive. Of course, many childfree people wind up making extraordinary accomplishments. Time not drained by parenthood is certainly conducive to creative work, business success, and social contributions. However, you should be able to make your own choices about your goals. Unreasonable expectations, whether yours or someone else's, aren't conducive to creative work. To be truly creative, you have to be willing to risk failure and relaxed enough to play around with ideas and possibilities.

4. You have as much right to be "ordinary" as anybody else. You have not committed a sin by not having children; you have nothing to atone for. Your talents will emerge more easily if you don't impose excessively high expectations on them.

5. Revel in solitude and quiet time. Ironically, some people who decide to remain childfree because they crave solitude never take advantage of it. They get caught up in a whirlwind of activities that precludes any quiet time. Why? They fear solitude because when there are no distractions, unwanted thoughts and fears can't be ignored or repressed as easily. Few of us like to face our problems head-on or admit that our marriage, our work, or other parts of our life are not as satisfying as we would like them to be. But solitude is a golden opportunity for growth and a rare commodity for new parents. Don't pass up your special opportunities to meditate, daydream, fantasize, pray, or plan. Sometimes just staring out the window or mindfully petting your cat can be sublime.

Don't overload yourself with activities that prohibit solitude and relaxation. Ironically, even pursuits that seem to encourage growth, such as journaling, or attending yoga or dream workshops, can actually hinder your development if you overdo them. You could wind up spending so much time rushing from one activity to another that you don't get that wonderful, slowing down, centering effect from any of them.

6. If you are in a relationship, make the most of it. You're lucky. Because you don't have children, you have time and energy to lavish on each other, and you'll both benefit from taking advantage of that fact. Research indicates that childfree couples are quite happy, possibly happier than those with children. Susan Lang's book *Women Without Children* gives many examples of couples with strong, enjoyable relationships. Set aside time for each other. Even though some couples choose to be childfree in order to protect their relationship, they may become so involved in various activities that they spend little time together. This could be due to some fear of intimacy, or it can happen if you don't prioritize couple time.

7. Share. One of the advantages of parenting is a satisfying, long-term project the couple engages in together. Consider a special project you can work on together. For many childfree couples, such projects evolve naturally. If this isn't the case for you, choose one consciously; for instance, consider environmental work or volunteer vacations.

8. Develop a family system. Who would you turn to if your partner died? With whom do you spend holidays? Do you have any ties with people under sixteen or over sixty? Family ties are important, and if you're not close to "blood" family—either physically or emotionally—create a "chosen" family with friends, colleagues, neighbors, and so on. (See Chapter 5, "Which Way Happiness.")

9. Let go of guilt. Do you feel that you are getting away with something, as if you are relaxing in a hammock while others are weeding the garden or mowing the lawn? No need to feel bad. You have avoided the burdens of parenthood, but your life has its own burdens.

10. Get together with other childfree people to socialize and share ideas and possibilities. See Appendix 2 for childfree resources.

Looking to the Future

Some people who make the childfree choice feel no need to make new decisions because they are concentrating on the good life they already have. But many of you who have just made this choice may be uncertain what you want to do next.

This can be a fruitful time of brainstorming and fantasies. Journaling, life planning workshops, meditation, and books such as Gregg

Levoy's *Callings: Finding and Following an Authentic Life* can jumpstart your explorations.

When Tamara was in her mid-thirtiess she realized that she wanted to go back to school for a doctoral degree in clinical psychology. This clearly felt like her life's mission, but she and her partner were also looking at the possibility of parenthood. They worked hard on this decision, including working with a therapist to review and weigh various choices. She concluded that while becoming a mother was something she was interested in doing, she was not yet ready to be a mother, especially as she recognized that the timing was such that doing both at the same time was not realistic. With heartfelt clarity, she made the choice to opt out of becoming a mother, but then she also made a personal promise to herself going forward to help children and their families. She added:

> At that critical moment in time, I dedicated myself to honor and express my mothering impulse in this way. To this day, I am filled with gratitude for the children and families whose lives I touch in my professional and personal life, and whose lives touch mine.
>
> Once I realized that I wasn't going to be a mother, I realized that through my clinical work with children, I could honor and express the mothering part of myself. I get to be close to my clients and their mothers in a way that is healing for them and satisfying for me.

For Katie, a health administrator, thinking about what to do next has been fun. She had thought she wanted to have children in order to be playful and do new things. Then she attended my workshop, did the exercises on her own and then with her husband. They decided to be childfree and have begun doing some of activities that she had been postponing, such as music, dancing, exploring nature, and studying mindfulness. She realized that she didn't need to have kids to do these activities.

Since she made her decision, she is swimming, preparing for a triathlon, and getting certified as a fitness instructor.

She has enjoyed her own decision process so much that she has become an advocate, encouraging friends to have a sense of adventure about the baby decision, whatever they decide.

Katie adds, "This is the happiest and number one fact that has guided me to remain childfree with my husband: There is no shortage of love in the world, and we can decide how and who we want to love. For us, this includes welcoming children of all ages into our lives."

To get a sense of the range and possibilities that men and women are enjoying in their childfree lives, I highly recommend the facetiously titled book, *Selfish, Shallow, and Self-Absorbed: Sixteen Writers on the Decision Not to Have Kids*, edited by Meghan Daum. And Laura Carroll's *Families of Two* and *The Baby Matrix* are also excellent.

Making It Final—Sterilization

Have you considered sterilization? The decision to be sterilized actually involves two *separate* decisions: first, the decision not to have a child; and second, the decision to close that option off forever.

Sterilization offers the following advantages:

1. An end to worry about contraceptive failure. Many couples report that their sex life improves after sterilization. Women in particular say they never realized how much fear of pregnancy affected their sex lives.

2. An end to anxiety about possible long-term effects of contraception and an end to contraceptive inconvenience.

3. A rite of passage. Sterilization can be a turning point that results in a burst of creativity in another area of your life. By closing the door to parenthood permanently, you may be more open to new possibilities and interests, and you will have more time and energy to pursue them.

4. A sense of closure: an end to a long, involved decision-making process. You have taken time to think things through. If you are in a relationship, you've spent time talking about the advantages listed above, as well as any disadvantages. The major disadvantage of sterilization is its irreversibility. Like a decision to have a baby, a decision to be sterilized is irrevocable. For this reason, I suggest the following guidelines.

If You Are Considering Making It Final

Be cautious about getting sterilized in your twenties.

Some people are so certain they would never want children that they undergo sterilization procedures while in their early or mid-twenties. If you and your partner are quite sure you will never want children, if you would find an accidental pregnancy or abortion totally unacceptable, if you are worried about contraceptive side effects, sterilization may be the contraceptive of choice. And more and more people in their twenties are making that choice. However, it is possible that you will change your mind about children when you're older. For that reason, it may be a good idea to wait awhile before making this decision.

Childfree television commentator Betty Rollin described to me her doubts about sterilization in the under-thirty crowd: "You can't assume your present feelings are going to be with you forever. People often change their attitudes as they get older. I think that choice is one of the great gifts of life and, in a sense, early sterilization deprives one of having that choice." Likewise, in my interview with Carol Nadelson, a Boston psychoanalyst and vice-chairman of psychiatry at Tufts New England Medical Center said, "I see a lot of people who decide to become parents in their late thirties or early forties."

One of the reasons people change their minds in their thirties or even early fortys relates to psychologist's Erik Erikson's concept of generativity—a concern with nurturing and guiding future generations. For many men and some women, this need generally doesn't surface until midlife. And although you can meet this urge in other ways through creative work or by associating with other people's children as many childfree people choose to do, you may wish to reconsider parenthood at that time.

For women, a change of heart is possible when they reach their late thirties or early forties, especially those women who embarked on a career at age twenty-two and have had fifteen years of professional success by age thirty-seven By that time, many are:

- Ready for a change. They want to try something new and different.
- Ready to shift from a work ethic to a family ethic. Whether they take a few years off, continue working full-time, or switch to part-time, they are ready to shift or widen their focus.
- So well-established in their work that it's easier to combine career and motherhood, and the frustrations of coping with a double life may seem less taxing when they're older and wiser.

Their partner may also shift their psychic energies from career achievement to personal relationships. If both partners are now willing to spend time parenting, having a baby becomes more feasible than it was when they were in their twenties and too busy establishing their careers to consider parenthood.

But suppose you're in your twenties, have given this matter quite a bit of thought, and want to be sterilized. Is there an acid test for sterilization readiness?

According to Maxine Ravech, sterilization counselor at Preterm in Brookline, Massachusetts, at the time I interviewed her in the 1980s, taking responsibility for oneself is the dividing line between the twenty-three-year-old who's mature enough to be sterilized and the one who isn't. "If I hear someone saying to me, 'I know I could be wrong, but I do understand that sterilization is irreversible, and I believe this decision is right for me,' I think that person is mature enough to understand the meaning of sterilization." If you can agree with this statement, if you think you could live with regret should it ever materialize, you are making a mature choice.

If you are in a relatively new relationship, consider postponing the procedure until you have been in a committed relationship for at least a year. Feelings about children are sometimes linked to our feelings about our mates or lovers. One woman who didn't want any children with her first husband couldn't wait to get pregnant with her second. In fact, happy parents who thoroughly planned their parenthood report that conceiving and giving birth was a way of celebrating their union and their love for each other.

Although your image of a child in the abstract may seem repulsive, the idea of making a baby with your loved one could become attractive as you and the relationship mature. Therefore, give yourself some time to ensure that your feelings about your partner and your relationship won't affect your feelings about a child.

1. Give yourself time to let the decision jell. If you are considering sterilization now, wait six months to a year before taking any action. Does your interest in the idea fluctuate depending on your moods or how you feel about your love relationship? Obviously, this should not be a spur-of-the moment decision. You'll be more certain about the plan if you have given it the test of time.

2. If your partner originally wanted a child, and would prefer that you not have a sterilization procedure, give yourselves some extra time. I've already stated my belief that you should never have a child unless you *both* want one. By the same token, it's probably best to postpone such a final sterilization decision until your partner has come to terms with the childfree decision. Your relationship will go more smoothly if your partner has a chance to express anger and disappointment, mourn, and find substitute ways to nurture. If you simply make a unilateral decision and top it off with an unalterable sterilization procedure, your partner is going to feel steamrolled. That extra time prepares your partner to support your choice, and to support you through any physical discomfort the procedure might cause.

3. The partner who is more committed to being childfree should be the one to undergo sterilization. I suggest this because the partner who has at least some positive feelings about parenthood might choose to have a baby with a future partner in the event of widowhood or divorce.

Even when both partners agree to remain childfree, typically, one will be more certain than the other. "I had a tubal ligation," Angela reported, "because I was more committed to being childfree than Doug. I've known ever since I was a child that I didn't want children so it makes more sense for me to be sterilized. He was willing not to have children for my sake. He enjoys the peace and freedom of our life and gets 'fatherly' satisfaction from his activities with his Boy Scout troop. But if something happened to me, or if we split up, it's quite possible that he would want a child with a different partner."

4. If you do get sterilized:

a. Don't panic if you have some qualms just before or after the procedure. It's natural to have a few regrets, but if you've made a careful decision, you'll probably live quite happily with it.

b. Seize the opportunity to make plans. Now that you don't have to use your nest egg for a nestling, how might you test your own wings? Perhaps it's time to realize your dream of owning your own business, or to take a less profitable, but more exciting job. Or perhaps you can take the trip you've always longed for, up the Himalayas, or down the Amazon.

c. Be choosy and careful in announcing your action. Should you tell, and if so, how and to whom? The advantage of an announcement is that it will put an end, once and for all, to all those tiresome questions and pressures. It also allows you to share your excitement, relief, and your sense of freedom, and it keeps your communication clear.

On the other hand, if you don't share the news, you won't have to deal with possible rejection, anger, and hostility, often in the form of endless lectures. And if you have any lingering doubts about the wisdom of your decision, these lectures can be intolerable.

If you're like most people, you'll probably start telling those people who will support your action and delay or avoid telling many who would disapprove. But there are some people, your parents, for example, who may have to be told even though the telling won't be pleasant. Even if you decide against sterilization, you may decide to tell your parents that you've decided to remain childfree, or you may choose to say nothing unless they ask. Either announcement may evoke shock, hurt, disappointment, and anger.

Now let's talk about telling your family regardless of whether you've undergone sterilization:

> **i. Try to keep the conversation current and focused on your respect and concern for them.** As we have previously discussed, you'll want to avoid slipping into old parent-child patterns. Your partner, a supportive sibling or a therapist could help you plan what to say if you are at a loss.
>
> **ii. Empathize with their feelings of disappointment, hurt, and anger.** Let them mourn. You've taken away what they had believed was their "right" to grandchildren. Don't take away their right to their own reactions. You don't have to agree with their attitude or feel guilty about it, but you can say, "I can understand why you feel that way." Or you might say, "I'm sorry to disappoint you." If they have other grandchildren, remind them of this.
>
> **iii. Listen carefully.** You and your parents may never agree, but you can offer each other compassion, understanding, and authentic conversation.
>
> **iv. Realize that their expectations of grandparenthood are understandable.** Society in general doesn't know enough about the childfree choice or fully accept it yet. When your parents raised you, they assumed they would have the pleasure of knowing your children. It's hardly surprising they're disappointed. Try teaching them about the childfree choice. Give them this book and offer other resources (see the Appendix). Share with them what you've learned from your own experience, from other childfree couples, and from your reading. If they are not

likely to pick up a book, offer them a few carefully selected excerpts.

v. Give them time. They may come to accept your decision once they get used to the idea, especially if they see that you and your partner are happy with your lives.

vi. Help them find other satisfactions. If they already have other grandchildren, or if you have siblings who might eventually have children, remind them of this. Try to help them find other ways to get involved with children. When you think they might be receptive, perhaps in a conversation a few weeks after the announcement, gently and tactfully suggest that they consider:

- Becoming substitute grandparents to a family whose "real" grandparents have died or live far away.
- Becoming special friends to the children or grandchildren of their friends and neighbors.
- Volunteering at a day care center or a Big Brother or Big Sister program.
- Spending more time with existing grandchildren even if it means traveling to another city. If they say, "That's too expensive," remind them that they won't be spending money on your children and therefore that trip may be more feasible.

vii. Help them unload their guilt. Your parents may feel that they are somehow at fault, that you've made this choice because they were rotten parents or because you've been soured on family life. Or they may perceive the decision as a way of rebelling against them and everything they stand for. To counter this, let them know your positive reasons for remaining childfree. Tell them there's no reason to feel guilty. Of course, they made some mistakes—who doesn't? But make sure they recognize that you've made the decision because it's right for you, not in reaction to them, assuming this is true.

viii. Get them to take pride in your generativity. If you tell them your positive reasons for remaining childfree, they'll be proud of you. They won't have grandchildren, but they can share, enjoy, and applaud your accomplishments. If their values, courage, or example led you to any of your chosen commitments, point this out so they can identify more fully with your choice.

ix. Realize that the relationship between your parents and your partner may change. If your parents believe (accurately or not) that your partner is more committed than you are to the childfree choice, they may resent him or her and say, "If only my child had married someone more traditional. That awful son-in-law [or daughter-in-law] led my child astray." Counter by describing your active participation in the decision and giving them a chance to vent their feelings. This may smooth over the relationship.

x. Tell them—if it's true—that you value them more than ever. Whether your relationship with your parents is terrific or just mediocre their importance to you may increase after you've made your decision. More than ever, the positive family ties you have could be a valuable resource.

xi. Don't make the mistake of thinking you've talked to your *parents* if you've talked to only one. Avoid these common tactics such as talking to one parent only (most frequently Mom) and letting her relay the message to the other parent or talking to both parents, but assuming that the situation is resolved when only *one* parent has actually expressed feelings about the subject.

Using What You've Learned About Yourself to Grow

In the process of deciding to be childfree, you may have recognized, even more fully than you had before, some positive characteristics or talents that you factored into your decision such as a strong sense of independence, valuing privacy and silence, perhaps being reflective, meditative, or introverted. You may also be a maverick thinker, a rebel, an enemy of the status quo. You may spend time as a writer or teacher urging others to be more questioning.

If you relate to these characteristics or your partner does, you might think about ways to use and honor them even more fully than you already have. Now that you have ruled out parenthood, you (and your partner) may have some satisfying conversations while brainstorming possibilities.

The Childfree Person—A New Kind of Pioneer

Congratulations on venturing into one of the new lifestyles of the twenty-first century. You're fortunate to live in the first age in which people whose talents and interests do not lie in child-rearing are able to say "no" to parenthood and "yes" to themselves. You are free to spend your time and energy on the pursuits that offer you the deepest satisfaction.

The self-awareness, risk-taking, and assertiveness you have developed during the decision-making process should stand you in good stead as you continue staking out new territories of childfree living. Although the childfree choice is more common and respected now than it was when *The Baby Decision* was originally published in 1981, you still have a chance to be a pioneer in modeling a viable alternative to parenthood.

✦ CHAPTER 14 ✦
SMALL PLEASURES:
LOOKING TOWARD PARENTHOOD

Now that you've made the decision to have a baby, you are ready to focus on bringing that child into your life. Don't worry if you feel a little confused or uncertain and asking questions like, "What are we getting ourselves into? Are we really going to do this? What if we can't get pregnant? What if we can't find child care?" There are a thousand "what ifs" that you can't answer today. These thoughts may make you worry whether you are making the right decision.

If you are over forty, have experienced infertility, pregnancy loss, or any problem in your reproductive system, even if you haven't tried for pregnancy, you may be afraid that you won't get to be a parent. You may wonder if you even belong among readers of this chapter who are focusing on when, not if, they become parents.

But this chapter is for you, too. You can seek medical care and do your best to become pregnant. You choose a clinic/doctor, you follow their treatment plans, and you can now leave that part to your medical team. Or you may have applied to adopt and be awaiting the next step from your adoption team. But while waiting for pregnancy or adoption, you can psychologically prepare yourself for parenthood. This gives you something constructive to do that is in your control, that makes you more confident that you will be ready to parent when the time comes.

Three's Company—Preparing for the Baby

1. **Don't expect to get pregnant the first night.** Many couples who struggle with the baby decision find it difficult to give up control.

Often, they are the kind of people who planned everything meticulously in the past, carefully choosing their colleges, their training programs, their jobs, and their partners. Now they unconsciously assume they can choose the baby's due date. They can't.

Moreover, once a couple has made the decision, particularly if they spent months or even years wrestling with it, they are so excited and so eager to act on the decision immediately that more waiting becomes extraordinarily painful. It seems so ironic that after finally deciding to have a baby, the baby doesn't quickly show up.

If you are over thirty and haven't gotten pregnant within six months, it *is* a good idea to seek medical help. But not the first month. Your body is not a machine; you can't just program it for conception! (For more information about infertility, see Chapter 10, "Solving Fertility Problems.")

2. Picture yourself enjoying your choice. Close your eyes and imagine yourself and your partner having a happy, healthy pregnancy and an easy childbirth. Now picture yourselves playing with the baby. Imagine yourselves being more in love than ever, finding that the child has added a new dimension to your relationship. Positive imagery can serve as a self-fulfilling prophecy.

3. Prepare for parenthood.

- Take a childbirth class to make birthing a more pleasant and loving experience for everyone involved. If you are single, choose a beloved friend or family member to be your birth partner.
- Learn parenting skills. Read now; it will be harder to find the time later. (See the appendices for a list of useful books.) Do you know what a newborn looks like? Do you know what a three-month-old can and can't do? Is it possible to spoil a six-month-old? Find out ahead of time.
- Look for role models. If you like the way your parents raised you, analyze their behavior. What specifically did they do well? Ask them about it. If you don't like the way they reared you, try to find other role models, couples you know personally who seem to be doing a good job with their children. Observe how

they handle various situations. Ask them to describe their parenting philosophy. Parenting books and classes can also offer alternatives to the way your parents raised you. If you are pressed for time, look for one-day or half-day weekend workshops.

4. **Consider ways of preserving something that matters from your previous life**. Focus on aspects of the childfree lifestyle that you have enjoyed, and try to find ways of meeting some of these needs. If you crave solitude, for example, can you and your partner spell each other so you can each have some quiet time alone? If dinner out once a week seems essential, can you cut some other corners to make it possible?

5. **Work on any emotional problems that might get in the way of parenting.** If you're worried or nervous about parenthood, seeing a counselor during pregnancy can be helpful. Here are some typical problems:

- You're absolutely terrified of parenthood even though you very much want a child.
- You realize you're expecting the baby to give meaning to your life. You're worried because you know you have to have some other meaning, too.
- You're convinced you're going to make the same parenting mistakes your parents did. This is especially serious if you were abused physically, sexually, or psychologically.
- You and your partner had a tug-of-war. The "baby person" won, but the "childfree person" gave in before working through all his or her concerns. This partner needs more understanding and preparation for parenthood.

6. **Zap all unrealistic expectations on sight!** Don't strive to be the perfect parent. There's no such thing. A Zen concept applies here: The harder you try to be perfect, the farther away from perfection you'll fall. If you *want* a child and you're relatively mentally healthy, you *will* be a good parent, despite your faults and failings. Take comfort in the knowledge that your child comes with natural

resilience. Children are more like rocks that chip than eggs that break. One of your most satisfying parenting tasks will be teaching your child to recognize, value, and boost her resilience even further.

Also, don't expect to create the perfect child. You cannot mold a child's personality because he or she is already born with one. Your guidance and support, though crucial, are only part of the equation. Letty Cottin Pogrebin in "Motherhood!" *Ms*, May 1973, describes her role: "I am not a sculptor who molds a child from clay. I'm the gardener who tends a seed that will grow to become itself."

Look Forward to the Creativity and Joy You Hope to Experience

According to some proponents of the childfree lifestyle, a child is, at best, a glaring stop sign on the road to growth and, at worst, a bundle of dynamite that shatters the road entirely. But parents who *value* children and who have, by definition, made a good baby decision, make a conscious trade-off: exchanging personal pleasure for parental pleasure—the pleasure of fostering the growth and development of another human being. Through that process, a parent can experience tremendous growth, too. In the words of Margaret Fuller, "The character and history of each child may be a new and poetic experience to the parent, if he will let it" (in *The International Thesaurus of Quotations*).

How Children Can Help You Grow

1. **Children tend to be "warm fuzzies" in residence.** They not only receive affection; they give it. Hugs, kisses, and smiles can make you feel loved and important. Of course, you cannot rely on your child for love and self-esteem, but he can be a delightful source of pleasure. Kids can cheer you up on days when work doesn't go well or when you and your partner are at odds. It is not a reason to have a child, but it's a nice fringe benefit.

Of course, there are days when their behavior exhausts or

exasperates you, and unfortunately, these can be the same days that work or your relationship are troubling you, too. The simultaneous problems may be interrelated or coincidental. For instance, a baby may fuss because he is reacting to a couple's fight. These are days to use other ways of feeling better: calling a friend, napping when the baby does, or putting on music that soothes you both.

2. Children offer new perspectives. They constantly challenge the status quo by asking "Why?" In their naiveté, they can offer fresh insights and new solutions—*if* you're open to your child's sense of wonder and creativity.

3. Children teach you about yourself. It's easy to be a textbook expert on child development. But it's truly an education to watch the development of a real child. This intensive course in child psychology is especially useful if you happen to work with children and families. Having your own child forces you to refine your theories of child development, your philosophies of child-rearing, and your beliefs about human nature.

4. Children offer comic relief. They are a vivid reminder that life goes on, no matter what. When adults are absorbed in a crisis, a child's silly giggles can provide some much-needed perspective.

5. Children force you to think about the future. They remind you that you will die someday. Even if you're good at deceiving yourself most of the time, it will occur to you, at least occasionally, that your children will outlive you. This realization can spur you to have a positive influence on the world that you eventually pass on to your progeny. For instance, you may want to participate in social action to deal with racism, violence, or the environment. Of course, you are not likely to have time or money to be involved, or very involved, in such work when your child is a baby, but you might be able to make a satisfying and meaningful contribution later.

6. Children keep you on your toes. You have to remain flexible and open to adjust to moment-by-moment and week-by-week changes in your children. You have to grow along with them.

7. Children help you develop self-discipline that you never before thought possible.
       a. In order to succeed as a disciplinarian, you have to learn

self-discipline first. You have to separate your need to vent your frustration (the urge to give him a good, hard whack, for example) from your child's need to learn to obey important rules.

b. Children force you to get organized. As parents, you'll be forced to do a given amount of work in less time. It's hard to goof off when you know your children need you or when every wasted moment raises the tab on the babysitter's bill. On the other hand, allow yourself some goof-off time. Everyone needs it, particularly parents.

Whether or not you enjoy parenthood depends on what *you* bring to it. If you embrace it openly and eagerly, with no unrealistic or idealistic expectations, you won't be disappointed. But if you expect it to provide all the meaning in your life or miraculously solve your problems, you will be disillusioned.

Like any other life experience, parenting has its highs and lows. It is both joyous and frustrating, stimulating and draining. But as long as you base your decision to become a parent on a full awareness of both sides, you will be able to take pleasure in the plusses and cope with the minuses.

Lessons from Room Nineteen:
How to Be a Mother Without Being a Martyr

I spent twelve years of my adult life working, *living my own life*. Then I married, and from the moment I became pregnant for the first time I signed myself over, so to speak, to other people. To the children. Not one moment in twelve years have I been alone, had time to myself. So now I have to learn to be myself again. That's all.

– Susan Rawlings, middle-aged heroine
of Doris Lessing's classic short story,
"To Room Nineteen."

Rawlings' words "That's all" are ironic because retrieving a self after so many years of denying that self is an awesome task. So awesome in fact, that Susan Rawlings can't do it. Over the years, she has not only lost her self but also her willingness to fight for its return. Once a week, Susan breaks away from household responsibilities to spend time in a hotel room. She rents a room, not with an affair in mind, but in hopes of self-discovery. But what she finds is that when she lost her self, she also lost her ability to care. In the end, she commits suicide out of apathy rather than despair.

Although few middle-aged women resort to suicide, many, like Susan, are overwhelmed by the difficulty of finding the lost threads of their pre-parent existence. However, should you become a mother you need never face such an awesome task, not if you adamantly hold onto those threads, letting them guide you through motherhood and through your continuing growth as an adult woman. You'll never have to search desperately for your identity if you never let go of it in the first place. In this section, we're going to look at some of the ways you can assure yourself that you'll never land in Room Nineteen because you'll have reserved room for growth right in your very own home.

The words "mother" and "martyr" start and end with the same letters, but the similarity should end there. Regardless of whether women stay home or work part-time or full-time, they often seem to fall victim to their own and to society's unrealistic expectations. As Angela Barron McBride says in *The Growth and Development of Mothers*, "[Motherhood] is an impossible job for all women as presently defined." No mother can be held responsible for making everyone in the family happy. No mother can be expected to repress or ignore her needs all the time in order to meet the needs of her family.

Survival Tactics

Take care of yourself, and your family will take care of itself. As Anais Nin said in *The Book of Quotes* compiled by Barbara Rowes, "When you make a world tolerable for yourself, you make a world tolerable for others."

Mothers' needs don't die; they simply go underground. A frustrated mother's interactions with her husband and children are polluted by her guilt and hostility. Anger and depression are the only responses to being squelched. Whatever your family's needs are, you're entitled to fulfill your own as well.

Advice for Full-Time, At-Home Mothers

1. You will need time away from the baby. Ask your partner or another relative to take the baby, hire a sitter, or exchange babysitting with a friend, or a local children's play group.

2. Choose one non-family-related goal that interests you and actively pursue it. It might be a class, an art project, a community activity, a freelance paid job—anything that you enjoy and in which you can take pride. However, it's generally best to choose something in which your progress will be visible. Although as a mother you make significant progress with your children, it isn't tangible. Come June, you'll still be diapering the same bottom you diapered in May. So it's nice to be able to observe and measure progress in another activity.

3. Get out of the house as often as you can, with and without the baby.

4. Spend time with other grownups when you can. When you can't, use your telephone or email to reach out to other adults.

5. Join a mother's group or cooperative play group to give both yourself and your baby a chance for fun and friendship.

6. Seek professional help if you feel frustrated and depressed. Try talking to your husband and your friends. If that doesn't help, see a counselor.

7. Consider going back to work if you haven't been happy at home. You might enjoy your time with your child if you also had the stimulation of your job. You may also find that work offers you a breather from your child, making your time together more fun.

Advice for Working Mothers

If you work, you have the advantage of getting a tangible pay-check and getting out of the house on a regular basis. But chances are you're overburdened, especially if you are a perfectionist or if your partner hasn't taken on a reasonable share of the household burdens.

1. Make a date with yourself. Set aside a block of personal time each week to do whatever you please. Don't skimp on this time because you have so much else to do. Your "for myself" time is no luxury; it's an absolutely essential form of burn-out prevention.

2. Be realistic. If your partner won't do his/her share, don't try to do it yourself. Better to let some dust pile up, than the resentment. If you are fortunate enough to afford it, hire child care or cleaning help, or barter these services.

Advice for All Mothers

1. Don't be shocked by your feelings. Occasional urges to throw the baby out the window or to run away from home are quite common in mothers of young children. If you sometimes have these feelings, you're neither neurotic nor "bad." There's a big difference between fantasizing about something and actually doing it. The temptation to strike out at the baby or to run away from him is a natural psychological response to the unnatural conditions of motherhood. I say "unnatural" because it is only in postindustrial Western culture that mothers of young children have been so isolated. For most of human history, mothers have had much more contact with and support from other mothers and from their own female relatives. They have also been able to stay more involved in adult activities. The problem is not you or even motherhood itself, but rather the isolation chamber our society makes of motherhood.

2. Get rid of your tension. There are two necessary steps in breaking out of your frustration. The first is to reach out to caring adults—your partner, your friends, a mother's group, a professional counselor, or a parenting class. The other is to release your tension. Leave the baby in a crib or playpen, go to your room, close the door, and do whatever will make you feel better—scream, cry, pound a pillow or bam it against a wall, count to ten, taking deep breaths. When the baby is napping or has gone to sleep for the night, meditate or do yoga or relaxation exercises. Leave the baby with someone else long enough to get some physical exercise. Running, swimming, bike-riding, and tennis are all great tension-releasers. If you are too exhausted to do any of these, perhaps you could take a quick walk around the block, try one or two yoga poses, or listen to a visualization or meditation or self-compassion recording. (See the Bibliography for mindful parenting books.)

3. Express your anger and ask for changes. Let your partner know when you are angry. Explain why as specifically as possible and focus on your feelings. Don't say, "You're inconsiderate. You don't care about anybody but yourself." Instead say, "You haven't paid attention for the last three nights when I've tried to tell you how frustrated I am with the baby." If you're not angry at him/her, but just want to let out your frustrations, be sure to tell him/her that.

Once you've talked about how you feel, discuss what you can both do about it. Make specific requests for change. Don't say, "I never have any fun and you do. I want to start having a good time for a change!" Instead say, "Will you stay with the baby on Monday nights and on Saturdays so I can paint, swim, and see my friends? I think I'll be a lot happier."

When your children are old enough, the two steps described above will work with them, too.

4. Don't force yourself to take your child to every activity that someone thinks is good for children. While it is important for children's development and self-esteem to plan activities that excite them, don't go overboard. Include your child in some things that you especially enjoy. If you love the woods, put the baby in a backpack and take her for a short hike. If you love to dance, put on music and move to the rhythm together. Your child will find your enthusiasm contagious. She'll be glad you care enough to share it with her. Of course, you should not try to make your child into a carbon copy of yourself or discourage her interest in other things, but also take your own interests into consideration. As your child gets older and develops her own interests, encourage her to pursue them on her own, with other children or other adults. You can provide the money, the materials, and the transportation required, but you don't have to provide your constant presence. Willing encouragement is better than unwilling participation.

5. Don't force yourself to be an earth mother. Your child needs warm hugs but not warm bread. She won't die of malnutrition if her milk comes from a bottle instead of a breast or if her carrots come from a squeeze packet instead of your garden. Baking, nursing, and making natural baby food are great if you do them because you love to. But if you're only doing them out of a sense of duty, you would be better off skipping them. Instead, use the time to have fun with your baby.

6. Don't let guilt get the best of you. Don't read child care books that make you feel guilty. The recycling bin is the rightful place for any child care book suggesting that one false move will land your child in prison or on the analyst's couch. Most children manage to survive a wide variety of parents and parenting styles. If you're reasonably happy, love your child, and respect her individuality, your child will probably turn out fine. A few emotional scars in the course of growing up are unavoidable, but endurable. In fact, with your guidance, a child's pain can stimulate his growth and understanding that some frustration and disappointment is part of life. This is excellent training for resilience and maturity.

You should be concerned if you're ignoring your child, yelling constantly, being cold or critical, or failing to discipline. But if you avoid such behavior, your guilt is unwarranted and will only interfere with your pleasure in parenting. Even if you do engage in some of these behaviors, you can change. Seek professional help promptly, and ask your partner and other mothers for support.

If you're suffering from counterproductive or immobilizing guilt, try a talking cure. Other mothers and family counselors are two of the best sources of help. You need someone who can be supportive and objective.

7. Insist on retaining your personhood. Never let go of the identity questions you dealt with before becoming a mother. Always seek and make the most of whatever meaning and mission you have in life in addition to motherhood. No matter how good a mother you are, no matter how satisfying you find this role, your children are going to walk out the door later on. Don't let them take your whole reason for living with them. As Susan Rawlings knew, "Children can't be a center of life and a reason for being. They can be a thousand things that are delightful, interesting, satisfying, but they can't be a wellspring to live from." If you find and enjoy other wellsprings, you'll enjoy motherhood more than ever.

✦ CHAPTER 15 ✦
GRAPE JUICE ON MOMMY'S BRIEFCASE, OR HOW TO COMBINE MOTHERHOOD AND CAREER WITHOUT LOSING YOUR MIND OR YOUR JOB

I had to ask myself why, when 90 percent of my manuscript was already in my editor's hands, did I keep postponing, again and again, the section I wanted to write on career and motherhood? I frowned at and crossed out much of the first draft. I just couldn't get it right.

The fact is I haven't really wanted to write this chapter because part of me rejects the reality. I want to write utopian science fiction of a society where mothers and fathers have the paid leave, quality day care, and other social supports that make it possible for both sexes to fully contribute to their jobs, fully enjoy nurturing their child, and not be overwhelmed by financial worries and time pressures. I believe I have been waiting for society to magically change before my book went to press! At the very least, I wanted, somehow, to find some brilliant, clever strategies for parents to live enjoyable, more leisurely lives balancing work and family time, and even personal time.

When I wrote the first edition of *The Baby Decision* in 1981, I had young daughters. I assumed that if either of them chose to have a child in the twenty-first century, there would be an abundance of day care, paid leave, flex-time, home, telecommuting, etc. I assumed that with the absence of sexism and advances in social supports for parents of both sexes, the struggles of the 1980s a thing of the past, a draconian tale that my daughters wouldn't even be able to imagine. Unfortunately, these problems are still making the work/family balance precarious.

Fortunately, some of the other predictions I made did come true, or at least are moderately trudging toward becoming true: greater acceptance of childfree people and of single and LGBT parents.

Also, working women are less likely to be told that they are neglecting their children or that day care is bad for them. Another positive change is that both studies and interviews with millennial men show how attached they are to their children; they do more child care and housework than previous generations, and they often report that they would work less outside the home if economics weren't a problem. However, despite their commitment as fathers and husbands, they are afraid to take paid paternity leave even if their company offers it for fear of being considered less committed to work. We still haven't arrived at the society I dreamed of for my daughters.

Recently, journalists have criticized women executives and professionals for quitting, assuming that they had little work commitment or that they were turning perfect at-home parenting into a career. But this is unfair and unrealistic. Countering the attitude that well-trained, successful women just whimsically abandon their careers to play with their children, Pamela Stone asserts in *Opting Out? Why Women Really Quit Careers and Head Home:*

> This decision is not a return to traditionalism. It is not women who are traditional; rather it is the workplace, stuck in an anachronistic time warp that ignores the reality of lives of high-achieving women . . . and resists and rebuffs their efforts to change it.

Ann-Marie Slaughter attacks these same critiques strategically and creatively. The author of the groundbreaking *Atlantic Monthly* article "Why Women *Still* Can't Have It All" and *Unfinished Business: Women, Men, Work, and Family,* Slaughter describes small breakthroughs that are currently happening and argues for more sweeping changes that families would require to be able to make their best career contributions to society, earn living wages, and be able to enjoy and care for their children. She goes on to recommend an "Infrastructure of Care,) a set of arrangements and institutions that allows citizens to flourish not only in the pursuit of their individual goals but also in their relationships to each other." Her recommendations address the needs of elders as well as young children and parents, who may be sandwiched between the needs of both generations while working demanding jobs and having little time to meet their own or their partner's needs.

Slaughter's infrastructure includes affordable child care, higher wages for child-care workers, paid leave for both parents, and job protection for pregnant workers.

Of course, American society is not likely to accept a higher tax structure to pay for the changes, but Slaughter also points to actions taken by corporations, motivated by attracting and retaining the superstar, hard-to-replace millennials, to offer paid leave for fathers as well as for mothers, flexible schedules, and telecommuting. She thinks that when CEOs of these companies take fatherhood leave, they will make it less terrifying for other fathers to actually use their leave. Currently, if fathers take a leave, they risk being written off as "not a serious player," more likely to find themselves derailed from the fast track.

While we can take a little heart in these changes, we are looking not only at too little too late, but also these corporate advances/ experiments have a long way to go before they fit Slaughter's infrastructure: only a handful of companies are offering paid leave, and they are typically offering it to their most elite employees and not to their secretaries or support staff. This method is ironic because the elite employees typically need these benefits less than the hourly employees since they could more easily afford leave of absence without pay than the lower-level employees.

How did you react to the "Swedish Family Hotel Exercise," in Chapter 2, "Secret Doors"? If you are leaning toward parenthood, how big a factor in your decision-making is the lack of family supports such as those that Slaughter recommends?

Slaughter points out that companies offering better family services and flexibility are rated higher financially and are more highly regarded. If companies thrive when they offer these benefits, attracting talented leaders and thinkers of childbearing age, she believes other companies will follow suit.

Juggling Career and Motherhood

Can you combine a career and motherhood?

1. You can if you get some form of support.

- A partner who shares the workload at home.
- High-quality, reliable child care.
- Role models in the form of other working families.
- A cheering section, including your partner, your friends, and also your children when they're old enough to admire you and appreciate the ways you contribute.

2. You can if you let go of perfectionistic expectations. You'll have to accept the fact that you probably won't be as outstanding a worker as a single, childfree colleague. You'll also have to accept the fact that you won't be as available to your child as a mother who is home full-time.

3. You can if you're willing to give up some of your leisure. Of course, it is essential to give yourself at least a little leisure time each week. Unfortunately, many of the women who successfully combine career and motherhood do so by skimping on their social life, exercise, recreation, and downtime.

4. You can if you don't have high housekeeping standards. Will nothing less than spotless floors and gourmet meals be acceptable? Unless you have someone to help, or a lot of energy, you're going to find the going rough. Some clutter in the form of toys and equipment is inevitable, but try to figure out the combination of standard-lowering and streamlining that works best for you.

5. You can if you want to badly enough. It's certainly hard to cover all the bases, but perhaps you would rather be overtired than forced to sit out the game. Some mothers who have tried both staying home and working, prefer working. They say they would rather be worn out from doing too much than depressed from not doing enough satisfying work. Similarly, many women who are already committed to their work decide to have children anyway because, even though they know they'll be overloaded, they think it will be worth it.

Journalist Letty Cottin Pogrebin, in "Motherhood!" *Ms.*, 1973, expressed this succinctly when her daughter asked her on a hectic day whether she regretted being a mother. Ms. Pogrebin answered: "Sometimes my life is a little too full because I have you children, but, for me, it would be much too empty if I didn't."

6. You can if you explore options. There are other options besides carrying your briefcase into the labor room and showing up at the office two hours postpartum. You can:

- Take a maternity leave of three to twelve months. Then decide whether to go back to work or stay home.
- Switch to part-time, or possibly share a job with someone else if your budget will allow it. Unfortunately, it is often impossible for low wage earners to cut back.
- Take a few years off.
- Switch to consulting, private practice, freelancing, part-time teaching, or volunteer work. These activities allow you to develop professionally while devoting large blocks of time to motherhood. Many women planning pregnancy strategically develop expertise that is indispensable to their employer and/or profession in order to prepare for consulting.

7. You can if you limit the size of your family. If you both want or need to continue working full-time, having an only child may be your best bet. For most two-career couples, two is the absolute limit.

8. You can combine career and motherhood more easily if you don't try to do it all at the same time. As Sherrye Henry, New York radio commentator, whom I interviewed on December 5, 1979 put it:

> I personally have been able to manage motherhood and feminism and do them both justice, as they have done me. The problem that lies ahead for my daughters, though, which did not burden me, is that they may think they have to accomplish all things at once. Impossible. The time required to fire up a career will not allow quiet nurturing moments with babes; high-powered executive actions are not consonant with lullabies. The women who try to put it all into one time-frame will pay a terrific price in terms of physical and emotional punishment. Just the time deciding how to make the trade-offs will be debilitating!

Unfortunately, thiry-seven years later, many families are doing it all in one time-frame, an economic necessity. And of course, women aren't the only ones who are suffering. Partners and children, too, are rushed. Relaxed family times are a rare commodity; despite the joys they provide.

One woman who decided not to try to do it all is Liz, who worked for twelve years as an occupational therapist before she married Eric and gave birth to Daniella. Liz had enjoyed her work, but she was ready for a change. She enjoyed staying home with Daniella for three years. During this time, to keep up in her field, she attended networking events and conferences and read some journal articles.

Gloria, a thirty-eight-year-old paralegal, had two conflicting realizations. The same year that she realized she wanted a baby, she also realized she wanted to go to law school. But she is the kind of person who gets caught up in whatever she does and prefers to savor one experience at a time. Her solution? She's going to stay home with the baby for a couple of years and then apply to law school. While she is reversing the typical chronology for professional women, her fertility cannot wait. And she really wants to settle into the motherhood role without being stressed by a rigorous training program. She is grateful to have the financial security to make staying home possible, even though she will take on the burden of education loans later on.

Although the difficulties of re-entry should not be underestimated, intelligent, motivated women can succeed at work even if they have spent several years at home. Volunteer work, part-time or contract work, and attending local networking meetings are ways that at-home mothers can stay connected in their fields. These activities may be unappealing or unfeasible in the first year or two, but some new mothers like to do them early on, "to not feel swallowed up by motherhood," as some women put it. (See "Resources, in Appendix 2 for organizations that help you with these issues.)

As you consider options open to you as a working mother, be flexible. You can't be absolutely certain which choice will be right for you. What is perfect in January may be intolerable by June. So don't paint yourself into a corner by saying, "I'd never dream of going back to work before the baby enters school," or, "I'll never stay home."

Who's Changing the Diapers—Parents as Partners

Many women have found the solution to their problems as overburdened working mothers in the person of their partner. Having it all is much easier if your partner is willing to assume an equal share of the household and child-care responsibilities.

Unfortunately, change happens very slowly. In *The Second Shift: Working Families and the Revolution at Home,* author Arlie Hochschild documents that working mothers still do more housework and child care than their partners. Both parents and children will be better off if we can change this. If they are sharing the burden, mothers will be less physically tired and more emotionally content. There would be less conflict and more time to enjoy family life.

Below, I offer some guidelines for making parenthood workloads more equitable.

Guidelines for Shared Parenting

1. **Tackle the obstacles to changing gender roles for an ideal work/family balance for all parents.** We tend to think we're so sophisticated and liberated that we can slither out of our old sex roles as

easily as a snake sheds its skin. But humans are more like snails than snakes. Role-changing is a slow and painful process.

Many couples who had an equal relationship pre-parenthood revert to more traditional patterns after the baby's birth. The main reason is that children strike a deeper cord in us than careers do. If they were raised in a traditional, heterosexual home, Dad brought home the bacon and Mom cooked it. Sometimes when you become a parent, you identify with your own same-sex parent more intensely than previously, and you may unwittingly slip into your parents' behavior patterns. But you can step out of these patterns if you're aware of them and if you're willing to try new ones.

The dynamics will be different if you were raised by a single parent or a gay couple, but you can still benefit from thinking about this issue. As you step into your new parent role, do you find yourself saying or doing things that your parent would have done? Which parent, if you had two? Do you remember any arguments about sharing the workload at home?

a. Have a chair dialogue with your mother/father (see Chapter 2, "Secret Doors.") You won't do this with your parent present. To discover some of the ways you're following in your parents' footsteps, pretend to tell your imaginary same-sex parent the ways in which you would like to emulate them. Then mention how you would like to parent differently. Explain how your friends, non-sexist beliefs, and psychological knowledge have influenced your parenting goals.

Suggest that your partner try the same exercise, having an imaginary conversation with his same-sex parent. You might also try a variation to broaden both your perspectives: Ask him to take your role while you play your mother or father, then take his role while he plays one of his parents. Stepping into each other's shoes in this fashion can be a playful, nonthreatening, maybe even fun way to discover some of the attitudes that may be blocking a smooth transition to shared parenthood. And you'll learn a lot about each other in the process.

b. Discuss this issue with your partner. Your family history influences not only your expectations of yourself as a parent but also your expectations of your partner. Just as a man may unconsciously slip into his father's patterns, he may also expect his wife to emulate his mother's. In fact, by taking his father's role, he may unconsciously even force his wife to step into his mother's role.

For example, Joel's father was overly stern with him and his brothers, and in reaction, his mother became overly indulgent. When Joel became a father, he was so strict that his wife, also in reaction, wound up being indulgent, too.

It's also possible to misinterpret your partner's behavior because you may react to him as if he were your opposite sex parent. When Dale let Tessie play in the backyard mud puddles, Janet was horrified. She associated Dale's lack of concern for the dirt with her stepfather's lack of concern for her. But when she realized that Tessie was having a great time and that Dale planned to bathe her afterward and change her clothes, she was able to able to distinguish her easygoing husband from her neglectful stepfather.

The point is that we tend to forget how deeply ingrained and how complex role behavior and expectations may be. Remember that your husband didn't invent sexism. Like you, he is merely a product of a sexist society. Because he's nearby, it may be tempting to put him on trial for all the ills men have perpetrated on womankind through the centuries. And it may be equally tempting to sentence him to hard labor. But he's more likely to participate enthusiastically as a partner than as a prisoner.

c. Seek out couples who are sharing parenthood successfully and use them as role models. Ask them for help and suggestions.

2. Don't consider your partner to be "helping" you with "your" work. After a while, according to Ellen Goodman in her *Boston Globe* column, "Being a Grateful Wife Means Always Having to Ask," the partner begins to "wonder why she should say thank you when a father took care of his children and why she should say please when a husband took care of his house." Remember, they're his children, and it's his house, too. You didn't marry a boss; you married a partner.

3. Don't divide the chore list rigidly in half. Take into consideration which tasks each of you actually likes to do; then divide up the ones neither wants. If he loves to cook and you hate it, it's silly for each of you to cook half the meals. But it is a good idea to rotate the chores you both hate, whether weekly or monthly, so neither of you is stuck with the same ones all the time. It can be helpful to vent your frustrations, then re-negotiate or experiment with alternative ways of coping.

4. Share the power as well as the responsibility. You can't expect to shed half the load and hang onto all the control. That means that both of you should have an equal say in housekeeping and child care.

5. Give your partner the trust and respect s/he deserves. You should not insist that everything be done exactly your way or perfectly. Nor should you confuse a legitimate difference in standards with irresponsibility or resistance on your husband's part. Have faith in his ability to learn. If he doesn't tape the diaper tightly enough, he'll learn quickly! As Nancy Press Hawley says in *Ourselves and Our Children*, "Mothers who want to share parenthood often need to hold their tongues."

Caryl Rivers, Rosalind Barnett, and Grace Baruch, suggest in *Beyond Sugar and Spice* that one way to deal with a wife's typically superior knowledge of domestic practices is for her to serve as a consultant. In a consultant-client relationship, the consultant provides information, but the client is free to decide whether and how to act on that information. This approach may work for some couples who would otherwise become hopelessly entangled in power struggles.

Father Power

Fathers are increasingly involved with their children, and researchers and society are more fully understanding the powerful influence they have on their offspring. Ideally you will both share the excitement and anticipation throughout the pregnancy, from the positive test, through both the miracle and ordeal of childbirth. The father's hand on the mother's belly when he feels the first kick is a favorite memory for many. Share your feelings during pregnancy, not only the joy but also the darker moments of anxiety and ambivalence. Take childbirth classes and read parenting books together. Spend bonding time, "skin to skin" (e.g., baby's bare chest held against the father's chest) with the baby immediately after birth.

Writer David Steinberg in The Future of the Family described the joys of fatherhood, and the growth that comes from taking on a new role:

> As a man, it's easy to always be in situations that call for aggressive, rational manipulative perspectives and skills. With Dylan I move out of that more completely than I ever have before. As a result, I feel myself growing in all kinds of new ways. The clear importance of these new skills in caring for Dylan helps me respect and value them as they develop.

Steinberg describes some of the special delights for fathers and their children now available, that were absent in the days when fathers worked long hours and were only minimally involved with their children. He enjoys discovering nurturing skills he didn't know he had as well as the pleasurable experience of dealing with Dylan.

Finding Your Own Path to Shared Parenthood

Nancy Press Hawley, in *Ourselves and Our Children* points out that "The 'ideal' of shared parenthood is not for everyone and should not be seen as yet another pressure on parents to perform." Some women seem to feel that the Feminist Bureau of Investigation is going to send Betty or Gloria over to charge that your husband resists too much and that you do not insist enough. But pressure to conform to the new stereotype of the absolutely equal couple is as counterproductive as pressure to conform to the old traditional role divisions.

For example, consider Renata, an engineer, who is being pressured by her husband Leonard to have a baby. Her response: "I tell him I'm just not cut out to stay home. And I can't see leaving a baby in day care. He says he would stay home with the baby and just work part-time. But I couldn't stand his doing that. How could I respect a husband who stayed home and changed diapers? What would people say about us?"

Although many career women would jump at such an offer, Renata won't take Leonard up on it. Despite her nontraditional career choice, she has very traditional attitudes toward motherhood.

Or look at Melissa, an ardent feminist, who has trouble finding time to paint because of her hectic schedule as a commercial artist. She and her husband Will are working on the baby decision. Will has suggested that she quit her more-than-full-time job to spend half her time with the baby and the other half in her studio. But Melissa won't even consider it. "If I had a baby, I'd have to work full-time. I can't stand the idea of Will's supporting me." While it is a challenge to maintain identity and a sense of autonomy if one doesn't have a job, there are ways to do so. Melissa's rigidity if preventing her from enjoying her art, and her good fortune to not be obligated to work full time.

While Renata felt that motherhood was possible only within a traditional framework, Melissa felt that it was possible only within a nontraditional one. And both women are victims of their own rigid thinking. Neither can ask, "What's best for me and for us?"

The moral of these stories: try to be flexible in considering options. That way you'll have more options to consider. All couples have to find their own unique solutions to the problems of parenthood and family life.

Day Care? Where?—Mother's Dream or Nightmare?

Before you start searching for day care, let's take stock of your thoughts on day care. You may have nothing but positive feelings about day care if you have friends whose children have thrived in centers or with nannies. These friends may tell you how comfortable they are at work knowing that their child is well-cared for. These arrangements can make children more confident, knowing that their parents aren't the only people who can take care of them. Socializing with other children and learning new skills may be additional benefits that your friends have reported. You may even have noticed, for instance, that a friend's child who used to cling to his parents is more relaxed and independent since he started day care.

But what if even with some of the above information in mind, you have some negative feelings about day care? See if you can relate to any of these feelings.

Guilt

You're afraid your child will suffer emotional damage because you aren't there all the time. Study after study (see the Bibliography, Appendix 1) has shown that children of working mothers are no more unhappy or emotionally scarred than those whose mothers are in the home. However, it is clear to mental health professionals that children of *frustrated* mothers often have emotional problems. If you would be frustrated at home, your child is much better off sharing a happy mother with the folks at the office than having a miserable mommy all to herself.

But even if you've read the studies, your guilt won't magically disappear. If your mother stayed home with you and you both enjoyed that, you may worry that a different choice may not work as well for you and your child. With time and conversations with other working mothers, you will be able to enjoy work as well as your child.

Jealousy

You may already be jealous of a potential day care teacher before you've even made the first phone call. Perhaps you're worried that your child won't know who her mother is. You're afraid she'll love the caregiver more. You want to be the most special person in your child's world. Will you earn that place if you don't spend most of your time together?

Rest assured that children save a special place in their hearts for their mothers and fathers. There's room in their lives and affections for two parents and a day care provider or nanny. Research and my own experience both as an infant day care worker and a day care consumer show that children know who their parents are, right from the first month. They feel the intensity of your love, sense the familiarity of your face and body, and respond accordingly.

Anger

It's only natural to feel anger about the incredible burden of arranging care for a child any time you're not going to be around. What a switch from being childfree! Some of your anger at day care may really be anger at the injustice of being on duty around the clock. And if your partner is not participating in the child care search, your sense of resentment may intensify.

I've been struck by the number of super competent women who don't bat an eyelash at all kinds of complicated arrangements at work but who feel completely incapable of finding a day care placement. While some women don't know where to begin, there can be psychological impediments. Common fears include not being able to find a good placement, fear their child won't be comfortable in day care, and fear of going back to work after the baby is born. Get help from your partner, friends, mothers' groups, or professionals so you won't feel so alone and you'll have perspective on any emotional obstacles in your way.

Now that you have sorted out your emotions, let's talk about day care logistics.

Choosing the Right Kind of Day Care

There are three main sources of child care for working parents:

1. Day care providers who care for a small number of children in their own homes

2. Day care centers that have infant sections (not all do). Some centers care for only infants and toddlers, and don't have preschoolers.

3. Babysitters or nannies who come to your home.

Day Care Homes

Advantages:

- Your child is cared for by an experienced parent.
- Your child may receive more individual attention than in a center.
- The environment is more homelike, and the experience more nearly approximates the mother-child relationship you would have at home.
- Your child has other children to play with.

Disadvantages:

- Your child may not get as much intellectual stimulation as he or she would at a center.

- The day care mother may not be as well-educated or as thoroughly trained as a day care teacher.

Day Care Center

Advantages:

- The center provides a program of education and stimulation. A good infant program includes indoor and outdoor activity, sensory and language activities, massage and physical exercise.
- The center provides a sense of stability. If the day care teacher quits, you still have a placement for your child, provided, of course, that you and your child like the new infant care employee.
- A center has knowledgeable teachers. Day care workers usually have a fair amount of college course work and/or training in early childhood education.

Disadvantages:

- The child may not get enough attention if the center is understaffed.
- There may be high staff turnover. Try to find out about this.
- Your child will probably have to be sent home if moderately ill, whereas a home-based day care might still keep him.

In-Home Care

The main advantage of in-home care is convenience. It's wonderful not to have to transport the baby to day care, especially in a snowstorm or downpour. It's also great for the child to be in familiar, comfortable territory. Many people are able to cut the costs of having a nanny by sharing the hours and costs with another household.

However, there are a few disadvantages.

- If an in-home caretaker quits or gets sick, you may be stuck at home for a while. It's not always easy to make new arrangements right away, and it is a good idea to have a contingency plan if you choose this type of care. If you use a nanny agency, they may be able to provide another caretaker quickly.
- Additionally, a nanny may be expensive.
- You may also experience a lack of privacy, despite the convenience, if she lives with you.
- Turnover is another problem. Many foreign nannies are enthusiastic and reliable, but they often stay only a year, so you and your child have to grieve the loss of a quasi-family member and get adjusted to and try to bond with someone new. This situation may repeat itself, year after year.

Guidelines for Evaluating Your Child Care Choices

1. Make a joint decision if you have a partner. Visit centers or conduct in-home interviews together. Discuss your reactions to people and places visited and the pros and cons of various possibilities. Brainstorm other possibilities. If you don't have a partner, use friends, relatives, or a mothers' group as your sounding board.

2. Trust your feelings. Give them more weight than any objective considerations. Strong positive feelings about a person are better indicators than any intellectual assessment. The reverse is also true. If you seem to have every reason to like a person, but you have an uneasy feeling in your stomach nonetheless, trust your gut. Back off and try somebody else. You don't have to be best friends with your child's caretaker, but if she doesn't show you any warmth, she probably won't have much for your child, either.

3. Observe the children already in the day care home or center. In a day care center, are the children moderately noisy and rambunctious? Is the place neither bedlam nor monastery but rather a happy medium? Do the children look happy? In a day care home, do the day care children and the day care parent's own children seem happy? Are they relaxed and engaged in play and interactions with other children?

4. Analyze the environment from the standpoint of the child's needs. Is it safe? Is it clean? Is it attractive and interesting? Are the facilities adequate? Would you be happy spending time there if you were a child? Are licenses and certifications up to date?

5. Bring your child with you. How do the child and the prospective caretaker interact? Is the caretaker relaxed and warm, unnaturally cheery, or chillingly distant? Bear in mind that your child may cry because the person is a stranger and might be quite happy with her once she gets to know her. Crying doesn't necessarily bode ill. In fact, crying can be a useful opportunity to see how the caretaker handles your baby's crying or discomfort. Does she know how to soothe? Does she take it in stride? Does she seem to treat the baby with respect? If you are visiting day care facilities before the baby's birth, watch how the caretaker interacts with the children, especially any babies.

6. How flexible is the caretaker? Does she seem willing to accept and carry out your wishes for the child's care? Is it easy to talk to her about this? If you and she have different attitudes about child-rearing, will she be adaptable enough to accept your views?

7. Discuss fees and hours in advance. Will you pay by the hour, the day, or the week? When are you expected to pay, and what forms of pay are accepted? If you're fifteen minutes late, will you have to pay extra? Will you pay for holidays, for days your baby is home sick with you?

8. Ask for references and follow up on them. Ask references what they like or don't like about this person or center. If they are no longer using this particular placement, find out why. It may be that they moved or that their child outgrew the need for the placement. But it's also possible that the placement was less than ideal, and you'll want to investigate this. You may wonder if you should bother with calling since the caretaker would only give you references she assumes will say good things. Nevertheless, you may garner information from the references by their tone of voice, their pausing before answering a question, or their seeming to choose their words carefully.

9. Talk to more than one person or center before making your final decision. If you meet a center director initially, be sure to meet the person who would actually care for your child. It helps to have a choice, and comparing two resources may give you insight into both possibilities. Be sure to write notes immediately after each visit so thoughts and impressions will be fresh in your mind. This is especially crucial if you visit two centers or interview two people on the same day.

10. Once it's time to start, try to ease the child in gradually. Spend an hour or two the first day, a few hours the second, and so on. It will give all three of you—baby, mother, and caretaker a chance to make a smooth transition.

11. Don't hesitate to start out on a trial basis. See how it goes. If you're not satisfied, talk to the caretaker about your concerns. How does she respond? Is she defensive or does she listen and consider making changes? Don't settle for second best because you can't bear the thought of making new arrangements, or because you're convinced you won't find anything better. If you're not comfortable, your child probably won't be comfortable either.

12. Be creative. Have you considered all the possibilities? If you've heard of a good day care home or center that's full, get on the waiting list and ask the mother or director to refer you elsewhere. Would a stay-at-home relative, friend, or neighbor be willing to care for your child? Could you and your partner stagger your schedules so that hired day care wouldn't be necessary or so that a responsible high school or college student could take care of the baby for just a few hours? These resources may also be useful as a backup if regular arrangements fall through.

13. Don't assume that the arrangement that satisfies a friend will satisfy you. Because you and your child are unique, a placement that's perfect for your friend's child may be less than ideal for yours.

14. Don't allow yourself to be so discouraged by a waiting list that you don't even bother to put your child's name on it. When an opening does occur, a center may find that many children on the list are now in other placements. What sounds like an impossible wait could actually be shorter than you think. Check mothers' listservs and community message boards and network with friends to find out if any new facilities are opening. Children's librarians are another source.

15. Keep in mind that the child's needs change as he gets older. Every child needs a mixture of nurturance and stimulation, but infants and toddlers need nurturance most of all since they get reasonable amounts of stimulation as they're held, cuddled, rocked, changed, and sung to. Older children, on the other hand, have more complicated needs, and require a wider variety of activities. They still need a nurturing caregiver, but their needs for intellectual stimulation and interaction increase. After all, they'll get plenty of hugs at home. For this reason, as your child's needs change, a switch from a day care home to a day care center may be beneficial.

16. Start exploring possibilities while pregnant or even before. You'll have more time and feel less pressured. And you may be able to put your name on a waiting list for a popular program, such as a university-run infant center. Day care referral sources include:

- Online or brick-and-mortar child care resource center.
- A parenting hotline.
- A general community information and referral center.
- Word-of-mouth—ask other working parents for names.
- Local churches, synagogues, schools, and community centers.
- Family service agencies or mental health centers.
- A local day care center that doesn't take babies but may refer parents to day care homes and, in some cases, supervises these homes.
- A nanny agency or a domestic employment agency.

It may help to discuss your concerns with a professional. Child care referral workers and counselors in family service agencies are likely to be sensitive to your needs, and can help you identify your needs, explore your concerns and help you with arrangements.

When you're feeling frazzled about the day care situation,

consider these less obvious benefits: arranging for day care can help you learn to conduct research, interview and assess people, make hiring decisions, and supervise. All of these skills will prove useful at work and may serve to increase your overall self-confidence.

Although finding day care is often logistically and emotionally difficult, you will master this passage, and your child will benefit from the experience of playing with and learning from other adults and children.

✦ CHAPTER 16 ✦
HOW TO MAKE THE MOST OF YOUR DECISION

Congratulations. You mustered the courage to make a conscious decision rather than to drift into one. You read this book, did exercises, talked to your partner (or a friend, if single), maybe even argued and negotiated. You sorted out logic and emotions to arrive at your decision. You may have reaped other benefits: such as feeling closer to your partner or discovering values that you or your partner may never have fully expressed. These changes may have positive effects on your life, which may or may not relate to the baby decision.

Let's look at some ways to make the most out of your accomplishments and of the life you have chosen.

1. Apply what you've learned about decision-making to other decisions. Be as critical, but not as cautious, about making other commitments. Because the consequences of most other major decisions are not as irrevocable, you cannot and should not spend as much time on every choice. But it is a good idea to ask yourself: Is this really best for me/us? Will we grow from this choice? Are we choosing safety over growth? Have we based the decision on an appropriate combination of logic and emotion? Have we considered all the practicalities? Does it feel right emotionally and make sense logistically?

2. Build on the intimacy you've developed with your partner while making the baby decision. If you were able to maintain an I-thou relationship, giving each other respect and understanding, even during a tug-of-war, you have a good foundation for future decisions and conflicts. These are the building blocks for a good life together regardless of your choice

3. Keep on taking risks. Your life will be more exciting and more rewarding. If you've chosen to be childfree, you've already faced the risks of your own regrets and others' hostility. It should, therefore, be a little easier to take some of the other risks that your choice allows you—a career change, taking up painting, or even a mountain-climbing expedition.

If you're going to have a baby, the physical risks of childbirth and the emotional risks postpartum are obvious, but later risks may be less so. Children tie you down to some extent, and to combat this, you need to venture out, both literally, with and without the children, and psychologically, by exploring new ways of parenting. You can give your children a sense of curiosity and adventure not just when you travel but in everyday activities.

4. Expect success. Now that you've made your choice, assume you'll be happy with it. Close your eyes and visualize your future. Picture your joys and your accomplishments. Imagine yourself with your partner in old age, looking back on your life and agreeing that you made the right choice.

5. "Steal" a little from the other choice. Consider what you'll miss most by giving up the other choice, and plan ways to capture some of that. If you're going to become a parent but crave exotic travel, plan ways to make that happen even if you have to wait a year or two. Give up some other less important activities if necessary. If you decide that you will interrupt a career that's important to you, make plans for how you will stay involved in it, such as working part-time or attending professional meetings. If you're going to remain childfree but want a warm relationship with a child, consider spending time with a friend's child or a niece or nephew, or do volunteer work and be a Big Brother or Big Sister.

Remember, as a childfree person, if you're not interested in children, no one expects you to spend time with them! If you enjoy nurturing adults, you might mentor younger people at work. You and your partner can also nurture each other, for instance, a surprise weekend trip, flowers, a massage, or a favorite meal.

6. Accept your ambivalence. Everyone wonders, "What would have happened if . . . ?" especially during rough times—a hectic day for a parent, a lonely one for a non-parent. We all have to sacrifice something in order to get something else. But like guilt, ambivalence only gets worse if you try to get rid of it. The decision-maker who can't stand uncertainty is forever out of breath chasing unwanted thoughts away. So it's important to accept that because you're human, you'll always have *some* regrets. Perhaps there can be some consolation in knowing that accepting ambivalence helps prepare you for other decisions and dilemmas.

7. Spend time with people who have made the same decision. They can serve as role models and provide needed emotional support and suggest coping techniques. It helps if some of them are a few years ahead of you in living with their choice. If most of your friends have made the other choice, seek out new people.

8. Spend time with people who have made the opposite choice. If you've really come to terms with your decision, you should not feel threatened by spending time with them. Try to respect your friends and their right to choose differently. Even though your friendships may be based on certain shared attitudes and beliefs, try to recognize and appreciate the differences, too. It can be refreshing and stimulating to learn about and share some of your friends' experience.

Your life will be enriched if you spend time with people who are different. Parents can offer childfree couples a sort of extended family and a chance to be with the kids without having to make huge sacrifices. They offer childfree friends who haven't made a final decision a built-in laboratory for testing out feelings and reactions. Childfree couples can, if they want to, offer parents occasional relief from the burdens of child care, and some vicarious satisfaction through tales of their work and travel. While it is hard for new parents not sleeping through the night yet to get past envy, taking a grown-up attitude can actually allow you to enjoy these conversations. Such conversations can lead to mental notes about future travel, or an idea to put into practice when one goes back to work.

Frequently, friends drift apart when one couple is having a baby and the other is not. In the first year, their plans to get together are often at odds. Childfree friends, for instance, would prefer to meet at an elegant restaurant while the baby stays home. Meanwhile the parents invite these friends to their home or meet at a family restaurant to save babysitting money and/or because they wrongly assume their friends want to hang out with the baby.

Although the people involved typically complain, "We have nothing in common anymore," the real reason might be that they have *too much* in common—unexpressed ambivalence. The prospective parents worry, "If they're so much like us and they're not going to have a baby, maybe we made a mistake." The childfree couple worries, "If they're so much like us and they're enjoying the baby, maybe we're wrong." And so each couple calls the other a little less often, and a worthwhile friendship may dissolve or be unnecessarily strained.

This phenomenon is by no means universal. Many people maintain close relationships with friends who made the opposite choice, unfailingly respecting and supporting their friends' decision. They even enjoy knowing someone who can offer them a bird's-eye view of a different existence. But for too many other couples, their own insecurity weakens their ties to friends who made the opposite decision.

Work on this problem by discussing it openly with your friends. Take the first step by saying, "Let's talk about our feelings. Let's not drift apart. If we pick up signs of jealousy or disapproval in ourselves or each other, let's talk about it. We're both going to have regrets sometimes, and if we don't share them, maybe we'll stop sharing other things. And our relationship is too valuable to let that happen!"

It's true that some childfree couples can't stand being around children. And it's equally true that some parents feel that their childfree friends' lives aren't very meaningful. But such people are in the minority. I believe that the doubts, rather than different interests or lifestyles, keep us away from those who chose the flip side of the baby decision.

9. Don't proselytize. Generally, the amount of time that people spend talking about the decision is in inverse proportion to their comfort with it. This is especially true for those who are trying to persuade everyone that their decision is best not only for them but also for everyone else as well.

Do you tend to harp on your baby decision at social or family gatherings, telling everyone and anyone why *your* decision is the right one for everybody? If so, ask yourself, "Who am I *really* talking to? Am I trying to convince myself?"

If the answer is yourself, then you may have more homework to do on your decision.

If the answer is "the other person," have you really considered this particular person's needs and interests or are you just imposing your own? Even if you're sincerely concerned about the other person's happiness, can you be sure that you know what's right for him or her? If you do feel that the person hasn't considered all the issues, you can point them out tactfully and objectively. But don't set yourself up as a judge.

Should You Announce Your Decision?

There is one advantage in telling the world: going public reinforces your decision. As people react, both positively and negatively, your commitment may solidify. You will feel bolstered by those who are enthusiastic, and you will gain more confidence in your choice when you come up with good answers for the people who criticize you or simply ignore them.

The disadvantage of an announcement is that it can invite criticism that you may not yet be prepared to face. The solution: be selective about who you tell.

If you're planning a baby, you may want to wait until you're pregnant before telling anybody. If you don't conceive right away, you won't have to put up with referrals to "just the right doctor" and the kind of unwanted advice that raises your anxiety level. Even when you're pregnant, you might want to wait until the second trimester, when losses are less likely. Be especially cautious about telling people at work. You don't want to be passed over for a promotion or a plum assignment because of this knowledge.

If you're planning to remain childfree, you may hear a lot of negative comments from pronatalists. If you've discussed the decision-making process publicly, this news won't come as a surprise. But if you haven't told a soul that you're even thinking about the baby question, it's wise to be prepared for criticism and even wiser to be selective about making the announcement.

At this point you may feel a sense of accomplishment and relief. People sometimes say, "I feel as if a burden has lifted off my shoulders." Others are happy to discover more energy, better concentration, and a creative flow of ideas about the next stage of your life. Even if you have chosen to be childfree, actively ruling out parenthood will probably give you a sense of energy and renewal for enjoying life.

✦ ACKNOWLEDGMENTS ✦

For review of the manuscript in its early stages, I thank Mara Altman, Phyllis Fitzpatrick, MSW, LICSW, Stephanie Morgan, MSW, Psy.D., Katie O'Reilly, Deborah Rozelle, Psy.D., Jenna Russell, Kayla Sheets, LCGC, Carol Sheingold, MSW, LICSW, Janet Surrey, Ph.D., and Bina Venkataraman.

Thanks to my colleagues at RESOLVE, the national infertility organization: Barbara Eck Menning, R.N., founder, Carol Frost Vercollone, Assistant Director, Diane Clapp, B.S., R.N., Medical Information Counselor. I thank Diane Clapp for the work we did together on the topics of grief and of helping members stop fertility treatments. I thank national RESOLVE board members Dr. Susan Cooper (in memoriam), Dr. Isaac Schiff, Dr. Veronica Ravnikar, Dr. Holly Simons, and Dr. Aline Zoldbrod. Other RESOLVE colleagues were Alma Berson, LICSW, my clinical consultant, and Ellen Glazer, LICSW.

A special thanks to Dr. Selwyn Oskowitz of Boston IVF, recently retired, with whom I shared many talks at the podium, and many cases in our practices. Our collaboration has been an honor and an education.

Other colleagues I wish to acknowledge are RESOLVE of New England, Ali Domar, Ph.D, Dale Eldridge, LICSW; Jane Feinberg-Cohen, LICSW; Davina Fankhauser; Ellen Feldman, LICSW; Annie Geogehan, LICSW; Leigh Gray, LICSW; Dr. Martha Griffin; Adele Kaufman, Ph.D.; Sue Levin, LICSW; Rebecca Lubens, LICSW; Abigail MacDonald, LICSW; Barbara B. McCauley, LICSW; Lisa Rothstein; and Ava Sarafan, LICSW. To Cambridge Center for Adult Education, for hosting The Baby Decision workshops since 1984.

To all of my psychotherapy clients, coaching clients, and workshop attendees whose intelligent questions, lively dialogues with classmates, along with their creativity, courage and humor have informed this book. May you all enjoy the lives you have chosen!

For urging me to write a second edition of *The Baby Decision*, deep thanks to author Colin Beavan, Dr. Janet Surrey, Barbara McCauley, LICSW, and Marilyn Yohe, Lic.Ac. For recent media attention to the book and my work, I thank Mara Altman, Ann Friedman and Corrie Pikul. Thanks also to Colin Beavan for featuring my work in his latest book, *How to Be Alive: A Guide to the Kind of Happiness That Helps the World*.

For sharpening my writing skills, I thank Grub Street teachers and consultants Becky Tuch and Jacqueline Sheehan, and my Grub classmates and community, especially Alyssa Haywoode, who helped with concepts, editing, and social media.

For insights that brightened the book, I thank Marcella, Vanessa, and Rocco Bombardieri, Dr. Paul Fulton and the Institute of Meditation and Psychotherapy, Dawn Davenport of Creating a Family, James Leahy, Dr. Stephanie Morgan, Dr. Judy Osher, Dr. Deborah Rozelle, Dr. Rebecca Shrum, Dr. Janet Surrey, Dr. Karen Tripitto, Dr. Liz Wolheim, Rabbi Susan Harris, and Katie Wilson. For enthusiastic support and contributions to my wellbeing, I thank Loocie Brown, M.A.; Malissa Wood, M.D.; Mary Ellen Rodman, M.D.; Lori Berkowitz, M.D.; Jose Donovan, P.T.; Kristin Eckler, M.D.; Susan Hopper, P.T. and Sue Guertin, P.T. assistant, both at Theraspring. For ongoing support, I thank Maxine Olson, Joyce and John Dwyer, Janet Buchwald and Joel Moskowitz, Rabbi David Thomas, Cantor Lorel Zar-Kessler, the members of Congregation Beth El, Louise Brown, Dee Dee Pike, Marcia Lewin-Berlin, and Suzanne Salter. Amber Garcia, Jean Ferro, Susan Milberg, Gail Sillman, Sally Plone, and Sherry Kauderer, James Maguaran, M.D., Luanna Devenis, Ph.D, and Dr. Tanya Korkosz, and Kathie McInnis and Trish Pratt. Thanks to family members Alan and Ann Malkoff, David Malkoff and Lesley-Anne Stone, Christine and Mark Malkoff, Alison, Tom, Beth and Aaron Drucker-Holzman, Louise Bombardieri, Rosemary Dykeman, Gina

Girouard, Rosemarie and Chris Dykeman-Bermingham, Marietta Bombardieri, and Vincent Nobile. Other close family members who have played important roles are Cyndy Marion, and Loretta Hunt Marion, and Karim Naguib. I thank my daughters, Marcella and Vanessa Bombardieri, my daughter-in-law Cyndy Marion, and my nephews David and Mark Malkoff not only for support but also for being extraordinary role models of creative chutzpah. In particular, Vanessa and Cyndy's round-the-clock dedication to White Horse Theater (off-off Broadway, New York City) is a great inspiration.

To my grandson, Sofyan, for the love, charm and humor that sustained me though this long project. Thanks also to his parents, my daughter Marcella Bombardieri and son-in-law Karim Naguib for demonstrating the joys and challenges of family life.

For encouragement and superb library services, thank you to Robin Demas, Cynthia DiRenzo, Patricia Diotte, and Maliha Quddus, and Gay Weiss of the Concord Free Public Library. Thanks also to the wonderful staff at the Acton and Stow libraries.

For an ad hoc writer's room in a café, I thank Andrew and Stacey Bluestein of Emma's Café in Stow, MA, for espresso, good food, and their warm welcome.

Thanks to all the talented midwives of the book itself, Jane Friedman, publishing consultant, Hillary Rettig, productivity consultant, Andi Cumbo-Floyd, editor, Barbara Aronica-Buck, cover and interior designer, Sharona Jacobs, photographer, Claire McKinney and her associate Larissa Ackerman, publicists, Jeremy Townsend, proofreader, and Cheryl Lenser, indexer.

For ongoing support through all difficulties, a special thank you to Phyllis Fitzpatrick, Rachel Sagan, Stephanie Morgan and Deborah Rozelle.

And to my husband Rocco, who has made this book possible with his constant encouragement, tireless work, and most of all, his love.

ACKNOWLEDGMENTS FOR THE FIRST EDITION

So many people have contributed to this book that it is impossible to thank everyone personally. I especially want to express my appreciation to the individuals and couples who shared so much of themselves during workshops or interviews.

Thanks to all the people whose enthusiasm and expertise added so much to the book:

To the psychotherapists who trained me: Elsie Herman, Nancy Leffert, Teresa Boles Reinhardt, and Ron Reneau.

To Elizabeth Bunce-Nichols and the Nashville YWCA for helping the project get started.

To the following people for sharing their professional knowledge: psychoanalysts Jean Baker Miller and Carol Nadelson; psychologist Glenn Larson; COPE workshop facilitators Ginny DeLuca and Randy Wolfson; gynecologist Kenneth Blotner; Miriam Ruben of the Association for Voluntary Sterilization; and Preterm staff members Pat Lurie, Mag Miller, Maxine Ravech, and Billie Rosoff.

To Nina Finkelstein, Sherrye Henry, Erica Jong, and Letty Cottin Pogrebin for their insights on feminism and motherhood.

A special thank you to author and television commentator Betty Rollin, whose explanation of her decision was both inspired and inspiring. This book is also easier to read thanks to Ms. Rollin's no-nonsense approach to writing. Imagining her reading over my shoulder and circling every bit of jargon guided my revisions.

To the National Alliance for Optional Parenthood (NAOP), especially Gail McKirdy of the National Resource Center, for helping me track down all kinds of information.

To the staffs of the Boston Public Library—Copley Reference Library and Roslindale Branch; of the Divinity, Psychology, Social Relations and Widener Libraries of Harvard University; and to Irene

Laursen and Debbie Smith of the Wellesley College Science Library.

To the following people for reading all or part of the manuscript: Rocco Bombardieri, Steve Cohn, Carol Conner, Judy Eron, William Farago, David Holzman, Glenn Larson, Sadie and Sol Malkoff, Marianne Perrone, Teresa Boles Reinhardt, and Martha and Steven Richmond.

To Judith Appelbaum and Nancy Evans for their skills and support, first in *How to Get Happily Published* and later through correspondence.

To Ginger Downing, who typed the manuscript, for her speed, patience, flexibility, and sense of humor.

To the women who provided loving care to my daughters while I wrote: Kathy King and Catherine Zirpollo in the early stages and high school students Dorothy Staffier, Jeannie and Joanne Varano on occasional weekends. A very special thank you to Alice Staffier, who took care of my children during most of my working hours. Without her intense dedication, this book would have taken twice as long to write.

To the following people for their enthusiastic support, which included resisting the temptation to say, "You've got to be crazy to write your first book the same year you have your second baby!" It was crazy, but it was also possible, thanks to Sandy and Tom Anderson, the members of the Arlington Street Church, John Baeder, Barbara Berger, Steve and Edie Cohn, Carol Conner, Emily Dunn, Zelda Fischer, Mimi Goss, Kathy Hearne, Susan Jordan, Marianne and Fred Perrone, Arthur and Betsy Purcell, Caryl Rivers, Beth Rotondo, Susan Schein, Barbara Sheedy, Barbara Sher, and Claire Willis.

To Judy Eron, for serving as a model of a woman who balances beautifully her two vocations: writing and psychotherapy,

To Glenn Larson, who helped me understand the meaning of self-actualization. The growth orientation of this book owes much to him.

To Marianne Perrone for her loving encouragement and for her artistic and conceptual fireworks which never failed to make my own imagination skyrocket.

To Rawson, Wade editors Eleanor Rawson and Sharon Morgan:

To Eleanor for her expertise and interest.

To Sharon for her dedication and skill. Thanks to Sharon, this is a stronger book.

To my agent Anita Diamant, for her support and commitment.

To my parents, Sadie and Sol Malkoff for their enthusiasm, and to Sadie for her editorial suggestions.

To my daughters, Marcella and Vanessa, for giving me firsthand knowledge of motherhood, contributing to the realism of the book, and also providing comic relief when the going got rough.

To my husband, Rocco, for believing in this book from start to finish and for making the enormous sacrifices it required. Without his loving support, *The Baby Decision* could not have been written.

✦ APPENDIX 1 ✦
BIBLIOGRAPHY

The Decision

Altman, Mara. *Baby Steps*. Kindle Single, 2014.

Ariely, Dan. *Predictably Irrational: The Hidden Forces that Shape Our Decisions*. New York: Harper Perennial, 2010.

Bardwick, Judith. *In Transition: How Feminism, Sexual Liberation and the Search for Self-Fulfillment Have Altered America*. New York: Holt, Rinehart and Winston, 1979.

Bombardieri, Merle. "Considering Parenthood." *Our Bodies, Ourselves*. New York: Simon and Schuster, 2005.

Daniels, Pamela, and Weingarten, Kathy. *Sooner or Later: The Timing of Parenthood in Adult Lives*. New York: Norton, 1992.

Davitz, Lois Lederman. *Baby Hunger*. Minneapolis, MN: Winston Press, 1984.

Dell, Diana L. and Suzan Erem. *Do I Want to Be a Mom? A Woman's Guide to the Decision of a Lifetime*. New York: McGraw-Hill, 2004.

Fabe, Marilyn, and Wikler, Norma. *Up Against the Clock: Career Women Speak on the Choice to Have Children*. New York: Random House, 1979.

Friedman, Ann. "What if You Just Don't Know If You Want Kids? *New York Magazine*, September 18, 2014, http:nymag.com/thecut/2014/09/what-if-you-just-don't-know-if-you-want-kids.html.

Gerson, Kathleen. *Hard Choices: How Women Decided About Work, Career, and Motherhood*. Berkeley, CA: University of California Press, 1985.

Kahneman, Daniel. *Thinking, Fast and Slow*. New York: Farrar, Strauss and Giroux, 2011.

Lehrer, Jonah. *How We Decide*. Boston: Houghton Mifflin Harcourt, 2009.

Leibovich, Lori. *Maybe Baby: Twenty-Eight Writers Tell the Truth about Skepticism, Ambivalence, and How They Made the Biggest Decision of Their Lives*. New York: Harper, 2007.

McKaughan, Molly. *The Biological Clock*. New York: Penguin, 1989.

Ostrander, Madeline. "How Do You Decide to Have a Baby When Climate Change Is Remaking Life on Earth?" thenation.com, April 11, 18th issue, http://thenation.com/article/how-do-you-decide-to-have-a-baby-when-climate-change-is-remaking-life-on-earth/.

Pikul, Corrie. "The Clock-Watcher: How Do You Know When—or if—You Should Have a Baby? *Elle*, February, 2011.

Rivers, Caryl. "The New Anxiety of Motherhood." *Women in a Changing World*. Uta West, ed. pp. 141–152. New York: McGraw-Hill, 1975.

Rubin, Theodore Isaac. *Overcoming Indecisiveness: The Eight Stages of Effective Decision Making*. New York: Harper and Row, 1985.

Whelan, Elizabeth. *A Baby? Maybe*. New York: Bobbs-Merrill, 1975.

Wills, Garry. "What? What? Are Young Americans Afraid to Have Kids?" *Esquire*, March 1974.

Wade, Donna. *I Want a Baby, He Doesn't: How Both Partners Can Make the Right Decision at the Right Time*. Avon, MA: Adams Media, 2005.

Yalom, Irvin. *Existential Psychotherapy*. New York: Basic Books, 1980. This book has an excellent chapter on decision-making.

Social Commentary

Badinter, Elizabeth. *The Conflict: How Modern Motherhood Undermines the Status of Women*. New York: Metropolitan/Henry Holt, 2011.

Beavan, Colin. *How to Be Alive: A Guide to the Kind of Happiness That Helps the World*. New York: Dey Street, 2016. With environmental concerns, discusses ways of nurturing children other than biological parenthood. Includes a chapter on this author's decision guidelines.

Carroll, Laura. *The Baby Matrix: Why Freeing Our Mind from Outmoded Thinking About Parenthood and Reproduction Will Create a Better World*. Live True Books, 2012.

Chatterjee, Keya. *The Zero Footprint Baby: How to Save the Planet While Raising a Healthy Baby*. Brooklyn, NY: Ig Publishing, 2013.

Crittenden, Ann. *The Price of Motherhood: Why the Most Important Job in the World Is Still the Least Valued*. New York: Metropolitan Books, 2001.

Douglas, Susan and Meredith Michaels. *The Mommy Myth: The Idealization of Motherhood and How It Has Undermined All Women*.

Glenn, Evelyn Nakano, Grace Change, and Linda Rennie Forcey. *Mothering: Ideology, Experience, and Agency*. New York: Routledge, 1994,

Golombok, Susan. *Modern Families: Parents and Children in New Family Forms*. Cambridge England: Cambridge University Press, 2015.

Hanauer, Cathi, ed. *The Bitch in the House: 26 Women Tell the Truth About Sex, Solitude, Work, Motherhood and Marriage*. New York: William Morrow, 2002.

Haningsberg, Julie E. and Sara Rudnick, eds. *Mother Troubles: Rethinking Contemporary Maternal Dilemmas*. Boston: Beacon Press, 1999.

Hartas, Dimitra. *The Right to Childhood: Critical Perspectives on Rights, Difference and Knowledge in a Transient World*. London: Continuum Books, 2008.

Holmes, Melanie. *The Female Assumption: A Mother's Story: Freeing Women From the View That Motherhood is a Mandate*. Create Space, 2014.

Hoschild, Arlie. *The Second Shift: Working Families and the Revolution at Home*. New York: Penguin, 2012.

Hewett, Sylvia Ann. *Creating a Life: Professional Women and the Quest for Children*. New York: Talk Miramax, 2002.

Ireland, Mardy S. *Reconceiving Women: Separating Motherhood from Female Identity*. New York: Guilford Press, 1993.

Jung, Courtney. *Lactivism: How Feminists and Fundamentalists, Hippies and Yuppies and Physicians and Politicians Made Breastfeeding Big Business and Bad Policy*. New York: Basic Books, 2015.

Kramer, Wendy and Naomi Cahn. *Finding Our Families: A First-of-Its-Kind Book for Donor Conceived People and Their Families*. New York: Avery/Penguin, 2013.

Morrow, Lance. "Wondering if Children Are Necessary." *Time Magazine*, March 5, 1979.

Ramsey, Patricia. *Teaching and Learning in a Diverse World: Multicultural Education for Young Children*. New York: Teachers College Press, 2011.

Reddy, M.T. *Crossing the Color Line: Race, Parenting and Culture*. New Brunswick, NJ: Rutgers University Press, 1994.

Richards, Sarah Elizabeth. *Motherhood Rescheduled: The New Frontier of Egg Freezing and The Women Who Tried It*. New York: Simon and Schuster, 2013.

Ruddick, Sara. *Maternal Thinking: Toward a Politics of Peace*. Boston: Beacon Press, 1989.

Schulte, Brigid. *Overwhelmed: Work, Love and Play When No One Has the Time*. New York: Sarah Crichton Books, 2014.

Senior, Jennifer. *All Joy and No Fun: The Paradox of Modern Parenthood*. New York: Ecco, 2014.

Selvaratnam, Tanya. *The Big Lie: Motherhood, Feminism, and the Reality of the Biolgoical Clock*. Amherst, New York: Prometheus, 2014.

Spar, Debora L. *The Baby Business: How Money, Science, and Politics Drive the Commerce of Conception*. Cambridge, MA: Harvard Business School Press, 2006.

Tsigdinos, Pamela Mahoney. *Silent Sorority: A Barren Woman Gets Busy, Angry,*

Lost and Found. BookSurge Publishing, 2009.

Valenti, Jessica. *Why Have Kids? A New Mom Explores the Truth About Parenting and Happiness.* Boston: New Harvest, 2012.

Van Ausdale, D. and J.R. Feagin. *The First R.: How Children Learn Race and Racism.* Landham, MD: Rowan and Littlefield, 2001.

Zoll, Miriam. *Cracked Open: Liberty, Fertility, and the Pursuit of High Tech Babies: A Memoir.* Northampton, MA: Interlink, 2013.

Personal Growth

Berne, Eric. *Games People Play: The Psychology of Human Relationships.* New York: Ballantine, 1973.

Bowen, Murray. *Family Therapy in Clinical Practice.* New York: Jason Aronson, 1978.

Brach, Tara. *Radical Acceptance: Embracing Your Life with the Heart of the Buddha.* New York: Bantam, 2003.

Bridges, William. *Transitions: Making the Most of Life's Changes.* 3rd ed. Cambridge, MA: Da Capo, 2009.

Buber, Martin. *Hasidism and Modern Man.* New York: Harper Torch Books, 1958. His quote on "mission" in "Which Way Happiness" appeared on pp. 139-40 of his book.

Carstensen, Laurie L. *A Long Bright Future: An Action Plan for a Lifetime of Happiness, Health and Financial Security.* New York: Broadway Books, 2009. Planning for healthy aging.

Erikson, Erik. *Identity, Youth and Crisis.* New York, W.W. Norton, 1968. Generativity quote pp.138–139.

Fromm, Eric, *Escape From Freedom,* New York: Avon, 1965.

Germer, Christopher. *The Mindful Path to Self-Compassions: Freeing Yourself From Destructive Thoughts and Emotions.* New York: Guilford Press, 2009.

Gilbert, Daniel. *Stumbling on Happiness.* New York: Knopf, 2006.

Hanson, Rick. *Hardwiring Happiness: The New Brain Science of Contentment, Calm and Confidence.* New York: Harmony, 2013.

Lifton, Robert J. *Boundaries: Psychological Man in Revolution.* New York: Random House, 1969.

Levoy, Gregg. *Finding and Following an Authentic Life.* New York: Harmony, 1998.

McAdams, Dan P. *The Redemptive Self: Stories Americans Live By.* New York: Oxford Univerity Press, 2006. A scholarly but fairly readable book relevant to life decisions and how we view and talk about our lives.

McKay, Matthew and David Harp. *Neural Path Therapy: How to Change Your Brain's Response to Anger, Fear, Pain and Desire.* Oakland, CA: New Harbinger, 2005.

Maslow, Abraham. *The Farther Reaches of Human Nature.* New York: Penguin, 1976. Jonah Complex quote, p. 34.

_____. *Toward a Psychology of Being.* Princeton, NJ: Van Nostrand, 1968. Growth versus deficiency quote pp. 21–59.

May, Gerald. *Will and Spirit. A Contemplative Psychology.* New York: Harper One, 1987.

May, Rollo. *The Courage to Create.* New York: Bantam, 1976. The sayings of the oracle quote pp.125–127.

_____. *Love and Will.* New York: Dell, 1974.

_____. *Man's Search for Himself.* New York: Signet, 1967.

Neff, Kristin D. *Self-Compassion: Stop Beating Yourself Up and Leave Insecurity Behind.* New York: Morrow, 2011.

Orsillo, S.M. and L. Roemer. *The Mindful Way Through Anxiety: Break Free From Chronic Worry and Reclaim Your Life.* New York: Guilford Press, 2011.

Rico, Gabrielle, *Pain and Possibility. Writing Your Way Through Personal Crisis.* Los Angeles: J.P. Tarcher, 1991.

Rogers, Carl. *On Becoming a Person.* Boston: Houghton Mifflin, 1961.

Sheehy, Gail. *Passages.* New York: Bantam, 1977.

Siegel, R.D. *The Mindfulness Solution: Everyday Practices for Everyday Problems.* New York: Guilford Press, 2016.

Marriage/Relationships

Buber, Martin. *I and Thou.* New York: Charles Scribner's Sons, 1958.

Campbell, Angus. *The Quality of American Life: Perceptions, Evaluations, and Satisfactions.* New York: Russell Sage Foundation, 1976.

Cockrell, Stacie, Cathy O'Neill, and Julia Stone. *Babyproofing Your Marriage: How to Laugh more, Argue Less, and Communicate Better as Your Family Grows.* New York: Harper-Collins, 2007.

Cowan, Carol Pape, and Philip A. Cowan. *When Partners Become Parents: The Big Life Change for Couples.* New York: Basic Books, 1992.

Feldman, Harold. "The Effects of Children on the Family," in Andree Michel, ed., *Family Issues of Employed Women in Europe and America.* Leiden, The Netherlands: E.J. Brill, 1971.

Gottman, John, and Julie Scwartz Gottman. *And Baby Makes Three: The Six Step Plan for Preserving Marital Intimacy and Rekindling Romance After the*

Baby Arrives. New York: Crown, 2007.

Howard, Jane. *Families.* New York: Simon and Schuster, 1978.

Jordan, Pamela L., Scott M. Stanley, and Howard J. Markman. *Becoming Parents: How to Strengthen Your Marriage as Your Family Grows.* San Francisco: Jossey-Bass, 1999.

Moustakas, Clark. *Creative Life.* New York: D. Van Nostrand, 1977. The quote at the beginning of "Tug of War" is from p. 42 of his book.

Parker, Kim. "Parenthood and Happiness: It's More Complicated Than You Think," www.pewresearch.org/fact-tank/2014/02/07/parenthood-and-happiness-its-more-complicated- than-you-think.

Raley, Patricia E., and Mel Roman. *The Indelible Family.* New York: Rawson, Wade, 1980.

Raskin, Valerie. D. *Great Sex for Moms: Ten Steps to Nurturing Passion While Raising Kids.* New York: Fireside/Simon and Schuster, 2002.

Senior, Jennifer. *All Joy and No Fun: The Paradox of Modern Parenthood.* New York: Ecco, 2014.

Smith, Manuel. *When I Say No, I Feel Guilty.* New York: Bantam, 1975. Includes assertiveness techniques useful for coping with pronatalist pressures.

Shem, Samuel and Janet Surrey. *We Have to Talk: Healing Dialogues Between Men and Women.* New York: Basic Books, 1998.

Squire, Susan. *For Better, For Worse: A Candid Chronicle of Five Couples Adjusting to Parenthood.* Garden City, New York: Doubleday, 1993.

Surrey, Janet and Samuel Shem. *The Buddha's Wife: Her Story and Reader's Companion/ The Path of Awakening Together.* New York: Atria, 2015.

Winks, Cathy, and Anne Seamans. *Sexy Mamas: Keeping Your Sex Life While Raising Kids.* Makawao, HI: Inner Ocean, 2004.

Childfree Choice

Books with an asterisk * are sensitive to and relevant for those choosing to be childfree after infertility and others who are childfree by chance, not by first choice. Listings with two asterisks ** were written specifically about choosing childfree after infertility.

While you may find all the listing below of interest, I identified the most relevant ones for readers whose first choice was not to be childfree.

Anton, Linda Hunt. *Never to be a Mother. A Guide for All Women Who Didn't—or Couldn't Have Children.* San Francisco, CA: Harper, 1992.*

Bombardieri, Merle. "Childfree Decision Making" (after infertility) fact sheet available from resolve.org.**

Burgwyn, Diana. *Married Without Children.* New York: Harper and Row, 1981.

Cain, Madelyn. *The Childless Revolution.* Cambridge, MA: Perseus, 2001.*

Carroll, Laura. *Families of Two.* Xlibris, 2000. (See also *The Baby Matrix* in the Social Commentary section.)

Daum, Meghan. "The Difference Maker" in Daum, Meghan. *Unspeakable and Other Subjects of Discussion.* New York: Farrar, Stauss and Giroux, 2014.

Daum, Meghan, ed. *Selfish, Shallow, and Self-Absorbed: Sixteen Writers on the Decision Not to Have Kids.* New York: Picador, 2015.

Carter, Jean and Michael. *Sweet Grapes: How to Stop Being Infertile and Start Living Again.* Indianapolis, IN: Perspectives Press, 1998.**

Casey, Terri. *Pride and Joy: The Lives and Passions of Women Without Children.* New York: Atria Books, 2007.

Faux, Marian. *Childless by Choice.* Garden City, New York: Doubleday, 1984.

Foster, Karen. *No Way Baby! Exploring, Understanding and Defending the Decision Not to Have Children.* Self-Published, no place given, 2012.

Greene, Gael. "A Voice Against Motherhood." *Saturday Evening Post,* 26 January 1963, p. 10.

Hughes, Aralyn. *Kid Me Not: An Anthology by Childfree Women of the 60's now in their 60's.* Austin, TX: Violet Crown, 2014.

Kamien, Marcia. "We'll Never Have Kids!" *Woman's Day,* 9 January 1978, p. 8.

Kramer, Lilly. "The No-Child Family." *New York Times Magazine,* 24 December 1972, p. 28.

Lafayette, Leslie. *Why Don't You Have Kids? Living a Full Life Without Parenthood.* New York: Kensington, 1995.

Lang, Susan. *Women Without Children: The Reasons, the Rewards, the Regrets.* New York: Pharos, 1991.*

Mantel, Henriette, ed. *No Kidding: Women Writers on Bypassing Parenthood.* Berkeley, CA: Seal: 2013.

Manterfield, Lisa. *I'm Taking My Eggs and Going Home: How One Woman Dared to Say No to Motherhood.* New York: Steel Rose Press, 2011. **

Notkin, Melanie. *Otherhood: Modern Women Finding a New Kind of Happiness.* Berkeley, CA: Seal Press, 2014.**

Peck, Ellen, and Senderowitz, Judith, eds. *Pronatalism: The Myth of Mom and Apple Pie.* New York: Thomas Y. Crowell, 1974.

Rollin, Betty. "Motherhood: Who Needs It?" *Look,* 22 September 1970, pp. 15–17.

Safer, Jeanne. *Beyond Motherhood: Choosing a Life Without Children.* New York: Pocket Books, 1996.

Schwartz, Pepper. "Para Dads and Para Moms." *New York Times,* 9 November, 1995.

Scott, Laura. *Two is Enough: A Couple's Guide to Living Childless by Choice.* New York: Seal Press, 2009.

Veevers, Jean. *Childless by Choice.* Scarborough, Ontario: Butterworth's, 1980.

Walker, Ellen L. *Complete Without Kids: An Insider's Guide to Childfree Living by Choice or Chance.* New York: Greenleaf Book Group. 2011.

Pregnancy

Armstrong, Penny and Sheryl Feldman. *A Wise Birth: Bringing Together the Best of Natural Childbirth with Modern Medicine,* 2nd ed. London: Pinter and Martin, 2006.

Bardacke, Nancy. *Mindful Birthing: Training the Mind, Body and Heart for Childbirth and Beyond.* New York: HarperCollins, 2012.

Bittmen, Sam, and Zalk, Sue Rosenberg. *Expectant Fathers.* New York: Hawthorn, 1978.

Boston Women's Health Book Collective. *Our Bodies, Ourselves: Pregnancy and Birth.* New York: Simon and Schuster, 2011.

Brott, Armin, and Jennifer Ash. *The Expectant Father: Facts, Tips and Advice for Dads to Be.* New York: Abbeville Press, 2010.

England, Pam and Rob Horowitz. *Birthing from Within: An Extraordinary Guide to Childbirth Preparation.* Albuquerque: Partera Press, 1998.

Gaudet, Tracy and Paula Spencer. *Body, Soul, and Baby: A Doctor's Guide to the Complete Pregnancy Experience from Preconception to Postpartum.* New York: Bantam, 2008.

Groenou, Aneema van. *The Active Woman's Guide to Pregnancy: Practical Advice for Getting Outdoors While Expecting:* Berkeley, CA: Ten Speed Press, 2004.

Hall, Nancy W. *Balancing Pregnancy and Work. How to Make the Most of the Next Nine Months on the Job.* Emmaus, PA: Rodale, 2004.

Jana, Laura A., and Jennifer Shu. *Heading Home with Your Newborn. From Birth to Reality,* Second Edition. Elk Grove Village, IL: American Academy of Pediatrics, 2005.

Kitzinger, Sheila. *The Complete Book of Pregnancy and Childbirth.* 4th ed. New York: Knopf, 2004.

Klaus, Marshall H., John J. Kennell, and Phyllis H. Klaus. *The Doula Book:*

How a Trained Labor Companion Can Help You Have a Shorter, Easier Childbirth. Cambridge, MA: Perseus Publishing, 2002.

Murkoff, Heidi. *What to Expect Before You're Expecting. The Complete Pre-Conception Plan.* New York: Workman, 2009.

Mykso, Claire and Magali Amadei. *Does This Pregnancy Make Me Look Fat?: The Essential Guide to Loving Your Body Before and After Baby.* Deerfield Beach, FL: Health Communications, 2009.

Noble, Elizabeth. *Essential Exercises for the Childbearing Year: A Guide to Health and Comfort Before and After Your Baby is Born.* 4th ed. Harwich, MA: New Life Images, 2003.

Ogle, Amy, and Liza Mazzullo. *Before Your Pregnancy: A 90-day Guide for Couples on How to Prepare for a Healthy Conception.* 2nd ed. New York: Ballantine, 2011.

Paul, Ann Murphy. *Origins: How the Nine Months Before Birth Shape the Rest of Our Lives.* New York: Free Press, 2011.

Piver, Susan, ed. *The Mindful Way Through Pregnancy: Meditation, Yoga, and Journaling for Expectant Mothers.* Boston, MA: Shambhala, 2012.

Puryear, Lucy J. *Understanding Your Moods When You're Expecting: Emotions, Mental Health, and Happiness, Before, During and After Pregnacy.* Boston: Houghton Mifflin, 2007.

Rabb, Diana and Errol Norwitz. *Your High Risk Pregnancy: A Practical Supportive Guide.* Alameda, CA: Hunter House, 2009.

Riley, Laura. *You and Your Baby Pregnancy: The Ultimate Week-by-Week Pregnancy Guide.* 2nd ed. New York: Wiley, 2012.

Romm, Aviva Jill. *The Natural Pregnancy Book. Herbs, Nutrition and Other Holistic Choices.* Berkeley, CA: Celestial Arts, 2003.

Simkin, Penny. *The Birth Partner: Everything You Need to Know to Help a Woman Through Childbirth.* 2nd ed. Boston: Harvard Common Press, 2001.

Simkin, Penny, Janet Whalley, and Ann Kepler. *Pregnancy, Childbirth, and the Newborn: The Complete Guide,* revised and updated edition. Minnetonka, MN: Meadowbrook Press 2000.

Sussman, John, and B. Blake Levitt. *Before You Conceive: The Complete Prepregnancy Guide.* New York: Bantam, 1989.

Tracy, Amy E. *The Pregnancy Bed Rest Book: A Survival Guide for Expectant Mothers and Their Families.* New York: Berkley, 2001.

Twenge, Jean. *The Impatient Woman's Guide to Getting Pregnant.* New York: Free Press, 2012.

Whelan, Elizabeth. *The Pregnancy Experience.* New York: W.W. Norton, 1973.

Wolfe, Maxine G., and Margot Goldsmith. *Practical Pregnancy*. New York: Warner Books, 1980.

Nursing

Huggins, Kathleen. *The Nursing Mother's Companion*. Boston, MA: Harvard Common Press, 2010.

Mohrbacher, Nancy, and Kathleen Kendall-Tackett. *Breastfeeding Made Simple: Seven Natural Laws for Nursing Mothers*. Oakland, CA: New Harbinger Publications, 2010.

Pryor, Gale. *Nursing Mother, Working Mother: The Essential Guide to Breastfeeding Your Baby Before and After You Return to Work*. Boston, MA: Harvard Common Press, 2007.

Postpartum

Bennett, Shoshanna. *Beyond the Blues: A Guide to Understanding and Treating Prenatal and Postpartum Depression*. 2nd ed. San Jose, CA: Moodswings Press, 2006.

Brink, Susan. *The Fourth Trimester: Understanding, Protecting, and Nurturing an Infant Through the First Three Months*. Berkeley, CA: University of California Press, 2013.

Karp, Richard. *The Happiest Baby on the Block: The New Way to Calm Crying and Help Your Newborn Baby Sleep Longer*. New York: Bantam: 2003.

Kendell-Tacket, Kathleen. *The Hidden Feelings of Motherhood: Coping with Stress, Depression and Burnout*. Oakland, CA: New Harbinger Publications, 2001.

Placksin, Sally. *Mothering the New Mother: Women's Feelings and Needs After Childbirth; A Support and Resource Guide*. 2nd ed. New York: New Market Press, 2000.

Klaus, Marshall, and Phyllis Klaus. *Your Amazing Newborn*. Reading, MA: Perseus Books, 1998.

Leach, Penelope. *The Essential First Year*. London: DK Publishing, 2010.

Wiegarz, Pamela S., and Kevin L. Gyoerkoe. *The Pregnancy and Postpartum Anxiety Workbook: Practical Skills to Help You Overcome Anxiety, Worry, Panic Attacks, Obsessions, and Compulsions*. Oakland, CA: New Harbinger Publications, 2009.

Parenting

Adair, Catherine Steiner. *The Big Disconnect: Protecting Childhood and Family Relationships in the Digital Age.* New York: Harper Collins, 2013.

Berends, Polly Berrien. *Whole Child, Whole Parent.* New York: Harper and Row, 1987.

Boston Women's Health Book Collective. *Ourselves and Our Children.* New York: Random House, 1978.

Chess, Stella, Thomas Alexander, and Herbert G. Birch. *Your Child Is a Person: A Psychological Approach to Parenthood Without Guilt.* New York: Penguin, 1977.

Choudhri, Nihara K. *Preparing for Baby: All the Legal, Financial, Tax, and Insurance Information New and Expectant Parents Need.* Chicago: American Bar Association, 2015.

Cohen, Lawrence J. *Playful Parenting: An Exciting New Approach to Raising Children That Will Help You Nurture Close Connections, Solve Behavior Problems, Encourage Confidence.* New York: Ballantine Books, 2002.

Ehrensaft, Diane. *Spoiling Childhood: How Well-Meaning Parents Are Giving Children Too Much, But Not What They Need.* New York: Guilford Press, 1997.

Eliot, Lise. *What's Going On in There? How the Brain and Mind Develop in the First Five Years of Life.* New York: Bantam, 1999.

Galinsky, Ellen. *The Six Stages of Parenthood.* Reading, MA: Addison Wesley, 1987.

Golinkoff, Roberta Michnick. *Einstein Never Used Flash Cards: How Our Children Really Learn-and Why They Need to Play More and Memorize Less.* Emmaus, PA: Rodale Press, 2004.

Gopnik, Alison. *The Philosophical Baby: What Children's Minds Tell Us About Truth, Love and the Meaning of Life.* New York: Picador, 2010.

Haelle, Tara and Emily Willingham. *The Informed Parent: A Science-Based Resource for Your Child's First Four Years.* New York: Tarcher/Perigee, 2016.

Hughes, Daniel and Jonathan Baylin. *Brain-Based Parenting: The Neuroscience of Caregiving for Healthy Attachment.* New York: W.W. Norton, 2012.

Kabat-Zinn, Myla and John. *Everyday Blessings: The Inner Work of Mindful Parenting.* New York: Hyperion, 1997.

Leach, Penelope. *Your Baby and Child: From Birth to Age Five.* New York: Knopf, 2010.

Lipman, Susan Sachs. *Fed Up with Frenzy: Slow Parenting in a Fast-moving*

World. Naperville, IL: Sourcebooks, 2012.

Lythcott-Haims, Julie. *How to Raise an Adult: Break Free of the Overparenting Trap and Prepare Your Kid for Success*. New York: Henry Holt, 2015.

Medina, John. *Brain Rules for Baby: How to Raise a Smart and Happy Child from Zero to Five*. Seattle, WA: Pear Press, 2014.

Mogel, Wendy. *The Blessing of a Skinned Knee: Using Jewish Techniques to Raise Self-Reliant Children*. New York: Scribner, 2008. Reviewers emphasize that this book is useful for people of all faiths, and atheists.

Napthali, Sarah. *Buddhism for Mothers: A Calm Approach to Caring for Yourself and Your Young Children*. Crow's Nest, New South Wales, 2010.

_____. *Buddhism for Mothers of Young Children: Becoming A Mindful Parent*. Crow's Nest NSW Australia: Inspired Living, 2009.

Siegel, Daniel. *The Whole-Brain Child: 12 Revolutionary Strategies to Nurture Your Child's Developing Mind*. New York: Bantam, 2012.

Stern, Daniel, and Tina Payne Bryson. *Diary of a Baby*. New York: Basic Books, 1990.

Sunderland, Margot. *The Science of Parenting: How Today's Brain Research Can Help You Raise Happy, Emotionally Balanced Children*. London: DK, 2006.

Stoppard, Miriam. *Complete Baby and Child Care*. New York: DK Publishing, 1995.

Taffel, Ron. *Childhood Unbound: Saving Our Kids' Best Selves: Confident Parenting in a World of Change*. New York: Free Press, 2009.

Motherhood

Edelman, Hope. *Motherless Daughters: The Legacy of Loss*, 2nd ed. Cambridge, MA: Da Capo Press, 2006.

_____. *Motherless Mothers: How Mother Loss Shapes the Parents We Become*. New York: HarperCollins, 2006.

Eheart, Brenda, and Susan Martan. *The Fourth Trimester: On Becoming a Mother*. E. Norwalk, CT: Appleton Lange, 1983.

Genevie, Louis, and Margolis, Eva. *The Motherhood Report: How Women Feel About Being Mothers*. New York: Macmillan, 1987.

Gore, Ariel. *The Hip Mama Survival Guide: Advice From the Trenches on Pregnancy, Childbirth, Cool Names, Clueless Doctors and Potty Training Toddler Avengers*. New York: Hyperion, 1998.

Gottman, John, with Joan DeClaire. *The Heart of Parenting: How to Raise an Emotionally Intelligent Child*. New York: Simon and Schuster, 1997.

Maushart, Susan. *The Mask of Motherhood: How Becoming a Mother Changes Our Lives and Why We Never Talk About It.* New York: Penguin, 2000.

McBride, Angela Barron. *The Growth and Development of Mothers.* New York: Barnes and Noble, 1974.

Nugent, Kevin. *Your Baby Is Speaking to You: A Visual Guide to the Amazing Behaviors of Your Newborn and Growing Baby.* Boston: Houghton Mifflin, 2011.

Peri, Camille and Kate Mosews, eds. *Mothers Who Think: Tales of Real Life Parenthood.* New York: Villard, 1999.

Rich, Adrienne. *Of Woman Born.* New York: Bantam, 1977.

Stern, Daniel N., and Nadia Bruschweiler-Stern, with Alison Freeland. *The Birth of a Mother: How the Motherhood Experience Change You Forever.* New York: Basic Books, 1998.

Balancing Careers and Children

Alcorn, Katrina. *Maxed Out: American Moms on the Brink.* Berkeley CA: Seal, 2013.

Bakst, Dina, Phoebe Taubman, and Elizabet Gedman. *Babygate: How to Survive Pregnancy and Parenting in the Workplace.* New York: Feminist Press, 2014. Focused on knowing your rights and negotiating.

Colburn-Smith, Cate and Andrea Serrette. *The Milk Memos: How Real Moms Learned to Mix Business with Babies—And How You Can, Too.* Los Angeles: J.P. Tarcher, 2007.

Elkind, David. *Parenting on the Go: Birth to Six, A to Z.* Boston: Da Capo, 2014.

Eschliman, Amy and Leigh Oshirak. *Balance Is a Crock, Sleep is for the Weak: An Indispensable Guide to Surviving Working Parenthood.* Avery Trade, 2010.

Evans, Carol and Christine Larson. *This is How We Do It: The Working Mothers' Manifesto.* New York: Hudson St. Press, 1996.

Friedman, Stewart D. *Baby Bust: New Choices for Men and Women in Work and Family.* Philadelphia: Wharton Digital Press, 2013

Gillespie, Becky Beaupre and Hollee Schwartz Temple. *Good Enough is the New Perfect: Finding Happiness and Success in Modern Motherhood.* New York: Harlequin, 2011.

Gerson, Kathleen. *The Unfinished Revolution: How a New Generation is Reshaping Family, Work, and Gender in America.* New York: Oxford Unversity Press, 2010.

Goodman, Ellen. "Being a Grateful Wife Means Always Having to Ask," Boston Globe, December 11, 1979.

Greenberg, Cathy and Barrett S. Avigdor. *What Happy Working Mothers Know: How New Findings in Positive Psychology Can Lead to a Healthy and Happy Worklife.* New York: Wiley, 2009.

Hawley, Nancy Press. "Sharing Parenthood." in Boston Women's Health Collective. *Ourselves and Our Children: A Book By and For Parents.* New York: Random House, 1978. Her quotes in Chapter 15 of this book appear on pp.138–139 in *Ourselves and Our Children.*

Levs, Josh. *All In: How Our Work-First Culture Fails Dads, Families, and Businesses—And How We Can Fix it Together.* New York: HarperOne, 2015.

Richards, Amy. *Opting In: Having a Child Without Losing Yourself.* New York: Farrar, Strauss and Giroux, 2008.

Sachs, Wendy. *How She Really Does It.* New York: Da Capo, 2005.

Slaughter, Anne-Marie. *Unfinished Business: Women, Men, Work, Family.* New York: Random House, 2015.

Stone, Pamela. *Opting Out? Why Women Really Quit Careers and Head Home.* Berkeley, CA: University of California Press, 2007.

Vanderkam, Laura. *I Know How She Does It: How Successful Women Make the Most of Their Time.* New York: Portfolio/Penguin 2015.

Williams, Joan and Rachel Dempsey. *What Works for Women at Work: Four Patterns Working Women Need to Know.* New York: NYU Press, 2014.

Fatherhood and Shared Parenthood

Bird, Caroline. *The Two-Paycheck Marriage.* New York: Rawson, Wade, 1979.

Fleck, Joseph, and Jack Sawyer. *Men and Masculinity.* Englewood Cliffs, NJ: Prentice-Hall, 1974.

Greenberg, Martin and Norman Morris. "Engrossment: The Newborn's Impact Upon the Father." *American Journal of Orthopsychiatry,* 44. July 1974.

Greenberg, Martin. *The Birth of a Father.* New York: Continuum, 1985.

Hall, Francine S., and Douglas T. Hall. *The Two-Career Couple.* Reading, Mass: Addison-Wesley, 1979.

Kotelchuck, Milton. "The Infant's Relationship to the Father: Experimental Evidence." *The Role of the Father in Child Development.* Michael Lamb, ed. New York: Wiley, 1978.

Levine, James. *Who Will Raise the Children? New Options for Fathers (and Mothers).* Philadelphia: S.B. Lippincott, 1976.

Meer, Sharon and Joanna Stroeber. *Getting to Fifty-Fifty: How Working Parents Can Have It All.* Berkeley, CA: Viva Editions, 2013

Pruett, Kyle, and Marsha Kline Pruett. *Partnership Parenting: How Men and Women Parent Differently—Why it Helps Your Kids and Can Strengthen Your Marriage.* Philadelphia: Da Capo Lifelong, 2009.

Raeburn, Paul. *Do Fathers Matter? What Science is Telling Us About the Parent We've Overlooked.* New York: Scientific American/Farrar, Straus and Giroux, 2014.

Ruddick, Sara, and Pamela Daniels, eds. *Working It Out: 23 Women Writers, Artists, Scientists and Scholars Talk About Their Lives and Work.* New York: Pantheon, 1977.

Steinberg, David, "Redefining Fatherhood: Notes after Six Months." *The Future of the Family,* L.K. Howe, ed. New York: Simon and Schuster, 1972.

Gresko, Brian, ed. *When First I Held You: 22 Critically Acclaimed Writers Talk About the Triumphs, Challenges, and Transformative Experience of Fatherhood.* New York: Berkley, 2014.

Adoption

Caughman, Susan and Isolde Motley, with *Adoptive Families* Magazine. *You Can Adopt: An Adoptive Families Guide.* NY: Ballantine, 2009.

Davenport, Dawn. *The Complete Book of International Adoption: A Step-by-Step Guide to Finding Your Child.* New York: Broadway Books, 2006.

Gilman, Lois. *The Adoption Resource Book,* revised edition. New York: Harper Perennial, 1998.

Falker, Elizabeth Swire. *The Ultimate Insider's Guide to Adoption: Everything You Need to Know About Domestic and International Adoption.* New York: Warner, 2006.

Gray, Deborah D. *Attaching in Adoption: Practical Tools for Today's Parents.* London and Philadelphia: Jessica Kingsley Publishers, 2012.

Gogen, Patty. *Parenting Your Internationally Adopted Child.* Boston: Harvard Common Press, 2008.

Hall, Beth and Gail Steinberg. *Inside Transracial Adoption. Strength-Based, Culture-sensitizing Parenting Strategies for Inter-Country or Domestic Adoptive Families That Don't "Match."* London: Jessica Kingsley, 2000.

Hopkins-Best, Mary. *Toddler Adoption: The Weaver's Craft,* revised edition. London: Jessica Kingsely, 2012.

Jarratt, Claudia Jewett. *Helping Children Cope with Separation and Loss,* revised edition. Boston, MA: Harvard Common Press, 1994.

Jarratt, Claudia Jewett. *Adopting the Older Child.* Harvard, MA: Harvard Common Press, 1978.

Johnston, Patricia Irwin *Adopting After Infertility*. Indianapolis, IN: Perspectives Press, 1992.

Johnston, Patricia Irwin. *Adopting: Sound Choice, Strong Families*. Indianapolis, IN: Perspectives Press, 2008.

Melina, Lois Ruskai. *Raising Adopted Children: Practical Reassuring Advice for Every Adoptive Parent*. New York: Harper Perennial, 1998.

Melina, Lois Ruskai and Sharon Kaplan Roszia. *The Open Adoption Experience: A Complete Guide for Adoptive and Birth Families—From Making the Decision Through the Child's Growing Years*. New York: Harper Perennial, 1993.

Newton, Ruth. *The Attachment Connection: Parenting a Secure and Confident Child Using the Science of Attachment Theory*. Oakland, CA: New Harbinger, 2008.

Pertman, Adam. *Adoption Nation: How the Adoption Revolution is Transforming Our Families—and America*. Boston, MA: Harvard Common Press, 2011.

Register, Cheri. *"Are Those Kids Yours?" American Families with Children Adopted from Other Countries*. New York: The Free Press, 1991.

Rothman, Barbara Katz. *Weaving A Family: Untangling Race and Adoption*. Boston: Beacon Press, 2005.

Varon, Lee. *Adopting on Your Own: The Complete Guide to Adopting as a Single Parent*. New York: Farrar, Strauss and Giroux, 2000. This is a great book on preparing to adopt regardless of marital status.

Gay, Lesbian, Bisexual, Transgender

Aizley, Harlyn, ed. *Confessions of the Other Mother: Nonbiological Lesbian Moms Tell All*. Boston: Beacon Press, 2006.

Ball, Carlos A. *The Right to Be Parents: LGBT Families and the Transformation of Parenthood*. New York: New York University Press, 2012. (Legal history).

Benkov, Laura. *Reinventing the Family: The Emerging Story of Lesbian and Gay Parenting*. New York: Crown, 1994.

Brill, Stephanie. *The New Essential Guide to Lesbian Conception, Pregnancy and Birth*. Los Angeles: Alyson Books, 2006.

Brodzinsky, David and Adam Pertman, eds. *Adoption by Lesbians and Gay Men: A New Dimension in Family Diversity*. Oxford: The Oxford University Press, 2012. Geared toward professionals.

Gamson, Joshua. *Modern Families: Stories of Extraordinary Journeys and Kinships*. New York: NYU Press, 2015.

Kaeser, Gigi, and Peggy Gillespie, ed. *Love Makes a Family: Portraits of Lesbian,*

Gay, Bisexual and Transgender Parents and Their Families. Amherst, MA: University of Massachusetts Press, 1999.

Levi, Arlene Istar. *The Complete Lesbian and Gay Parenting Guide.* New York: Berkley Books, 2004.

Martin, April. *The Lesbian and Gay Parenting Handbook: Creating and Raising Our Families.* New York: HarperCollins, 1993.

McGarry, Kevin. *Fatherhood for Gay Men: An Emotional and Practical Guide to Becoming a Gay Dad.* New York: Harrington Park Press/Haworth, 2003.

McIntyre, Casandra. "Two Ubermoms Are Better Than One." *The Other Mother* (see *Confessions of the Other Mother: Nonbiological Lesbian Moms Tell All.* Harlyn Aizley, ed. Boston: Beacon Press, 2006.

Pepper, Rachel. *The Ultimate Guide to Pregnancy for Lesbians: How to Stay Sane and Care for Yourself from Preconception Through Birth.* San Francisco: Cleis Press, 2005.

Pies, Cherie. *Considering Parenthood: A Workshop for Lesbians.* San Francisco: Spinsters Ink, 1985.

Priwer, Shan, and Cynthia Phillips. *Gay Parenting: Complete Guide for Same-Sex Families.* Far Hills, NJ: New Horizons Press, 2006.

Schulenburg, Joy. *Gay Parenting: A Complete Guide for Gay Men and Lesbians with Children.* New York: Anchor Books, 1985.

Sembler, Brette McWhorter. *Gay and Lesbian Parenting Choices: From Adopting or Using a Surrogate to Choosing the Perfect Father.* Franklin Lakes, N.J: Career Press, 2006. An outstanding guide that manages to be exhaustive and concise. Invaluable legal and medical information, and consumer advocacy. A gem.**

Shelton, Michael. *Family Pride: What LGBT Families Should Know about Navigating Home, School and Safety in Their Neighborhoods.* Boston: Beacon Press, 2013.

Infertility

Includes listings on donor conception and surrogacy. For considering the child-free choice after infertility, please see the "Childfree Choice" section. Starred items are relevant.

Barbieri, Robert, Alice Domar, and Kevin Laoughlin. *Six Steps to Increased Fertility.* New York: Simon and Schuster, 2000.

Bombardieri, Merle. "Childfree Decision-Making" {if you've been through infertility} http://www.resolve.org/resources/fact-sheets.html.

_____ "Coping with the Stress of Infertility," part of a packet on the topic available from resolve.org (see above).

_____ "The Twenty Minute Rule for Couple Communication About Infertility." This article is bundled into the "Coping With Stress" article above.

Cooper, Susan, and Ellen Glazer. *Beyond Infertility: A New Path to Parenthood.* New York: Lexington Books, 1994.

Debano, Patty Doyle, Courtney Edgerton Menzel, and Shelly Nicken Sutphen. *The Conception Chronicles: The Uncensored Truth About Sex, Love, and Marriage When You're Trying to Get Pregnant.* Deerfield Beach, FL: Health Communications, 2005.

Domar, Alice. *Conquering Infertility: Dr. Alice Domar's Mind/Body Guide to Enhancing Fertility and Coping with Infertility.* New York: Viking, 2002.

Douglas, Ann. *Trying Again: A Guide to Pregnancy After Miscarriage, Stillbirth, and Infant Loss.* New York: Taylor, 2000.

Ehrensaft, Diane. *Mommies, Daddies, Donors and Surrogates.* New York: Guilford Press, 2005.

Fleming, Anne Taylor. *Motherhood Deferred: A Woman's Journey.* New York: GP Putnam, 1994.

Glazer, Ellen Sarasohn and Evelina Weidman Sterling. *Having Your Baby Through Egg Donation.* London: Jessica Kingsley Publishers, 2013.

Griswald, Zara. *Surrogacy Was the Way: Twenty Intended Mothers Tell Their Stories.* Gurnee, IL: Nightingale Press, 2005.

Jaffe, Janet, Martha Ourieff Diamond, and David J. Diamond. *Unsung Lullabies: Understanding and Coping with Infertility.* New York: St. Martin's Griffin, 2005.

Jansen, Jani R. and Elizabeth Stewart, eds. *Mayo Clinic Guide to Fertility and Conception.* Boston: Da Capo Lifelong, 2015.

Magnacca, Kristin. *Love and Infertility Survival Strategies For Balancing Infertility, Marriage, and Life.* Washington, D.C: Lifeline Press, 2004.

Menning, Barbara E. *Infertility: A Guide for the Childless Couple.* Englewood Cliffs, NJ: Prentice-Hall, 1977. Pioneering work on emotional factors of infertility by the founder of RESOLVE, the national infertility organization. Although the medical information is outdated, this is a classic with timeless insights.

Orecchio, Christa and Willow Buckley. *How to Conceive Naturally and Have a Healthy Pregnancy after 30.* New York: Grand Central: 2015.

Orenstein, Peggy. *Waiting for Daisy: A Tale of Two Continents, Three Religions, Five Infertility Doctors, an Oscar, an Atomic Bomb, a Romantic*

Night, and One Woman's Quest to Become a Mother. New York: Blooms-bury, 2008.

Peoples, Debby and Harriette Rovner Ferguson. *Experiencing Infertility: An Essential Resource*. New York: W.W. Norton, 1998.

Raupp, Aimee. *Yes, You Can Get Pregnant: Natural Ways to Improve Your Fertility Now and into Your Forties*. New York: Demos, 2014.

Salzer, Linda. *Surviving Infertility. A Compassionate Guide Through the Emotional Crisis of Infertility*. New York: Harper Perennial, 1991.

Seckin, Tamer. *The Doctor Will See You Now: Recognizing and Treating Endometriosis*. New York: Turner, 2016.

Simons, Harriet. *Wanting Another Child*. Lexington, MA: Lexington Books, 1995.

Teman, Elly. *Birthing a Mother: The Surrogate Body and the Pregnant Self*. Berkeley, CA. University of California, 2010.

Twenge, Jean. *The Impatient Woman's Guide to Getting Pregnant*. New York: The Free Press, 2012.

Vercollone, Carol Frost. *Helping the Stork: The Choices and Challenges of Donor Insemination*. Hoboken, NJ: Wiley, 1997.

Williams, Christopher. *The Fastest Way to Get Pregnant Naturally: The Latest Information on Conceiving a Healthy Baby On Your Timetable*. New York: Hyperion, 2006.

Zoldbrod, Aline. *Men, Women and Infertility: Interventions and Treatment Strategies*. New York: Lexington Books, 1993.

Pregnancy Loss

Abbey, Amy L. Ed. *Journeys: Stories of Pregnancy After Loss*. Boulder, CO: Woven Word Press, 2006.

Berman, Michael. *Healing the Pain After Miscarriage, Stillbirth and Infant Death*. Westport, CT: Bergin and Garvey, 2001.

Friedman, Rochelle and Bonnie Gradstein. *Surviving Pregnancy Loss.*, 2nd ed. Secaucus, NJ: Carol Publishing Group, 1996.

Gray, Kathleen and Anne Lassance. *Grieving Reproductive Loss: The Healing Process*. Amityville, NY: Baywood Publishing, 2003. For Professionals.

Gross, Jessica Berger, ed. *About What Was Lost: Twenty Writers on Miscarriage, Healing and Hope*. New York: Penguin, 2007.

Kohn, Ingrid and Perry-Lynn Moffitt. *A Silent Sorrow: Pregnancy Loss—Guidance and Support for You and Your Family*. 2nd ed. New York: Routledge, 2000.

Lanham, Carol Cirulli Lanham. *Pregnancy After a Loss*. New York: Berkley Books, 1999.

Layne, Linda L. *Motherhood Lost: A Feminist Account of Pregnancy Loss in America*. New York: Routledge, 2002.

Lothrop, Hannah. *Help, Comfort and Hope after Losing Your Baby in Pregnancy or the First Year*. Tucson, AZ: Fisher Books, 1997. An excellent resource offering depth, compassion, excellent questions for self-care and communication.

Panuthos, Claudia and Catherine Romeo. *Ended Beginnings: Healing Childbearing Losses*. South Hadley, MA: Bergin and Garvey, 1984.

The One-Child Family

Falbo, Toni, ed. *The Single Child Family*. New York: Guilford, 1984.

Hawke, Sharryl, and Knox, David. *One Child by Choice*. Englewood Cliffs, NJ: Prentice-Hall, 1977.

McGrath, Ellie. *My One and Only: The Special Experience of the Only Child*. New York: Morrow, 1989.

McKibben, Bill. *Maybe One: A Case for Smaller Families*. New York: Simon and Schuster, 1998.

Nachman, Patricia Ann and Andrea Thompson. *You and Your Only Child: The Joys, Myths and Challenges of Raising an Only Child*. New York: HarperCollins, 1997.

Peck, Ellen. *The Joy of the Only Child*. New York: Delacorte, 1977.

Siegel, Deborah and Daphne Vuiller, eds. *Only Child: Writers on the Singular Joys and Solitary Sorrows of Growing Up Solo*. New York: Harmony, 2006.

Sandler, Lauren. *One and Only: The Freedom of Having an Only Child and the Joy of Being One*. New York: Simon and Schuster, 2013.

White, Carolyn. *The Seven Common Sins of Parenting an Only Child: A Guide for Parents, Kids and Families*. New York: Jossey-Bass, 2004.

Single Parents, Single Women

Alexander, Shoshana. *In Praise of Single Parents: Mothers and Fathers Accepting the Challenge*. Boston: Houghton Mifflin, 1994.

Anderson, Carol, Susan Stewart, and Sona Dimidjian. *Flying Solo: Single Women at Midlife*. New York: W.W. Norton, 1994.

Ashdown-Sharp, Patricia. *A Guide to Pregnancy and Parenthood for Women on*

Their Own. New York: Random House, 1977.

Bolick, Kate. *Spinster: Making a Life Of One's Own*. New York: Crown, 2015.

Greywolf, Elizabeth. *The Single Mother's Handbook*. New York: Morrow, 1984.

Hertz, Rosanna. *Single by Chance, Mothers by Choice: How Women are Choosing Parenthood Without Marriage and Creating the New American Family*. New York: Oxford University Press, 2006.

Kennedy, Marge, and Janet Spencer King. *The Single Parent Family: Living Happily in a Changing World*. New York: Crown, 1994.

Lamott, Anne. *Operating Instructions: A Journal of My Son's First Year*. New York: Pantheon, 1993.

Lehmann-Haupt, Rachel. *In Her Own Sweet Time: Unexpected Adventures in Finding Love, Commitment, and Motherhood*. New York: Basic, 2000.

Mattes, Jane. *Single Mothers by Choice: A Guidebook for Single Women Who Are Considering or Who Have Chosen Motherhood*. New York: Times Books, 1994.

Miller, Naomi. *Singles Parents by Choice: A Growing Trend in Family Life*. Insight Books, 1992.

Morrissette, Mikki. *Choosing Single Motherhood. The Thinking Woman's Guide*. New York: Houghton-Mifflin 2008.

Schwartz, Pepper. "Para Dads and Para Moms." *New York Times*, 9 November, 1995.

Traister, Rebecca. *All the Single Ladies: Unmarried Women and the Rise of an Independent Nation*. New York: Simon and Schuster, 2016.

Varon, Lee. *Adopting on Your Own: The Complete Guide to Adopting as a Single Parent*. New York: Farrar, Strauss, and Giroux, 2000.

Step-Parenting

Bernstein, Anne C. *Yours, Mine and Ours: How Families Change When Remarried Parents Have a Child Together*. New York: Norton, 1991.

Bray, James and John Kelly. *Step Families: Love, Marriage and Parenting in the First Decade*. New York: Broadway Books, 1998.

Burns, Cherie. *Step motherhood: How to Survive Without Feeling Frustrated, Left Out, or Wicked*. New York: Three Rivers, 2001.

Burt, Anne., ed. *My Father Married Your Mother: Writers Talk About Stepparents, Stepchildren, and Everyone in Between*. New York: W.W. Norton, 2006.

O'Connor, Anne. *The Truth About Stepfamilies; Real American Stepfamilies Speak Out.* New York: Marlowe and Company, 2003.

Oxhorn-Ringwood, Lynne Louise Oxhorn and Marjorie Vago Krausz. *Stepwives; Ten Steps to Help Ex-Wives and Stepmothers End the Struggle and Put the Kids First.* New York: Simon and Schuster, 2002.

Papernow, Patricia. *Surviving and Thriving in Stepfamily Relationships: What Works and What Doesn't.* New York: Routledge, 2013.

Penton, John and Shona Welsh. *Yours, Mine, and Hours. Relationship Skills for Blended Families.* Charleston, SC: BookSurge, 2007.

Roosevelt, Ruth, and Jeannette Lofas. *Living in Step.* Briarcliff Manor, NY: Stein and Day, 1976.

✦ APPENDIX 2 ✦
RESOURCES

Organizations & Websites

For more resources, please see the resources sections of the books in the bibliography as well as the websites listed here.

Childfree

Laura Carroll
https://www.lauracarroll.com
Author of *Families of Two* and *The Baby Matrix* offers support and information.

Childfree Meetup
http://www.meetup.com/topics/childfree
Meet locally with other childfree people.

Childfree.Net
http://www.childfree.net
This website connects you to many childfree websites and resources.

No Kidding!
http://www.nokidding.net
An international social club for childfree couples and singles.

Birth and Postpartum

American College of Nurse-Midwives
8403 Colesville Rd. Suite 1550, Silver Spring, MD 20910
240.234.8068.
www.midwife.org

American College of Obstetricians and Gynecologists (ACOG)
www.acog.org

Birthing from Within
www.birthingfromwithin.com

Boston Women's Health Book Collective
www.ourbodiesourselves.com
    This website offers more resources than can be included in their wonderful *Our Bodies, Ourselves* books, plus a blog.

Childbirth and Postpartum Professionals Association
PO Box 491448, Lawrenceville, GA 30049
888.692.2772
www.cappa.net

Conceivable Future
http://conceivablefuture.org
    A woman-led network bringing awareness to the threat of climate change to reproductive health and justice.

Doulas of North America
PO Box 626, Jaspar, IN 47547
888.788.3662
www.dona.org

Genetic Alliance, Inc.
http://www.geneticalliance.org
    Genetic education.

March of Dimes
http://www.marchofdimes.com
    Prevention of premature birth.

Mindfulness-Based Childbirth and Parenting Education Program
www.mindfulbirth.org

Postpartum Support International
6706 SW 54th Avenue, Portland, OR 97219
Support Helpline 800.894.9452
www.postpartum.net
> Nationwide telephone support referral to local help

Vibrant Gene
http://www.vibrantgene.com
> Kayla Sheets is a genetic consultant and genetic counselor who can help with planning and preconception care. Her website is full of information, including access to her talk shows. See my interview with her, Appendix 3.

Infertility and Pregnancy Loss

American Society of Reproductive Medicine (ASRM)
1209 Montgomery Highway, Birmingham, AL 35216
205.978.5000
e-mail **asrm@asrm.com**
patient/consumer website
www. fertilityfacts.org
> Professional organization of reproductive endocrinologists and allied professionals. The patient consumer website above is useful. Referrals provided.

Kristen Darcy
http://www.kristendarcy.com
> Life coaching blog often focused on infertility.

Domar Center
http://www.domarcenter.com
781-434-6578
> Stress management services including mind/body workshops

Endometriosis Association
8585 N. 7th Place, Milwaukee, WI 53223
414.355.2200
> **http://www.endometriosisassociation.org**
> Support and information

Health Journeys
http://www.healthjourneys.com
Relaxation and visualization downloads for stress management, healthy pregnancy, other relaxation and health needs.

Hope After Loss (formerly Hygeia Foundation, Inc.)
PO Box 3943, 264 Amity Rd, Woodbridge, CT 06525
800.893.9198
www.hygeiafoundation.org.
Bereavement Support.

RESOLVE
7918 Jones Branch Rd. Ste. 300, McLean, VA 22102
703.556.7172
www.resolve.org
A national organization for consumer advocacy, education on medical and emotional aspects of infertility and pregnancy loss. Local chapters have support groups, meetings and conferences. (I used to be their Clinical Director.)

Organization of Parents Through Surrogacy
P.O. Box 611, Gurnee, IL 60031
847.782.0224
e-mail bzager@msn.com
www.opts.com
Non-profit educational, networking, and referral organization serving prospective parents, surrogate mothers, and professionals.

SHARE Pregnancy Loss Support/St. Joseph's Health Center
402 Jackson St. St. Charles, MO 63301
800.821.6819
www.nationalshare.org
National support information, telephone support, chapters nationwide.

Stirrup Queens
http://stirrup-queens.com
Melissa Ford, author of *Navigating the Land of If*, offers insight and humor in her blog and gives you links to other infertility blogs.

Adoption

Adoption.Net
23161 Lake Center Drive, Ste. 209, Lake Forest, CA 92630
info@Adoption.NET
www.adoption.net
A goldmine of support of everyone involved in the adoption process including birthmothers and pregnant women. In addition to community sharing, social worker Kathy Brodsky contributes articles.

American Academy of Adoption Attorneys
PO Box 33053, Washington, DC 20053
202.832.2222
http://www.adoptionattorneys.org/aaaa-page/home
National organization of attorneys who specialize in adoption. In addition to referrals, the academy works on adoption reform.

Adoptive Families Magazine and Website.
http://www.adoptivefamilies.com/faq.php
In addition to the magazine, the website offers referrals to agencies, attorneys and parent groups, online community, blogs.

Building Your Family
New Hope Media LLC
39 West 37th St. 15th Fl., New York, NY 10018
646.366.0842
www.buildingyour family.com.
Online information and a guidebook for adopting or pregnancy.

Creating a Family
www.creatingafamily.com
Offers online adoption courses, information and referral for adoption and infertility and a radio show. Principal contributor is Dawn Davenport, author of *The Complete Book of International Adoption* (see bibliography section, Appendix A).

Families for Private Adoption
202.722.0338
http://ffpa.org
   Mission is to serve prospective parents who are interested in adoption outside of traditional agencies. Volunteers are adoptive parents.

National Adoption Center
1500 Walnut Street, Philadelphia, PA 19192
215.735.9988
800.TO-ADOPT
e-mail: **nac@adopt.org**
www.adopt.org
   Mission is to find homes for children in foster care, providing information and referral to prospective parents.

Treehouse
http://www.resca.net
   This is a community of foster families living together along with elderly people. An exciting new model in which the children enjoy emotional and academic success. New communities are opening in a number of cities.

Parenting

Brain, Child: The Magazine for Thinking Mothers
888.304.6667
www.brainchildmag.com

The Fatherhood Project
http://www.fatherhoodproject.org
   Research, education, and support, empowerment.

Literary Mama
www.literarymama.com

Mamazine
www.mamazine.com
   Feminist mothering.

Mocha Moms, Inc
http://mochamoms.org
    Local and online support for women of color in any stage of mother-hood.

Lauren Sandler
http://www.psychologytoday.com/blog/one-and-only
    Blogs about the one child family.

Single Mothers by Choice
http://www.singlemothersbychoice.com
    National organization with local meetings for those considering or try-ing to be single mothers or already mothers.

Sister Song Women of Color Reproductive Health Collective
http://www.sistersong.net
    A network of many organizations.

Well Family
http://well,blogs.nytimes.com/
    This is the new name for the popular The Motherlode parenting blog. columns by *New York Times* journalists and lively comments from readers.

Breastfeeding

KellyMom
www.kellymom.com
    A nurse/mother offers insights on nursing, parenting, and baby sleep patterns.

La Leche League International
957 N. Plum Grove Rd., Schaumburg, IL 60173
800.525.3243
www.llli.org

Step-Families

National Stepfamilies Resource Center
www.stepfamilies.info
Clearinghouse of information and support for stepfamilies and professionals.

StepMom Magazine
http://www.stepmommag.com
Online information and blog, as well as a monthly online paid subscription.

Gay Resources

Family Pride Coalition
http://www.familypride.org.
Advocacy for gay families.

GLAD
http://www.glad.org
Legal defenders and advocates.

Proud Parenting
http://proudparenting.com
Advocacy.

Our Family Coalition
http://www.ourfamily.org
Advocacy, support groups, education and parenting resources.

✦ APPENDIX 3 ✦
INTERVIEW WITH KAYLA SHEETS,
GENETIC COUNSELOR

Kayla Mandel Sheets, LCGC, is a board-certified and licensed genetic counselor and founder of Vibrant Gene Consulting. She specializes in preconception genetic care for individuals and couples who desire guidance in having a healthy pregnancy.

Much of the information in this interview is medical or scientific and therefore will change rapidly. Readers should consult experts for current information and use the information here only as a starting point in thinking about these important issues.

1. What self-care should people be considering before they try to get pregnant? How far ahead of trying for pregnancy should genetic counseling start? What if you want to have a baby, but don't think you'll start trying for a year or two? Should you start all this preventive stuff now because it's good for your health anyway?

a. There are many things that women and their partners can do to prepare for a healthy pregnancy. It is a little known fact that ACOG (American College of OB/Gyn) recommends every woman take time to create a reproductive health plan. I recommend that couples spend 3–6 months (or however long it takes) to get themselves into optimal health. Even if they are not planning on having a baby for a while, these health guidelines can help them get into healthy habits and with the luxury of having time on their side.

b. Research into the field of *epigenetics* (the expression of genes) shows that diet, exercise, and mental health are all important factors in the health and wellbeing of the baby, not just at birth but throughout his lifetime. Amazingly, the baby's health in utero can impact its health well into adulthood, and some of these epigenetic markers are passed on to the next generation. So the lifestyle of the couple can affect not only their baby's health, but the health of their grandchildren, too!

c. My recommendations depend on the client's needs and situation, but on the whole I suggest people consider the following appointments:

i. Find and plan a meeting with your OB or care provider

ii. Consider meeting with a nutritionist or registered dietician to formulate a diet plan, or optimize your current plan. Request information regarding foods that can promote the health of your microbiome (i.e., pre- and probiotics). They can also help with clients who need to lose or gain weight in order to meet the ideal BMI range of 18.5–26. (I wouldn't necessarily recommend speaking with your doctor about your diet because in the US, most are not formally trained in nutrition.) If you are unable to find a nutritionist, I recommend looking into web-based education, perhaps a web-based course such as Chris Kresser's **www.healthybabycode.com.**

iii. Make an appointment with a dentist. I recommend getting your teeth cleaned, cavities fixed, and x-rays done (while you're not pregnant!) These things are important to your oral health, which can have substantial impact on the health of your pregnancy. Poor oral health has been associated with preterm babies and other prenatal complications. We recently learned that the womb is not sterile (as once believed) and that the microbes that populate the placenta have the closest resemblance to the microbes of your mouth. We are still unclear about the process of how this happens, but for now suffice to say keeping good oral hygiene is clearly important.

iv. If you have a long-term injury, this might be your chance to heal it before becoming pregnant and putting more stress on it. I had a slipped disc that was not fully resolved, and worried me that it would become crippling during pregnancy. With the help of a massage therapist and physical therapist, I now am pain free and stronger than before my injury.

v. Before you start taking prenatal vitamins, I recommend getting a baseline blood assessment for vitamin and iron deficiencies. Either your OB, PCP or naturopath can help with this.

- As for prenatal supplementation, I recommend one that contains a natural form of folate ("folate," "5-methyl-tetrahydrofolate," "L-methylfolate" or "Metfolin") in lieu of the synthetic version, folic acid. Not everyone can metabolize folic acid well. There is a genetic test for how readily someone metabolizes folic acid into its active form of folate. The gene that encodes the enzyme is called methylenetetrahydrofolate reductase (MTHFR, for short). Some clients chose to be screened for this, while others choose to simply take the bioavailable form of the vitamin.
- You also get folate from foods such as dark leafy greens, chicken liver, and fruits. In total (food plus supplementation) aim for 800–1200 mcg per day. If you have a family history of birth defects (such as spina bifida or other open neural tube defects) or follow a vegetarian/vegan diet you should aim for the higher end of that range.

vi. Attempting pregnancy can be a stressful endeavor if it takes a while to conceive. Doing things that combat stress is essential to keeping your cortisol levels low (high cortisol levels can diminish fertility!). I recommend integrating yoga, tai chi, or meditation into your weekly schedule. Therapeutic massage and acupuncture can also help tremendously. If you have never meditated and want to learn, look into Mindful-Based Stress Reduction (MBSR) programs, notably ones that implement Jon Kabat-Zinn's work because they have been scientifically validated.

2. Why do you recommend that everyone, not just those with known genetic disorders see a genetic counselor before trying for pregnancy?

a. Genetic testing is changing rapidly and not every prenatal healthcare provider is able to keep abreast of the latest in genetic testing, and few have formal training in genetics to begin with. It's not their fault, it's just simply not their specialty. If you want to know all of your testing options, it's best you go to the source. Speak with a genetic counselor, ideally *before* you are pregnant so all of your options are on the table. Once you're pregnant, it will be a race against the clock to get your genetic testing needs met. From years of experience, I can say it's infinitely less stressful getting testing done without the pressure of time.

b. Folks often have important family history information that can impact how they manage their pregnancy. It's quite common for me to uncover something during a family history session, and for the couple to need more time to investigate further. Again, if they're already pregnant, it's a race to get this information together. Contacting relatives, tracking down old medical records, etc., can take quite a bit of time.

c. Genetic testing, especially for rare variants or complex tests can take weeks to get completed and results interpreted. It can also take time to get a complete family medical history. Calling Aunt Bertha, making sure of what conditions she's had and when she was diagnosed is only one phone call of many that you may need to make. If you're already pregnant, it is a race against the clock and you'll do the best you can, but couples regularly run short on time. This is completely avoidable! Why not have the luxury of time on your side?

d. Some couples have experienced recurrent miscarriages either with their current partner or a previous one. Genetic counselors have a number of tests that they can offer a couple in this situation, and help get them a possible explanation. If they are able to diagnose their condition, they have a better chance at overcoming it.

e. If you are attempting pregnancy, but have not had any result in 6–12 months, you may want to have a fertility consult with a genetic counselor along with an OB, or reproductive endocrinologist if your insurance permits it.

3. How does a pre-pregnancy genetic consult with people with no genetic history differ from a consult with those who do?

a. The consultation itself won't change, you will still discuss your family health history. When a couple has a more complicated history, it may take more time, and follow-up communications to get a complete picture of their risks. If the family gene (and variant) is known, then this will open options for the couple. One or both members might want to get screened for the gene, it depends on the scenario and the type of inheritance. These details can be provided by a genetic counselor, who can also coordinate follow-up testing for the couple.

b. In the event that their future pregnancy is at risk of a disorder, there are many options for the couple. They can consider IVF, and genetic screening for each embryo, and only implant the healthy ones. They can conceive naturally, and test the pregnancy directly. Gamete donation is another possibility, as well as adopting a chid. There are so many options for couples, we are very fortunate to live in this modern era where society is more supportive than ever before.

4. What recommendations or advice would you especially like to share?

a. Genetics is the ultimate form of preventative healthcare. Knowing your genes can save your life. But the key lies in getting the *right* test at the *right* time and having it interpreted *correctly*—all of which a board-certified genetic counselor can help you with.

5. Do you have any patient materials you created that are available for our readers?

a. I am hosting and producing a bi-monthly genetic health talk show. For folks who want to optimize their health, and stay on the cutting-edge, they can tune in to our YouTube channel: The Vibrant Gene Talk Show (**https://www.youtube.com/channel/UCER-HlPrpaclwMdcKcYyXUA**). Topics we have covered so far include "What Everyone Needs to Know About the Zika Virus," and "Genomic Sequencing for Newborns?"

b. I have a number of blogposts and links to important resources on my website. In particular, I address issues surrounding direct-to-consumer genetic testing, and propose a number of thought-provoking questions for people to ask themselves before pressing the "purchase" button.

c. I encourage people who are interested in learning about genetics and things they can do to improve their health to join my social media e-learning community.

6. Do you have recommended readings, e.g., a recent book, articles published by your professional association, websites other than ACOG, your association?

a. Mother to Baby, **http://www.mothertobaby.org/** is a national teratogen hotline, and free service. Anyone can call them with questions about exposures to chemicals, medications, vaccines, etc., while pregnant or breastfeeding.

b. To get more information on genetic counseling or to find a local genetic counselor: **www.nsgc.org**.

c. March of Dimes is also a good one.

d. Genetic Alliance—for online support groups, client advocacy and reliable information **http://www.geneticalliance.org/?gclid=CLrpmaHIi8gCFYiQHwodQeYAhQ**.

e. Books tend to become dated before they're published, so in genetics, we rely heavily on peer-reviewed journal articles on pubmed: (**http://www.ncbi.nlm.nih.gov/pubmed**)

7. When you were a guest lecturer in my class, you went into great details about the various kinds of tests. Is there a book, brochure or publication that maybe has all of this in a table?

a. These tests change and develop at an unprecedented rate, the information changes so quickly that I'd hate to put anything into print. For the latest information concerning genetic testing, I recommend readers visit with a genetic counselor.

8. How worried should couples be about autism and schizophrenia?

a. Autism Spectrum Disorders (ASD) and schizophrenia are both complex conditions that can have genetic and environmental factors attributed to them.

b. If there is a family history of autism, it is certainly worth looking into the details of the condition. In particular, it's important to find out if the individual has a *genetic diagnosis*. It depends on the circumstance, but it may be helpful to pursue genetic testing for the client, too, and determine if they are also at a higher risk of having children with autism. If they are at an increased risk, they have many options to promote their having a healthy baby.

c. What can be done to moderate this risk? Couples have many options. For all couples, I recommend that they take care of their health. Diet and exercise can both alter the expression of their genes. Also avoiding teratogens like drugs, alcohol, tobacco can help to create healthier eggs and sperm. A fifty-five-year-old who exercises, eats plenty of leafy greens, and does not smoke is a very different personal health presentation than a fifty-five-year-old who doesn't take care of themselves.

d. If a couple perceives that their risk of ASDs and/or schizophrenia is too high for their liking, whether it be due to a family history or concern about age-related risks, then gamete (egg and/or sperm) donation is a possibility. Adoption is another option. I think it is also important to realize that we are learning a lot about both conditions, and by the time this generation of babies are adults, we will have novel technologies and personalized treatments that may prevent the conditions from occurring altogether.

9. How can readers find you? What services can clients receive in person and remotely?

a. I am reachable through my website: **www.vibrantgene.com** (press the "contact us today" green button). I may take up to 48 hours to respond.

b. Readers can also benefit by joining my e-learning communities on Twitter (**@vibrantgene**), Facebook (**www.facebook. com/vibrantgene**), and Google+ (Private Support and Information Group, "Healthy Pregnancy and Genetics").

c. I provide private genetic counseling to individuals and couples. Through the use of telemedicine, I provide personalized consultations for preconception and prenatal care to clients locally, nationally and internationally.

✦ APPENDIX 4 ✦
MY OWN BABY DECISION

I was nineteen and working as a camp counselor in Michigan when the idea of remaining childfree first occurred to me. On a cool summer night when my eleven-year-old charges were finally asleep, I basked in the silence and asked myself, "Do I *really* want to be a mother some day?" I had come to realize that my least favorite part of the day was the time I spent with my campers while my favorite part was the time I spent reading—alone. I wondered if I was unfit to be a mother because I preferred quiet study to rowdy kids. Perhaps motherhood and I were not compatible.

A year later I met my husband-to-be, and as we began to consider marriage, it quickly became clear that the baby question would have to be resolved *before* the marriage question. Although the idea of children had some appeal, I wasn't prepared to sacrifice my career or my precious solitude, and I was seriously considering remaining childfree. Rocco, on the other hand, was eagerly looking forward to fatherhood. One of the oldest of six children, a member of a warm, vivacious extended family, Rocco considered children and happiness inextricably linked.

We agreed not to marry if we couldn't reach a mutually acceptable decision. It wouldn't be fair for Rocco to have to give up fatherhood or for me to submit to motherhood only to please him.

Since I was ambivalent rather than committed to the childfree choice, I set about to resolve that ambivalence, ever aware of the danger that I might foolishly give up my freedom in order not to give up Rocco. Over a year passed before our eventual engagement. During that time the women's movement was picking up momentum, and both social science research and feminist literature reassured me that women could combine careers and motherhood. I also worked in a day care center where I had a chance not only to enjoy being with young children, but also to meet their parents—flesh-and-blood role models of successful two-career families. These parents were enthusiastic about their children despite the frustrations and sacrifices involved in two-career family life. Rocco and I also discussed his commitment to child care and the crucial role he could play in preserving my career and my quiet time. The upshot was that I reached a point where I truly looked forward to becoming a mother.

We waited five years after marrying before having our first child. We wanted to enjoy more freedom, finish our education, and establish our relationship. In the five years between our wedding and Marcella's conception we earned two graduate degrees, lived in Brazil and Mexico, and traveled in Europe. We enjoyed lots of friends and activities, some shared, others apart.

We're now in our sixties. Our two daughters are grown and married. We have a two-year-old grandson. We enjoy these relationships immensely.

Looking back, there were certainly days of overwork punctuated by temper tantrums; days when being childfree would have been easier. But our decision worked out very well for us. It has been fun seeing who are daughters have turned out to be, and encouraging their interests, passions, and creativity.

I'm happy to say I managed to build and develop my career as a psychotherapist and even start a new one as a writer, and enjoy reasonable amounts of solitude as well. All of this has been possible because of Rocco's firm commitment to fathering his daughters and to making motherhood enjoyable for me.

I'm not sorry I waited those five years and questioned motherhood as carefully as I did. Not only did I learn about myself, my marriage, and my intense commitment to both career and motherhood, but I also learned a great deal that has contributed to my happiness as a mother. Rather than ignoring my childfree side, I used it as an ally. By talking with Rocco about the needs I thought motherhood would thwart we were able to begin working out acceptable solutions even before we married.

Had I married a different man I think I could have remained childfree and lived a happy life. I would have missed something by not having a child, but I would also have enjoyed many experiences that motherhood precludes.

✦ INDEX ✦

✦ ABOUT THE AUTHOR ✦

Merle (Malkoff) Bombardieri, is a clinical social worker/ psychotherapist who specializes in parenthood decision-making, infertility, adoption, and making the most of a childfree life. Although she is the mother of two grown children, she has also been an advocate for childfree people since 1979. She has been in private practice for thirty-plus years in Lexington, MA. In 1981, she published the first edition of *The Baby Decision* based on interviews and reviews of scholarly research. Then, in 1982 she became Clinical Director of RESOLVE, the national infertility association. There she wrote guidelines for infertility patients making decisions on new techniques such as in vitro fertilization and donor egg, as well as adoption and surrogacy. This revised second edition of *The Baby Decision*, is based on thirty-five more years of work guiding decision-makers in educational workshops, long-distance coaching for people around the world and psychotherapy. Merle brings a sense of humor and compassion to her work. She helps clients and readers get curious about themselves and uncover new discoveries that make life more fun.

Merle's writing has appeared in *Our Bodies, Ourselves, Brides, Glamour, Self,* the *Boston Globe Magazine, Boston Magazine* and psychology blogs. She has lectured at Harvard Medical School, M.I.T., Wellesley College, and the Cambridge Center for Adult Education. She has appeared on national radio and television news shows, talk shows and documentaries, including the *Leeza Show.* Merle has been quoted in *The New York Times, Time, Newsweek,* the *Boston Globe* and the *Huffington Post.* She has also written medical journal articles and a chapter in a medical textbook.

Merle is married and the mother of two grown daughter and the grandmother of a two-year-old boy. She enjoys creative writing, yoga, hiking, and travel.

She is working on a novel, *Don't Ask*, about two sisters and a surrogate pregnancy. Sign up on her contact page to hear more about it and to receive her newsletter.

✦ CONTACT INFORMATION ✦

Please go to **www.thebabydecision.com** to sign up to receive further information on the baby decision, Merle's newsletter, information on online courses, and news about her upcoming novel, *Don't Ask*.

Feel free to contact Merle via **www.thebabydecision.com** to inquire about baby decision coaching. Technology allows her to coach people remotely.

Follow Merle on Twitter @thebabydecision and like us on Facebook: www.facebook.com/thebabydecision.

Made in the USA
Las Vegas, NV
13 June 2021